Beyond the Betrayal

T0308817

The George and Sakaye Aratani Nikkei in the Americas Series

SERIES EDITORS
VALERIE MATSUMOTO AND TRITIA TOYOTA

This series endeavors to capture the best scholarship available illustrating the evolving nature of contemporary Japanese American culture and community. By stretching the boundaries of the field to the limit (whether at a substantive, theoretical, or comparative level), these books aspire to influence future scholarship in this area specifically and Asian American studies more generally.

Barbed Voices: Oral History, Resistance, and the World War II Japanese American Social Disaster, Arthur A. Hansen

Beyond the Betrayal: The Memoir of a World War II Japanese American Draft Resister of Conscience, Yoshito Kuromiya, edited by Arthur A. Hansen

Distant Islands: The Japanese American Community in New York City, 1876–1930s, Daniel H. Inouye, with a foreword by David Reimers

Forced Out: A Nikkei Woman's Search for a Home in America, Judy Kawamoto

The House on Lemon Street, Mark Howland Rawitsch

Japanese Brazilian Saudades: Diasporic Identities and Cultural Production, Ignacio López-Calvo

Relocating Authority: Japanese Americans Writing to Redress Mass Incarceration, Mira Shimabukuro

Starting from Loomis and Other Stories, Hiroshi Kashiwagi, edited and with an introduction by Tim Yamamura

Taken from the Paradise Isle: The Hoshida Family Story, edited by Heidi Kim and with a foreword by Franklin Odo

BEYOND

The Memoir of a World War II Japanese American Draft Resister of Conscience

THE BETRAYAL

Yoshito Kuromiya

EDITED BY Arthur A. Hansen

UNIVERSITY PRESS OF COLORADO

Louisville

© 2021 by University Press of Colorado

Published by University Press of Colorado
245 Century Circle, Suite 202
Louisville, Colorado 80027

 The University Press of Colorado is a proud member of
the Association of University Presses.

The University Press of Colorado is a cooperative publishing enterprise supported, in part, by Adams State University, Colorado State University, Fort Lewis College, Metropolitan State University of Denver, Regis University, University of Alaska, University of Colorado, University of Denver, University of Northern Colorado, University of Wyoming, Utah State University, and Western Colorado University.

∞ This paper meets the requirements of the ANSI/NISO Z39.48–1992 (Permanence of Paper)

ISBN: 978-1-64642-183-1 (hardcover)
ISBN: 978-1-64642-372-9 (paperback)
ISBN: 978-1-64642-184-8 (ebook)
https://doi.org/10.5876/9781646421848

Library of Congress Cataloging-in-Publication Data

Names: Kuromiya, Yosh, author. | Hansen, Arthur A., editor.
Title: Beyond the betrayal : the memoir of a World War II Japanese American draft resister of conscience / Yoshito Kuromiya ; edited by Arthur A. Hansen.
Other titles: George and Sakaye Aratani Nikkei in the Americas series.
Description: Louisville : University Press of Colorado, 2021. | Series: Nikkei in the Americas | Includes bibliographical references and index.
Identifiers: LCCN 2021034799 (print) | LCCN 2021034800 (ebook) | ISBN 9781646421831 (hardcover) | ISBN 9781646423729 (paperback) | ISBN 9781646421848 (ebook)
Subjects: LCSH: Kuromiya, Yosh. | Heart Mountain Relocation Center (Wyo.) | World War, 1939–1945—Draft resisters—United States—Biography. | Japanese Americans—Forced removal and internment, 1942–1945. | Japanese Americans—Civil rights—History—20th century. | Draft resisters—United States—Biography. | Internment camps—Wyoming—20th century. | World War, 1939–1945—Japanese Americans.
Classification: LCC D810.C82 K87 2021 (print) | LCC D810.C82 (ebook) | DDC 940.53/177787—dc23
LC record available at https://lccn.loc.gov/2021034799
LC ebook record available at https://lccn.loc.gov/2021034800

This publication was made possible, in part, with support from the University of California Los Angeles's Aratani Endowed Chair in Asian American Studies.

Cover illustration by Yoshito Kuromiya. Title-page illustration by Yoshito Kuromiya, ca. 2018.

To the memory of Fred Homi Iriye, whose life was cut short two days before his release from prison. Although he never regained his wrongly taken citizenship rights, his integrity was never questioned. Fred Homi Iriye was indeed a true patriot.

—YOSHITO KUROMIYA

In honor of militant Japanese American journalist James Matsumoto Omura for courageously exercising his freedom of the press rights to support, on constitutional grounds, the military draft challenge of Yoshito Kuromiya and his fellow resisters of conscience at the World War II Heart Mountain concentration camp.

—ARTHUR A. HANSEN

The war challenged Japanese Americans to justify themselves before an America more interested in revenge against the Japanese enemy than in an emerging minority just entering its second generation. The question is, Did it emerge?

—FRANK CHIN, *BORN IN THE USA* (2002, xvii)

CONTENTS

FOREWORD

LAWSON INADA

From out of the abuses,
From out of the cruelties,
From out of the losses,
From out of the tragedies,
Emerges this lucid voice
Of this honorable person.

https://doi.org/10.5876/9781646421848.c000a

PREFACE

ERIC L. MULLER

The book you are holding is an important document.

The past couple of decades have seen the long-overdue emergence of a significant literature on the Nisei draft resistance movements in the War Relocation Authority (WRA) camps of World War II. Nearly all of it, though, has been from the perspective of "outsiders" to those movements—people like myself who were not present to witness them. What is special about this memoir is that it is a detailed account "from within": the penetrating narrative of the draft resistance movement at the Heart Mountain concentration camp in northwest Wyoming from the perspective of a thoughtful and brilliant man who actually participated in it.

Several things distinguish Yosh Kuromiya's account of this important chapter in American history. First, Yosh—and I will speak of him in the present tense, as he lives on through this memoir—is an extraordinarily gifted writer, a natural if ever there was one. When I first interviewed him in the late 1990s, it was evident to me that he had a remarkable command of language; he chose his words carefully and deployed them with precision. But the experience of reading Yosh exceeds even the experience of listening to him. The prose in this volume is crisp and evocative and wry and compelling from first word to last. The draft resistance movement at Heart Mountain relied on the words of its most senior members, pronouncements that could sometimes be stilted and ponderous. They would have done very well to enlist Yosh as their speechwriter.

Second, Yosh is willing to acknowledge dissension and disagreement among the ranks of the young resisters who went to jail and between that group and their

https://doi.org/10.5876/9781646421848.c000b

leadership, the somewhat older men who organized the resistance movement. I can't emphasize enough how new and important this is, or how much richness and humanness Yosh's account adds to our understanding of the dynamics of resistance. For decades the Japanese American community and the scant academic literature have been largely satisfied with caricatures of the young Nisei on both sides of the question of complying with or resisting military service. On this account, those who served were, to a man, heroes and patriots. When the story of the resisters finally began to emerge from the shadows, it followed the same pattern: every man who resisted was cast as a "resister of conscience," motivated by carefully formulated and deeply held convictions about moral and constitutional principle. Yosh is too keen an observer of human nature for such caricatures. He says what no other resister has dared publicly admit: that there were tensions within the movement, that some of the resisters and even some of the leaders occasionally did things that led him to wonder whether everyone was acting for the same reasons and the right reasons. Yosh's memoir reminds us that these men were beset by the sorts of conflicts in motive and interest that would naturally emerge in any group of human beings. We would be well served by a memoir from a Nisei veteran that comparably breaks the caricature of every single Nisei soldier as a heroic patriot, though I do not expect to see one.

Third, Yosh characterizes the wartime and postwar experiences of the larger Japanese American community with uncommon perceptiveness. There is a trope that the community experienced its sufferings with the stoic, noble spirit of *shikata ga nai*—the notion that one endures that which cannot be changed and then emerges with dignity. Yosh suggests that *shikata ga nai* became for many Japanese Americans "a debilitating Pandora's Box of unresolved emotional trauma," a "personal hell." This is a stunning insight, rare if not unique in the literature.

————————

There are few people I've known whom I admire more than Yosh Kuromiya. I had the honor several years ago to invite him to return to Wyoming to participate in the dramatic reading of a play documenting the actions of the Heart Mountain resisters and their kangaroo-court prosecution in the federal courts. Yosh was ninety-one years old. He had been reluctant to return to the scene of his wartime incarceration and persecution, but a key feature of this particular script was its inclusion of Yosh's own words decrying the injustice in how he had been treated. Old Yosh had the opportunity to play young Yosh, and he seized it. Due to his advanced age, he was unable to join the other actors on stage. A floor lamp was brought to his shadowed seat in the auditorium so that he could read his part from there.

This is how I will always remember Yosh: seated in the warm glow of light in the darkness, speaking words of courage and truth.

ACKNOWLEDGMENTS

YOSHITO KUROMIYA

My eternal gratitude to all who, although too numerous to name, played an important role in my being who I am today, for better or worse. And while the outward signs may be far from the image of perfection that we all seek, it is the peace within the soul that ultimately determines the success of each and all our endeavors.

I owe special recognition to those who, while aware of my academic shortcomings, nevertheless encouraged me to express my thoughts in words:

To professor and poet Lawson Inada, who brings music and poetry to all our senses and thereby shares a language common to all mankind.

To journalist Martha Nakagawa for actively searching out key personalities involved in the rarely publicized aspects of our wartime history, that we might better understand who we are.

To Dr. Art Hansen, who consistently and patiently held the doors of public awareness open to us while we struggled to find our voices. It took the better part of a lifetime, but we could not have had a more prestigious doorman than the professor emeritus.

Also, to my four daughters, Suzi, Sharon, Gail, and Miya, without whose constant moral support and unquestioning faith the project may well have suffered an early demise.

I shall be forever indebted to my wife, Irene, for her extreme patience, diligence, and perseverance in typing and retyping the manuscript from my frequently illegible longhand scribbles. A special thanks to Sharon, daughter number two, who unscrambled my jumbled thoughts for clarity and credibility, but without streamlining to the extent that the words were no longer mine. I take full responsibility for any lack of clarity and/or lack of academic sophistication, as well as any grammatical errors or factual discrepancies in this manuscript.

ARTHUR A. HANSEN

Beyond the Betrayal was in a profound sense a collective undertaking. Yoshito "Yosh" Kuromiya's widow, and my longtime friend, Irene, merits much credit and thanks for devotedly assisting Yosh in preparing the original iteration of his autobiographical manuscript. When it was submitted for publication consideration to a reputable West Coast university press, adroitly edited by Professor Diane Fujino of UC Santa Barbara, it was peer-reviewed by two anonymous academic readers. Because only one of the two of them accorded it a positive assessment, the press decided against it being published. Although Fujino expressed a willingness to resubmit the manuscript, with appropriate revisions, to another university press, Kuromiya, then a nonagenarian, favored instead, in the interest of saving time, to issue his memoir as a self-published volume in a limited edition targeted for family members and friends. Fortunately, his four daughters by an earlier marriage (Suzi, Sharon, Gail, and Miya), drew upon their shared appreciation for fine writing as well as their common professional background in graphic design to convert the manuscript into a stunningly attractive book that met with their father's approval before his death in 2018. For voluntarily assuming this labor of filial love, the Kuromiya sisters deserve a great deal of credit as well as my immense appreciation. Gail Kuromiya, who afterward served as her sisters' point person in communications with me, became, in fact if not in name, my indispensable editorial associate.

I am much indebted to the distinguished Sansei poet Lawson Fusao Inada, who encouraged me to write an introduction to the family version of *Beyond the Betrayal*, because this act led me to boldly suggest to the Kuromiya sisters that I be permitted, with Diane Fujino's gracious collegial blessings, to edit the manuscript so that it could be offered for publication to the University Press of Colorado (UPC) and, if accepted, reach the enlarged reading audience of both scholars and the general public that it so rightly warranted (and which, at bottom, Yosh very much desired). The late Lane Ryo Hirabayashi (1952–2020), a giant in the field of Asian American studies, then championed the cause of *Beyond the Betrayal* being included within his well-regarded UPC's Nikkei in the Americas series, a final act of collegiality and friendship rendered to me personally and historical scholarship at large before he added two of his UCLA colleagues, historian Valerie Matsumoto and anthropologist Tritia Toyota, as coeditors for his series. My thanks also go to the two anonymous peer reviewers of *Beyond the Betrayal*, who favored it with overall positive appraisals that were both insightful and constructive.

There are a number of contributors to the final form of *Beyond the Betrayal* who combined to make it an even more special book than it would have been without their intervention. One of these is Frank Chin, the author of the book's powerful epigraph. It was he, more than anyone, who was responsible for the World War II Japanese American draft resisters of conscience—including Yosh Kuromiya—pulling their heroic wartime acts of conscience out of their postwar closets into the harsh light of public debate and, further, preserving their stories for the sake of posterity through his epic documentary novel *Born in the USA* (2002). Another contributor is the aforementioned Lawson Inada, the imaginative writer of *Beyond the Betrayal*'s foreword and afterword—the latter, "Drawing the Line," is dedicated specifically to Yosh Kuromiya—and someone who was allied from the beginning with Frank Chin in giving voice to the draft resisters of conscience. Still a third contributor of note is Eric L. Muller, the author of the most authoritative historical account of the World War II draft resistance movement, *Free to Die for Their Country* (2001), who not only penned the lyrical preface to *Beyond the Betrayal* but also drew upon his legal acumen as an endowed professor of law at the University of North Carolina to correct some misleading factual errors in Yosh Kuromiya's memoir.

To three other people, all of them notable Japanese American journalists who have been critical to the preservation and publicization of the Nisei draft resisters of conscience story and prominent boosters of Yosh Kuromiya, I extend my heartfelt thanks for their assistance with *Beyond the Betrayal*: Martha Nakagawa, whose detailed obituaries of draft resisters are legendary; Kenji Taguma, whose father, Noboru, was an outspoken WWII draft resister; and Frank Abe, whose documentary film *Conscience and the Constitution* (2000) and website resisters .com have together done so much to bring worldwide attention to the Heart Mountain Fair Play Committee and the Heart Mountain inmates who resisted the draft in accordance with that organization's principled position. Another person whose work on the Heart Mountain draft resistance movement that was exceedingly helpful to me in editing *Beyond the Betrayal* was Mike Mackey, especially his too often overlooked but extremely important edited anthology appropriately titled *A Matter of Conscience* (2002). In this same vein, I would like to register my sincere obligation to two filmmakers who featured the Heart Mountain draft resisters in their productions, Emiko Omori for *Rabbit in the Moon* (1999) and Momo Yashima for *A Divided Community* (2012).

I was indeed fortunate to have had the opportunity to informally interview Takashi "Tak" Hoshizaki, who, along with Yosh Kuromiya, was among the contingent of Heart Mountain men who resisted the draft in June 1944 and then were forced to spend two years of a three-year prison sentence at the McNeil Island Federal Correction Institute near Steilacoom, Washington, before being released and later pardoned by President Harry Truman.

Two people who merit special recognition for always having my back in my life and in my work are my historian wife, Debra Gold Hansen, and my closest friend, Kurtis Nakagawa.

Finally, it has been my great privilege to receive the encouragement, support, and guidance of the University Press of Colorado staff, most particularly two very exceptional people, former acquisitions editor Charlotte Steinhardt and current acquisitions editor Rachael Levay. Other UPC staff members that I thank for their respective contributions to the success of *Beyond the Betrayal* are Darrin Pratt, director; Laura Furney, assistant director and managing editor; Daniel Pratt, production manager; Alison Tartt, copyeditor; Beth Svinarich, sales and marketing manager; and Lee Gable, indexer.

EDITOR'S NOTE

ARTHUR A. HANSEN

Owing to Yoshito Kuromiya's manuscript, which was originally authored (but never released) by him for the consumption of family members and selected friends, being now intended as an edited document for a general readership, its title has been slightly modified from "Beyond the Betrayal Lies the Real America: A Personal Account" to "Beyond the Betrayal: The Memoir of a World War II Japanese American Draft Resister of Conscience." Otherwise, apart from minor changes in spelling, word choice, and sentence structure, Kuromiya's manuscript has been faithfully reproduced. All such alterations were transacted "silently," both to avoid being a distraction to readers and for aesthetic reasons. In no cases have the names of people and places provided by the author been changed for the sake of anonymity.

Although the author supplied only a scant number of bibliographical and discursive notes, it was necessary to devise a means of clearly distinguishing these notes from my own editorial notes. Accordingly, the memoirist's notes appear as footnotes, while my far more abundant notes are indicated by arabic numerals and appear as endnotes at the back of the book. Within the memoir proper, all insertions by Yoshito Kuromiya are enclosed in parentheses, while all bracketed insertions are mine.

In respect to my notes, some of them consist in whole or part of corrections or clarifications of Yoshito Kuromiya's information and interpretations that, in 2015, were rendered by Eric L. Muller, an endowed professor of law at the University

https://doi.org/10.5876/9781646421848.c000c

of North Carolina, Chapel Hill, and the author of the most authoritative book on the subject of World War II Nisei draft resistance, *Free to Die for Their Country: The Story of the Japanese American Draft Resisters in World War II* (2001). Muller's insightful and detailed critical assessment of a final draft version of the manuscript prepared by Kuromiya, which was passed along to me by his four daughters after his death in 2018, has been of incalculable value to me in safeguarding the historical accuracy of the present volume's contents.

To avoid possible confusion by readers over the use of Japanese American generational terms, their respective meanings are as follows: *Issei*, immigrant generation, denied, until 1952, US citizenship; *Nisei*, US-born citizen children of Issei; *Kibei*, Nisei educated in Japan; *Sansei*, third-generation Japanese Americans; *Yonsei*, fourth-generation Japanese Americans. As for the term *Nikkei*, it is employed generically to designate all Americans of Japanese ancestry.

Beyond the Betrayal

INTRODUCTION

A Remarkable Man of Consciousness, Conscience, and Constitutionalism

ARTHUR A. HANSEN

There are many different types of memoirs. That authored by Yoshito "Yosh" Kuromiya (1923–2018), *Beyond the Betrayal*, is primarily a transformational one. Its dominant theme is how during his lifetime he repeatedly overcame challenging circumstances, the most significant of them by far being his 1944 decision as a World War II Japanese American inmate at Wyoming's Heart Mountain concentration camp to resist the military draft. Although a total of some 300 other inmates in the ten War Relocation Authority (WRA)–administered incarceration centers made the same choice as Kuromiya, he alone has produced an autobiographical volume that explores in depth the short- and long-range causes and consequences of his fateful wartime action.

When reading Kuromiya's memoir, I was powerfully struck by three interwoven strands of his personality expressed within it that help to explain why he is especially well suited to convey to the public the generic plight of the Nisei draft resisters, notwithstanding that each resister's experience is necessarily distinctive. As foreshadowed in the title of this introductory essay, the three salient components of Kuromiya's character showcased in *Beyond the Betrayal* are consciousness, conscience, and constitutionalism.

While eluding precise definition, "consciousness" has been characterized in common parlance as the state or quality of being aware of an external object or something within oneself, or put a slightly different way, as the fact of awareness by the mind of itself and the world. As for "conscience," it has been ordinarily

https://doi.org/10.5876/9781646421848.c000d   3

construed to mean the inner sense of what is right or wrong in one's conduct or
motives, impelling one toward right action. In the case of "constitutionalism," it
essentially describes one's belief in and support for the basic principles and laws
of a nation or state that determine the powers and duties of the government and
guarantee certain designated rights to the people.

With such operational definitions for this trio of behavioral qualities now formulated, we can next proceed to delineate how Kuromiya has exemplified them
within the text of his life-review narrative.

In respect to consciousness, although Kuromiya does not mention this word
per se until chapter 10, upon reading the four-paragraph segment of his initial
chapter about the first days he spent in August 1942 as an inmate at the Heart
Mountain concentration camp in Wyoming, we are made acutely mindful that
our narrator is a complex person, both a writer and an artist, one who assays
his surroundings, scrutinizes his place (and that of others) within them, and
explores the nexus between these two processes. "As in a strange dream," records
Kuromiya, "my US citizenship had vanished and in its place were rows upon rows
of tar-papered barracks encircled by a barbed wire fence with guard towers at
intervals, manned by armed soldiers barely visible in the wind-driven dust. It was
all so surreal; I wasn't sure what to make of it." Fortunately for readers, the stream
of such manifest consciousness as revealed in this passage suffuses the remaining
pages of Kuromiya's redolent memoir.

While direct and indirect references to consciousness in *Beyond the Betrayal* are
few in number, they are nonetheless quite significant in illuminating how exceedingly Kuromiya prized this quality. His initial allusion to consciousness in chapter
10 relative to the new consciousness of the so-called "Age of Aquarius" of the 1960s[1]
is enlarged upon four chapters later, wherein he links this epoch to "a revolutionary
transformation of man's collective consciousness" and foretells that this development would be a "long, arduous one . . . [with] no turning back." In between these
two references, and more relevant to his education and budding career in landscape architecture, Kuromiya makes mention of environmental consciousness, a
concept that he was introduced to in one of his assigned texts at California State
Polytechnic University, Pomona. This book, authored by Garrett Eckbo (who later
employed Kuromiya in his noteworthy firm), was a landmark publication entitled
Landscape for Living.[2] This volume impressed upon Kuromiya that environmental
consciousness "was everyone's responsibility, and the landscape architect must play
a pivotal role in bringing about that awareness through his work." Moreover, when
he was hired by Eckbo's progressive company, Kuromiya viewed this opportunity
as symbolic of "a new awakening of environmentalism," a fortuitous development
that was magnified in significance because of being coincident with the political
stirrings of a new generation of human rights consciousness that swept the US and,
in the process, "upset the status quo and challenged smug apathy."

It is perhaps one direct and two indirect references to consciousness by Kuromiya in the latter sections of *Beyond the Betrayal* that serve best to penetrate to the core significance of this state of heightened awareness for him. In recalling the letter and telephone exchanges he had with his much-admired friend Michi Nishiura Weglyn[3] in the waning months of her life, Kuromiya writes: "We agreed that our spiritual nature was our true identity, and that our physical manifestation was the means through which we relate to the dimensional world that is essentially an illusion. Illusions end once they serve their purpose in the dimensional realm, and the spirit moves on to further enhance universal consciousness."

The two indirect references that Kuromiya makes to consciousness both revolve around a group known as The Prosperos.[4] Members of this school of thought believe that God is pure consciousness. It was through his second wife, Ruth, that Kuromiya, who was never a member of any church, encountered The Prosperos. He became "intensely interested" in this group, primarily because its general philosophy was "based on the premise of teaching one *how* to think as opposed to *what* to think." Kuromiya was so enamored with this philosophy, in fact, that he chose to end his memoir's epilogue with a poetic stanza he attributed to The Prosperos:

The truth is that which is so.
That which is truth is not so.
Therefore, Truth is all there is.

While consciousness was assuredly the backdrop milieu and psychological precondition for everything that transpired in Yoshito Kuromiya's creative life, including the writing of his memoir, what assumes the foreground in *Beyond the Betrayal* are his profound respect for and fierce allegiance to conscience and constitutionalism. The coupling of these two items in terms of the World War II Japanese American experience were accorded prominence most openly in Frank Abe's 2000 documentary film, *Conscience and the Constitution*, in which Kuromiya appeared. But this pair of elements was also spotlighted in five other extraordinary productions that surfaced at approximately the same time and in all of which Kuromiya played a significant part: Emiko Omori's documentary film, *Rabbit in the Moon* (1999); William Hohri's edited compilation of commentaries, *Resistance: Challenging America's Wartime Internment of Japanese-American* (2000); Eric L. Muller's historical monograph, *Free to Die for Their Country: The Story of the Japanese American Draft Resisters in World War II* (2001); Frank Chin's documentary novel, *Born in the USA: A Story of Japanese America, 1889–1947* (2002); and Mike Mackey's edited anthology of essays, *A Matter of Conscience: Essays on the World War II Heart Mountain Draft Resistance Movement* (2002).[5]

Even though Kuromiya overwhelmingly invokes the matter of conscience in his memoir in relationship to his 1944 decision at the Heart Mountain camp to resist being drafted into the military, he sometimes employs it in a different context. For example, his very first utilization of the term, which appears in chapter 1, is summoned in connection with an incident involving his Issei father, Hisamitsu, which had occurred well before his own birth in 1923. When Hisamitsu discovered with great certainty that one of his heretofore trusted Issei business partners had been bilking the firm's treasury, he found himself in a dilemma. On the one hand, he could confront his friend and alert the others partners, but he reasoned that to do so would result in the offending friend being humiliated and himself having to bear the disgrace of being a snitch. On the other hand, he could simply remain silent and resign from the partnership. His wife, Hana, without hesitation, advised him to "Reveal all!" But, as Yoshito Kuromiya surmised in his memoir, "for Hisamitsu it wasn't that simple. Certainly, he was outraged at being duped, especially by a trusted friend, but the issue was neither about the friend nor even the money. It was about honor. It was about the age-old tradition of a samurai and his sense of honor—or, if you will, his own conscience and personal integrity. His, not theirs." So Hisamitsu, acting on his conscience, promptly turned in his resignation. Toward the end of his memoir, Kuromiya returns to the subject of his father's conscience when commemorating his death in 1969. As expressed in his words, Hisamitsu "never preached virtue [but] . . . merely followed his conscience." This, then, was the family legacy that Kuromiya inherited, to utilize throughout his life as his own conscience dictated. Coming increasingly to believe that "one's conscience is in a sense the language of one's soul," Kuromiya drew unfailingly upon his conscience during the darkest days of his imprisonment at Heart Mountain and the McNeil Island Federal Penitentiary when it was his "constant companion and solitary counsel."

On another occasion in *Beyond the Betrayal*, Kuromiya utilizes the term conscience in the service of a species of gallows humor that bears upon his imprisonment and that of other Japanese American draft resisters and conscientious objectors at the McNeil Island prison. "One morning," writes Kuromiya, "the warden arrived to find a large banner strung across the second-story dorm windows which read: 'If Warden Stevens had a conscience, he would be a CO' (conscientious objector). He immediately ordered the confinement to the dorms of all the COs, which was about one-fourth of our population. He questioned them individually. One CO told us later that he had asked the warden why he was accusing only the COs. The warden retorted angrily, 'You're the only bastards on this island who know how to spell "conscience"!'"

Kuromiya's other references to conscience in his memoir are anything but a laughing matter. In chapter 6 he relates that when, in early 1944, at Heart Mountain he was informed that the US government had changed his draft classification, along with that of other Nisei, from 4-C (enemy alien ineligible for conscription) to 1-A (eligible for conscription), he was gladdened that he was "no longer considered sinister," but was dismayed that the reinstatement of his civil rights had not accompanied this change of draft status. He thus became determined that he "could not in good conscience bear arms under the existing conditions." Later in this chapter Kuromiya enlarges upon the rationale for his intrepid decision. "Had the mainland United States been threatened with invasion," he reasoned, "I would not have taken this stand. But to join in the killing and maiming in foreign lands, not because they were the enemy but in order to prove my loyalty to a government that imprisoned me and my family without hearings or charges, I felt would be self-serving, irresponsible, and totally without conscience."

Then, in chapter 8, having allowed that he had thought the name of the organization that coalesced at Heart Mountain to champion the draft resistance movement on constitutional grounds, the Fair Play Committee, was "rather silly," Kuromiya quickly added that "there was nothing silly about the issues it would soon challenge, nor the compelling principles it would invoke to jar the conscience of all who believed in the sanctity of citizens' rights."

Two chapters farther along, after Kuromiya reveals that in 1947, just a few days before he and his fellow draft resisters at the McNeil Island Federal Penitentiary were to be released, one of the most intelligent and respected of them, Fred Iriye—to whom he dedicates *Beyond the Betrayal*—was "accidentally" electrocuted when training the inmate who was to assume his vacated position as supervisor for the penal facility's entire electrical power system. On the train that took the released draft resisters from Washington to California, reflects Kuromiya, they were absorbed by silently trying to fathom a possible deeper meaning for the "unfortunate accident" suffered by Fred Iriye. Seeking to give retrospective voice to their collective questioning on this occasion, Kuromiya offers this reverie: "Was it some sort of *bachi* [retribution]? Was it instead punishment for self-righteous arrogance? Why Fred? He certainly wasn't guilty of arrogance. And if not Fred, then who? Maybe all of us—and Fred paid the price. Yet, why should we be punished for what our conscience demanded of us as the only honorable choice, given the circumstances? And where indeed is the arrogance in defending the constitutional principles we swore to uphold?"

In chapter 15 Kuromiya first reflects back on the onset of the war when among Japanese Americans "ethics became a matter of political expedience rather than one of personal integrity guided by one's conscience," and then observes how astounded he was in the aftermath of the war to find out how many of his fellow resisters not only "felt it best to let sleeping dogs lie" but also even suggested that he "not be so outspoken about civil justice, constitutional responsibilities, and matters of conscience." Ultimately, he concluded that "one's conscience . . . is a very personal matter." As a consequence, he was very transparent about his prison experiences and on one occasion talked freely and candidly about them to his young daughters, after which they good-naturedly presented him with a tiny doll attired in a convict's striped suit with a ball and chain attached to one of its ankles. Regarding this doll as a medal of honor, it hung from Kuromiya's desk lamp until the day he died.

In the penultimate chapter of *Beyond the Betrayal* Kuromiya pays homage to three special people he interacted with among many other extraordinary personalities in the post-WWII "psychological and spiritual recovery period of the Japanese American people": James "Jimmie" Matsumoto Omura,[6] Michi Nishiura Weglyn, and Ehren Watada.[7] For him, "all of them, in their own time and in their own way, refused to remain silent." Although cognizant of Weglyn's strict adherence to conscience, Kuromiya makes particular reference to Omura and Watada in this regard. Echoing what he had previously written about his father, Kuromiya extols Omura by noting that, "like Papa, Jimmie never spoke of high moral standards, nor of always following his conscience. He merely lived by them. That is, no doubt, why I knew he was a man of impeccable integrity. He reminded me of Papa." With respect to First Lieutenant Watada, who in November 2006 refused on the grounds of conscience to deploy his troops to Iraq and faced the possibility of both a court martial and prison time because he saw no legal or moral justification for the US attacking that country, Kuromiya felt a powerful experiential bond with him. What linked their two acts of resistance, which spanned a period of more than six decades, was that both could bear witness to the same hard truth—"conscience sometimes comes at a high price."

In his epilogue, Kuromiya turns from those individuals he raptly admires to the Japanese American Citizens League, an organization that he roundly condemns. To his mind, the JACL owed an apology to the entire Japanese American community for "falsely claiming" to represent their interest while in actuality "conspiring with our government to surrender our civil and human rights." Moreover, when the JACL leadership urged the mandatory induction of male Japanese Americans from behind the barbed wire of their wartime concentration camps under "the pretext of proving their loyalty," it effectively prevented each man from exercising his right as a citizen "to serve or not according to his conscience."

As for constitutionalism, while Kuromiya never refers in his memoir to this specific term as such, it is pervasively evoked by him through other words with a common base, such as constitution, constitutionality, constitutional, and unconstitutional. For example, in chapter 3, he employs this language in conjunction with the JACL. In wantonly providing the FBI with the names of supposedly "dangerous" Issei in the wake of Japan's attack on Pearl Harbor on December 7, 1941, charges Kuromiya, this older Nisei-dominated organization "apparently regarded the need to prove *their* loyalty to the US as a higher priority than the defense of the constitutional and human rights of their own people." This action made it evident to him that the JACL could not be trusted to assume the leadership of the Japanese American community, since it demonstrated starkly that the group's leadership too readily set aside "constitutional principles" when "confronted with issues of political convenience." Indeed, these self-appointed Nisei leaders were so anxious to accommodate government orders, however unjust, as a safe survival course for Americans of Japanese ancestry that, in the process, "the US Constitution was abandoned."

In chapter 5, in reference to his incarceration experience at Heart Mountain, Kuromiya resorts to scathing irony when reacting to the War Relocation Authority's plans to build a new high school in the middle of the camp: "Thus, our white captors could teach our children the beauty of our United States Constitution while in captivity." Later in this chapter he communicates to readers of *Beyond the Betrayal* what he believes to be the inescapable issue, then and now, of the World War II Japanese American incarceration experience: "*What is the citizen's rightful response to constitutional transgressions?*"

Within the succeeding chapter, Kuromiya discusses his responses to the two key questions on the highly controversial and contested "loyalty questionnaire" administered to all Japanese American adult inmates in early 1943 by the US government and endorsed by the JACL. He explains that he answered a somewhat reluctant yes to question 28 (Will you swear unqualified allegiance to the United States of America and faithfully defend the United States from any or all attacks by foreign or domestic forces, and foreswear any form of allegiance or obedience to the Japanese emperor, or any other foreign government, power, or organization?), precisely because he had never ever sworn allegiance to the Japanese emperor. On the other hand, he states that his response to question 27 (Are you willing to serve in the armed forces of the United States on combat duty wherever ordered?) was a conditional yes, the condition being that he "first be accorded equal constitutional rights as Caucasian American citizens."

Farther along in chapter 6, when recollecting his attendance during the dawning of the 1944 year at a mess hall meeting of the newly formed Heart Mountain Fair Play Committee, Kuromiya recounts that he was "captivated" by its chair, the middle-aged Nisei from Hawai'i, Kiyoshi Okamoto, not merely because of his direct demeanor and "brutally crude" language, laced with expletives, but also, and perhaps chiefly, because "he seemed to have an impressive knowledge of constitutional law, indispensable in any civil-rights forum." During attendance at future FPC meetings, he came to respect the other members of the group's steering committee, seeing them as principled men "who knowingly jeopardized their own and their families' welfare in an effort to regain dignity, if not justice, for all inmates." Thus, on or about March 16, 1944, and not altogether surprisingly, when Kuromiya received his notice to report for his physical exam prior to induction, he refused to comply. This message reverberated in his mind: "NO! This is *my* country! This is *my* Constitution! This is *my* Bill of Rights! I am here finally to defend them. I regret that I had surrendered my freedom. I shall not continue to surrender my dignity nor the dignity of the US Constitution!"[8]

At the beginning of chapter 8, when ruminating about the spirit that gave rise to the Heart Mountain draft resistance movement, Kuromiya opines that it was rooted in "the ancient samurai tradition of honor, commitment, and perseverance." But in America these values were not, as in Japan, rendered on behalf of a sovereign state or lord but in support of the "Constitution and the Bill of Rights." Then, when taking up the six-day mass trial that he participated in during June 1944 as a defendant with sixty-two other Heart Mountain draft resisters of conscience at the federal district court in Cheyenne, wherein they were declared guilty of draft evasion by the presiding judge and sentenced to three years in federal prison, Kuromiya characterizes it as a "travesty of justice" representing "yet another blow to our now fragile hope of ever establishing credibility in the idea that the Constitution and the Bill of Rights are the supreme law of the land." Still, he reasoned, an appeal of the verdict would have to be made and a precedent set, "if, in fact, the constitutional integrity of our case was our ultimate goal."

Following a sprinkling of references to constitutional matters throughout the next nine chapters, in chapter 18 these matters occupy center stage. What arguably sparked Kuromiya's active involvement in the post–Civil Liberties Act of 1988 campaign to redress the World War II mistreatment of the Heart Mountain draft resistance movement—an activism that had been retarded by his "temporary self-imposed exile" from the Japanese American community—was his participation in the February 21, 1993, dramatic program, *Return of the Fair Play Committee.* Scripted by Frank Chin, the fourth-generation Chinese American playwright and civil rights champion, it was held at the Centenary Methodist Church, located in the heart of Los Angeles' Little Tokyo district. This event, which brought together the leaders of the FPC and draft resisters from Heart Mountain and some of the other WRA camps with others who supported their actions during (and even) after the war, provided the catalyst for the development of *Conscience and the Constitution,* the documentary film by Chin and Frank Abe (which Abe alone brought to completion in 2000).

It was hoped by Kuromiya that this program and film and similar progressive happenings, building upon the efforts of a select number of reform-minded Nisei and Sansei a decade or more earlier, would bridge the "monstrous chasm" between the mainstream community and "all who protested the inhumane, unconstitutional treatment we were subjected to by the government—abetted by the insidious mind-control tactics of the Japanese American Citizens League." While he was guardedly skeptical that this healing process would occur, Kuromiya took heart that the reform movement within his racial-ethnic community, in which he was increasingly taking part, had as its focus "the legal and moral supremacy of the US Constitution and a citizen's fundamental duty to defend it." He was also inspired by the corresponding upsurge nationwide in cultural diversity, which in concert with technical advancement, had the potential to propel America to world leadership "under the humanitarian principles of our Constitution." At the same time, he was intensely aware that if his community and his country were to experience future redemption, people like himself who had "witnessed the catastrophic barrage of violations of citizens' rights, the very principles upon which our Constitution is based and is the heart and soul of our country, must not remain silent."

Beyond the Betrayal

The Memoir of a World War II
Japanese American
Draft Resister of Conscience

FIGURE 1.1. *The Mountain.* Watercolor by author, 1943 (Division of Political and Military History, National Museum of American History, Smithsonian Institution).

I

IN THE BEGINNING

August 1942. We arrived at Heart Mountain in the middle of a dust storm and none of us knew what to expect. We certainly didn't know some of us would become prisoners of war, war heroes, draft resisters, or even deportees. As a nineteen-year-old junior college student from California, I was awestruck to suddenly find myself somewhere in Wyoming as a "person of Japanese ancestry." As in a strange dream, my US citizenship had vanished and in its place were rows upon rows of tar-papered barracks encircled by a barbed wire fence with guard towers at intervals, manned by armed soldiers barely visible in the wind-driven dust. It was all so surreal; I wasn't sure what to make of it.

The wind howled all that night and the dust crept in through the cracks of our unfinished barrack room, but by daybreak all was eerily quiet. I stepped outside as if awakening from a bad dream. Then I saw it. There on the not too distant horizon to the west stood the mountain for which the camp was named, Heart Mountain in all its glory, with the rising sun reflecting off its distinctive eastern face on this cloudless morning, as if to apologize for the rude "greetings" of the night before. The mountain was majestic.

In the following days I did several sketches of the mountain in its various moods, which often reflected my own moods. It was the only sanity I was experiencing at the time. It was the only reality I could rely on. All else had to be an illusion, and in time would all blow away with the dust storm, and only the mountain would remain—or so it seemed to be telling me.

https://doi.org/10.5876/9781646421848.c001

I tried to convey its message to my parents, who must have been questioning the wisdom of immigrating to this "land of freedom and opportunity" which had turned into twenty-six years of hard labor, insults, humiliation, and finally a concentration camp in the middle of nowhere.

I picture them as newlyweds in the lush green countryside of Japan, a far cry from the desolate, windy plains of Wyoming.

———————————

The year was 1916 in Takamatsu, a small village in the prefecture of Okayama-ken, Japan. Here the primary occupation, as one would guess, was the tending of rice crops, evidenced by the endless paddies flooding the land between raised dikes, the glistening surfaces reflecting the sun's rays not unlike the panes of a gigantic window covering the earth as far as the eye could see. Indeed, it would seem the harvest of this humble but dedicated enterprise could feed all the hungry of the world and still have enough for the annual local *mochi* (cooked and pounded glutinous rice) festival.

But on this day the unfortunate demise of the world's hungry was the least concern of Hisamitsu Kuromiya. Hisamitsu was twenty-nine, and finally able to meet the *baishakunin* (matchmaker) who had painstakingly searched family records to find a suitable and willing bride for him, a bride who was graced with the highest form of feminine elegance, poise, character, and charm, as befitted a man of his samurai heritage. After all, hadn't he shown courage in venturing across the fearsome ocean to America at the young age of nineteen to seek his fortunes on his own terms, and in spite of being the eldest son and therefore heir to the family wealth had he remained in Japan? Hisamitsu was a proud man with profound respect for tradition, but he would never allow tradition to define him. He would never accept rewards he hadn't earned by his own sweat. Neither would he ever surrender to poverty—to hard times perhaps, which seemed the norm in his young life, but never to poverty. In a sense, Hisamitsu was his own worst enemy. But he would abide by his own high standards, for he was an honorable, if stubborn, man.

Later that same day clouds would gather and the once joyful rice paddies would darken, obediently reflecting the gloom of the skies and becoming ominous bottomless pits ready to devour any unsuspecting soul careless enough to venture too close to the edge of the road. The *baishakunin* assured him that he had faithfully fulfilled all conditions of their agreement, except one, that the prospective mate be of no higher education than high school. The *baishakunin* considered it a minor condition, but Hisamitsu found this unacceptable. In America he had already suffered the humiliation of being regarded as of a subhuman race by the general public, a public which *he* regarded as culturally inferior. He was determined not to be humiliated in his own household by a spouse who would regard herself his intellectual superior. Alas, the girl that the hapless *baishakunin* had selected did indeed meet all the conditions Hisamitsu had requested and more, but she also had just completed a highly respected college course and had graduated with honors. Out of fear of losing his fees, the *baishakunin* begged for time to find a suitable replacement, but Hisamitsu had to return to his "important" responsibilities in America (which turned out to be that of a houseboy/gardener on the estate of a wealthy though kindly businessman).

Unbeknownst to the *baishakunin*, however, there was no need to fret. Even though Hisamitsu was adamant regarding the terms of their agreement and was bitterly disappointed in the agent's oversight, he had no intention of stiffing the poor soul of his anticipated fees. For Hisamitsu was an honorable man who would pay his debts, even if it meant returning to America empty-handed, and even though it might be another six to eight years before he could muster the funds to resume his search for a bride.

Hisamitsu happened to spot an attractive young woman in the village square and was so intrigued with her apparent innocence and charm he beckoned the *baishakunin* to check out her background. As fate would have it, Hana Tada was sixteen years old and was expected to enroll in college the following year. She had a brother two years older and a personal handmaid who attended to all her needs. The family was of samurai stock, highly respected in the small village, quite well-to-do, and had no intention of giving up their only daughter to a renegade from America. Somehow through the incessant, desperate pleadings of the *baishakunin*, and perhaps additional monetary incentives from the *baishakunin* himself, the reluctant parents relented, much to Hisamitsu's delight. The sun reappeared for Hisamitsu. But for Hana that day was especially dark and grew darker in the days and years to follow. Little did she suspect her carefree days of laughter and joy had vanished with the sunlight. Womanhood was thrust upon her like a Grim Reaper. But Hisamitsu was not the villain. Hisamitsu was a lonely man seeking a companion who would provide him with a family to share in the richness and promise of America, *Land of the Free! Land of Opportunity!* Or so he dreamt.

The samurai warriors were a product of the feudal era in ancient Japan. They were the defenders of the nobility, from whom they received honors and were encouraged to elevate their skills as an art form. Some samurai pursued a philosophical path of insight and self-discipline in an effort to transcend the mundane limitations of the human condition. The samurai were also protectors of the common populace, the merchants, the craftsmen, the artisans, the educators, the healers, the entertainers, the fisherman, and most of all the farmers who opened their doors to them in times of impending invasion from hostile enemy thugs. It was in the interest of the nobility that the samurai protect the villagers on whom they themselves depended to provide all the services, comforts, necessities, and amusement for their elite lifestyle.

The basic stabilizer for this symbiotic relationship was a social caste system which limited everyone to the preestablished occupational level of the family of birth. Thus, once a farmer, always a farmer; once a samurai, always a samurai. The samurai seemed to enjoy a freedom and privilege few others were allowed. He could become a craftsman or a farmer and who would complain? Could it be the samurai was the Joker in the ancient Japanese cultural deck of cards? In any case, perhaps because of the uniquely superior role of the samurai in the caste system, the hiring of a *baishakunin* to attest to the purity of a samurai family bloodline became a tradition which was still common practice in 1916, long after the samurai himself became extinct.

And so it was that Hana Tada became the latest victim of this ancient custom which robbed her of the innocence of her childhood and perhaps her dreams of meeting and being courted by one of her own choosing. But, of course, tradition is no one's fault, while at the same time everyone's fault. How was a sixteen-year-old girl in 1916 Japan to understand that?

After a hasty but properly elaborate and ritualistic wedding ceremony and reception (where Hana no doubt felt more like a spectator than the main attraction), quick good-byes were exchanged with a few close friends and classmates who also seemed to be in a bit of a daze as events happened so suddenly and unexpectedly. It would take them and Hana's parents and brother a few days to realize that Hana was leaving them, perhaps forever, and it wasn't Hana's fault. Hisamitsu with his new bride would embark for America within the next few days.

———————

Hana was amazed at the huge liner moored at the harbor in Yokohama. It seemed incredible that so much steel could float on water. She looked at Hisamitsu for reassurance and received a look of impatience and exasperation. "Of course, it'll float! Haven't I crossed the ocean twice without so much as getting wet?"

The first time was when he ventured to America at nineteen, and the second when he traveled back to get Hana. Yet, he had to admit to himself the memory of his own terror when he first saw the vast ocean and almost decided to turn back.

Hana's apprehensions would soon turn to humiliation and disgust as they carried their handbags down each set of narrow metal steps, down, down deeper into the bowels of the steel monster until they came upon a large open arena with a thousand cots neatly lined up. *"Nan-da, shir-do cu-ra-su?"* (What, third class?) She openly expressed her shock and dismay and silently thought to herself, "Samurai, indeed!"

In spite of Hana's apprehensions, the ship did not sink. And though the accommodations were crude, they proved to be less depressing than anticipated. Many of the travelers turned out to be newlywed couples like Hana and Hisamitsu. Others were "picture brides" eager to meet their handsome princes and future husbands in distant America. Among the women, mostly in their late teens or early twenties, there was an air of optimism and anticipation of a new adventure free of the social constraints of Japan. But after a few days of exchanging personal backgrounds, much of which were, no doubt, gross exaggerations or outlandish fabrications tailored to impress new friends, a double sickness overwhelmed many of the women. The twin ailments were seasickness and homesickness. All the gaiety and socializing came to an abrupt end and was replaced with incessant sobbing and moping between frantic dashes to the communal bathroom. The dinner halls were almost empty. Of course, the choppy seas were of no help. But later as the seas calmed down and equilibrium was somewhat restored, the tittering and occasional shrieks of laughter gradually resumed. The ship was not sinking after all, although some had been so miserable that they would not have cared if it did, or perhaps had hoped that they would have to turn back due to some mechanical glitch that made it unwise to continue the long voyage still ahead.

To the delight of the already travel-weary passengers, land was eventually sighted in the far-off haze of the horizon. The exciting news beckoned all to scamper to the deck as the land mass became larger and larger. "Is this America?" many asked hopefully. "No," was the disappointing reply, "It's just the halfway point, but we will get to go ashore for a few hours while they replenish the ship's fuel and our kitchen supplies."

They entered a calm, safe harbor on the coast of an island that one day would play a critical, historic, and painfully personal role in the life of each passenger. The island was O'ahu, Hawai'i. The harbor was most likely Honolulu Harbor, just south of Pearl Harbor.

Hana firmly gripped Hisamitsu's hand while her other hand had some difficulty unclenching its hold on the rope handrail. The narrow strip of black water far below the gangplank appeared ominous, much like the rice paddies of Takamatsu on a cloudy day. Yes, like that day that had changed her life forever. With the impatient pushing from behind they finally reached the wooden dock, which seemed surprisingly stable. The way everything was supposed to be, thought Hana.

Suddenly a dark-skinned, heavyset woman threw a flowery, sweet-smelling necklace over Hana's head. Grinning from plump cheek to plump cheek, she joyously exclaimed "Aloha!"

Hana thought in bewilderment, *"Nan-da, aho-da?"* (What? Stupid?). Hisamitsu quickly explained to her that it was the traditional Hawaiian welcome, and that the lei was a symbol of friendship. Hana, embarrassed, bowed an apology to the lady and murmured *"Arigato gozai masu"* (thank you very much) as the crowd rudely pushed her along. They spent most of the afternoon visiting the small shops that were filled with gifts and souvenirs. Hana eagerly bought trinkets for her friends in Japan until Hisamitsu reminded her it would be a long time before she would see them again. What a spoilsport, she thought to herself.

Hana was delighted to discover many of the people there spoke Japanese, and some were recent immigrants from Japan themselves. To her, most of the darker-skinned people seemed friendlier, more open, and had a spontaneity and sincerity about them. They appeared less affluent in their attire, but didn't seem to care. And even though they held a respectful awe of that which was regarded as traditional or sacred and not to be questioned, they were always eager to pull out all the stops when it happened to involve a luau or other joyful celebration.

On the other hand, the lighter-skinned people seemed more self-contained, aloof, and at times even pompous, obviously confident of inherent superiority as providers of commerce and Christianity to the heathen islands. This, of course, turned out to be exploitation and not salvation, much like what had almost occurred in Japan sixty years earlier. They had little interest in the native customs and traditions, but tolerated them as harmless, primitive indulgences. As Hana mused over the apparent disparity, Hisamitsu hustled her along as it was almost time to reboard the ship.

That night she dreamt she heard a baby crying. Groping about in the half-light amid a chorus of off-key snoring, she followed the sobbing sound between the steel cots and came upon an infant girl with dark, chubby, tear-stained cheeks. She was wearing the lei that Hana had received earlier that day. Upon seeing Hana she broke out in a wide grin, stood up, and started swaying her hips in a hula dance, laughing all the while. Then she suddenly disappeared. Hana awoke with a start and realized it was Hisamitsu snoring beside her. She instinctively uttered to herself softly, "Aro-ha" [Japanese-accented "Aloha"]. Hana lay awake the rest of that night wondering what it all meant. What important message was she missing? Could it be a dark omen of what awaited her in America? Suddenly she felt cold.

Hana shared her dream with no one, not even Hisamitsu, fearful they might think her strange or a little "different." She spent more time alone on deck, absorbed with the vastness of the ocean. So much of nothing, she thought, just water, lots of water. She wondered how long it would take to reach the bottom if she somehow slipped over the rail and fell into the ocean. Indeed, how long would it take to even hit the water, she wondered, as she viewed the waves that lapped against the side of the ship far below as if beckoning her to join them.

She wondered also about Tomoye-san, her nursemaid-confidante and best friend, who had raised her since she was a baby. Her brother, as the firstborn son, seemed to get all the parental attention. She was, after all, just a girl-child. Tomoye was like a big sister. But in the rush and confusion, Hana had had little time to exchange tearful good-byes with her. Surely, they wouldn't keep her there, as Hana was the only reason for her to be there and now Hana was gone, perhaps forever. She must write to her as soon as they reached America. Who cared how deep the ocean was?

Hisamitsu came running up to her, sweat pouring down what appeared to be a new wrinkle on his face. He was almost twice her age and she had wondered why her parents would marry her off to such an old man, but being an obedient child, she never openly questioned their decision. Looking after her seemed to have caused new wrinkles on Hisamitsu's face. He tried to cover up his panic, but nonetheless admonished her for wandering off alone. Even in Hisamitsu's presence Hana had felt very alone, but she obediently bowed her head in apology for her thoughtlessness.

The rest of the voyage was somewhat uneventful. Hana stayed close to Hisamitsu except when she or he had to visit the bathroom. Observing his interactions with other passengers and crew members, Hana realized her husband, while far from a dashing Lothario, and not even remotely romantically inclined, held a dignity and self-assurance about himself, exuded sincerity and honesty in his affairs, and was compassionate and generous to a fault. Even though he exhibited traces of the traditional gender superiority of all the men of Japan, especially those of samurai heritage, he never used it to degrade or disparage his fellow man (or woman).

Hisamitsu was truly a gentle, humble, and, yes, honorable man. She no longer saw him as old, but rather, patient and wise. She silently thanked the clumsy *baishakunin* for bringing him into her life and vowed to entrust herself to his better judgment until such a time that *she* would have to care for *him*. Hisamitsu, meanwhile, sensed an affirmation of his instincts about the hidden treasures lying within the outwardly frivolous teenager he had spotted in the village square. Thus, their relationship became one of personal choice, not of tradition and obligation. Although their voyage may have seemed uneventful to the casual observer, the inner voyage was far greater than the depth of the ocean and the span between Japan and America. With few words spoken and against all odds the spirit of Hisamitsu and spirit of Hana had merged into one.

Hisamitsu, though not a highly educated man, was compassionate enough to realize that Hana would be totally vulnerable to the many slights and insults she would encounter in America, just as he himself had been shocked and confused to discover a somewhat different America than he had envisioned. Hana, who knew only the security of a social structure in Japan that favored her family in almost all respects, would be faced with the senseless hostility and humiliation Hisamitsu had endured, being perceived as subhuman. The lust for money which brought him here initially would prove to be the very demon that would cause

others to treat him thus, viewing him as a sly, cunning competitor. His very diligence and industriousness would threaten those who viewed him as coveting that
which they considered theirs and theirs alone, namely the entire country. Hana
would now become fair game for the same hostility.

Hisamitsu must somehow prepare Hana and protect her from her own despair
that could overtake her eventually, a despair he felt he was responsible for expos-
ing her to. But fear was the last thing he wanted to introduce into her heretofore
unchallenged innocence. Perhaps the *baishakunin* was right. Perhaps Hisamitsu
had been overprotective of his own frail ego. Nevertheless, he must now warn her
of the disillusionment that surely lay ahead for her, that she should not get her
hopes too high as the reality might be quite devastating to her.

Do not despair, he admonished her. He suggested to her that whatever her initial reaction when they reached America, to remember *shikataganai* (that's how
things are and there is nothing we can do about it). Fatalistic perhaps, but realistic
under the circumstances. He implied hope by imploring her to *gambare* (to per-
severe, bearing the pain of disappointment). "The power to overcome lies within
you, but will require your forbearance until the time is right and you will see the
real America which will reinstate your hopes. Have faith in yourself! Have faith in
America—the *real* America!"

Hisamitsu had no evidence that his words were understood by the naïve, fun-
loving teenager. Indeed, he wasn't sure he understood them himself. But somehow in his desperation to soften the blows that he knew lay ahead for her, he
found the words tumbling from his mouth. Little did he realize how prophetic his
words would be in their seemingly impossible search for the American dream.

Hana, of course, had no idea as to what Hisamitsu was alluding. She only
sensed there was something about which he was extremely agitated. Why did he
always insist on spoiling her day? Why couldn't he just let her be the carefree teenager she had always been? And so they continued their voyage on the choppy sea,
with Hana gradually acquiring her "sea legs" like an old sailor, and occasionally
surprising Hisamitsu with glimpses of the sturdy stuff of which this deceptively
skinny teenager was made.

Eventually they sighted land again. This time it was the real thing, America,
at last. *"Ah-me-li-ka, Ah-me-li-ka!"* came the joyful chanting throughout the
ship, again mostly from the younger women, as it passed through the Golden
Gate between San Francisco and Marin County. The ship would moor in the
dock in San Francisco and the new immigrants would be transported by ferry to
Angel Island for processing. Once on the island they would undergo a series of
tests to determine their physical and mental health and fill out reams of reports
and questionnaires.

One of the earlier questions Hana was asked was "Are you Chinese or Japanese?"

"Nihonjin desu!" she stated emphatically.

"I guess you mean Japanese. We'll just put down 'Jap' for short."

"Nan-da, Jap-pu?" Hana retorted, glaring at the agent. The agent quickly moved on to the next question thinking, how quaint and sensitive, these Japanese.

Hisamitsu thought to himself, she's really quite the spitfire. Perhaps it was he who needed moral support rather than she. Why had he worried so much? He felt great relief from this unexpected display of assertiveness. His initial intuition about the hidden strength and endurance of this feisty teenager he had discovered in the village square had been, yet again, confirmed. *Gambare*, indeed!

After several days on the island, awaiting the endless processing of paperwork, she was finally and officially accepted for entry into America. After hasty good-byes to her newfound shipmates still stranded on the island, she and Hisamitsu boarded a ferry that took them to Oakland, where they would catch a train to Los Angeles for the last leg of their transformative journey. On alighting from the ferry in Oakland, Hana suddenly felt very small. Had she shrunk during the long trip over the ocean? How could that be? In reality it was everything around her that was so huge. The buildings were taller and had larger doors and windows than those in Japan. The roads were wider (but definitely dirtier) and even the people were larger; giants by her standards. Even the train they boarded seemed larger, noisier, and more menacing than those she was accustomed to when traveling with her family in Japan during summer vacations.

They passed through acres and acres of farmlands and vineyards. So much of everything, she thought, not like the rice paddies of Japan. They stopped in small towns occasionally to let off some passengers and board new ones. They seemed to pass by people's backyards instead of the front. The only time she saw the front of houses was when the street happened to cross the tracks. Whenever she heard the loud clanging of bells, sure enough, there appeared a line of horse drawn carts or a motorized van, truck, or passenger vehicle waiting patiently for the train to pass. The people in the cars and wagons ogled the train's passengers, and they in turn ogled back as if to say, "How dare you slow us down." But some, especially children, waved. And Hana waved back.

Once out of the city and small towns, Hana was amazed at the open land that went on and on without so much as a farmhouse or tilled land to interrupt the vast open spaces as nature had planned. Indeed, it was only the railroad tracks and the smoke-belching locomotive that seemed strangely out of place. And she herself was now a part of that intrusion.

The sun was setting beyond the distant mountains. She was glad they had chosen seats on the west side of the train. Even though the afternoon sun was warm, the beauty of the sunset more than made up for it. Hana watched the red ball slowly sink behind the far-off peaks. As night fell, they were given snacks to eat and soft drinks as well as pillows and blankets for those who wished them. With the rocking of the train and the rhythmic clickety-clack of steel wheels on steel rails, Hana soon fell into a deep sleep. Her first day in free America had certainly been an awe-inspiring one. She was happy to be in America. Someday perhaps she could become a citizen and truly lay claim to her share of the bountiful richness of this beautiful land. She could hardly wait.

Soon, too soon it seemed to Hana, Hisamitsu was tugging at her to awaken. They had arrived at Union Station in Los Angeles[9] and must disembark or be carried all the way to San Diego (which meant little to Hana). Sleepy-eyed, they struggled with their bags into the waiting area of the station. Hana was astounded at the height of the ornate ceiling and scale of the furnishings. It seemed that the huge space could easily accommodate the locomotive that had brought them there, including the coal car behind it. They settled into the large leather chairs to await the transportation that Hisamitsu's master had arranged for them on hearing of their arrival. Hana felt so tiny in the huge chair she felt she and Hisamitsu should share a single seat as the station became crowded with early-morning commuters. Ignoring her pleas, he placed one of their bags beside her to fill the empty space. He suggested she stop wasting her energy bowing to everyone passing in front of them.

Soon their car arrived. A tall dark-complexioned gentleman in a uniform which made him appear as a dignified foreign emissary searched the crowd until he spotted the familiar face of Hisamitsu. After a hearty handshake and mutual slaps on the back, Hisamitsu introduced him in broken English to his new bride. The driver spontaneously thrust out his hand in a sincere welcoming gesture. Hana, somewhat unsure, reached out to meet his grasp while asking Hisamitsu in Japanese if it was all right for her to bow now—which she did with a broad impish smile.

The chauffeur grabbed not one or two pieces of their luggage but all of them at once and led the way to the limousine parked in a No Parking zone at the front of the station. He dropped the luggage at the red painted curb, and with a flourish and a deep bow he opened the rear door for Hana and Hisamitsu to enter. Once they were safely inside, he placed the luggage in the trunk, got behind the wheel, and headed for the busy streets with his horn blaring. In that instant Hana had fallen in love with America. She had unexpectedly got her belated honeymoon ride, American style.

The drive took them to the foothills of the Sierra Madre Mountains, where they entered the rambling hilltop estate of Hisamitsu's employment. On approaching the mansion, they bypassed the imposing Italian-style villa and continued toward a large garage that housed four shiny vehicles, much like the one that had brought them there. Stopping the car, the driver opened the door for them to exit, grabbed the luggage from the trunk, and led them on a narrow concrete path some distance behind and beyond the garage. Hisamitsu seemed rather confused and annoyed and wondered where the driver was taking them. Hana was enjoying the walk and admiring the colorful flowers along the pathway and across the expansive lawn. Soon they arrived at a low-roofed wooden structure that showed signs of recent structural adjustments and a fresh coat of paint. To Hisamitsu's consternation the driver explained that this would be their new home. The master had converted the former servant's quarters in the mansion into a den to house his many trophies. He had thought that Hisamitsu wouldn't mind, anyway, because this place would give them more privacy. Although the quarters seemed rather tight, even for small people such as Hana and Hisamitsu, Hana had no objection. She thought it was rather cute and cozy until she noticed the chickens. After escaping their nearby pens, they pecked at the door and windows as if to demand entry. She suddenly realized what Hisamitsu and the chickens were so upset about. But they never discussed it. *Shikataganai! Gambare!*

This was only the beginning. Within a few days she discovered that she was expected to care for the upkeep of not only the tiny "cottage," but also the large mansion, and do most of the cleaning, mopping, dusting, scrubbing, and all of the laundering and ironing. In fact, she was expected to perform all the duties she had relied on others to do in her sheltered childhood in Japan. Hisamitsu, meanwhile, took care of all the outdoor chores, mainly the gardening of the extensive grounds. Hana was extremely unhappy with the arrangement and felt betrayed by her own "honorable" husband. But the tradition of Japan, the only tradition she knew, demanded her obedience. So she complied in silence. She suppressed her outrage and humiliation.

The following month she was beset with spells of nausea and dizziness. Alarmed, Hisamitsu implored the master to have their family physician look in on her. The doctor immediately guessed what Hana's problem was, and with the help of the wife of one of Hisamitsu's friends who spoke both English and Japanese, she announced that she was pregnant. For some reason both Hana and Hisamitsu appeared surprised. The doctor suggested she get plenty of rest and avoid all strenuous activity. He had to be kidding, thought Hana, who was determined to do her share of what had been assigned to her. When the fetus became so large that she had difficulty maintaining her balance, she insisted on completing her chores, even into the wee hours of morning when necessary. She asked for no help and received very little, even from Hisamitsu. In December 1916, baby Masami was stillborn. *Shikataganai? Gambare?* Suddenly the words sounded hollow.

Her sadness over their loss was overwhelming. But the guilt of having endangered the life of her baby to demonstrate her indomitable spirit was one she shared with no one and suffered in silence. Hisamitsu, meanwhile, had to grapple with his own guilt for having exposed her to the unreasonable conditions that had brought on the tragedy. Everyone in the household secretly felt some guilt for having profited in one way or another by exploiting her obvious naïveté. They offered their condolences, but Hana suffered alone. After several weeks of depression and frightening bouts of disorientation, Hisamitsu realized he had to get Hana away from the environment that had brought so much grief into their lives.

Within a few months, however, Hana announced to Hisamitsu that she was pregnant again. They were to be given a second chance. They both agreed the added stress of moving and starting anew would be unwise at that time and that they should focus on the future baby's needs and their own health and welfare. So they vowed to save their money as best they could until the baby was born, and by then some opportunity would surely present itself. Hiroshi, a son, was born in October of 1917. His arrival would erase much of the self-imposed anguish and guilt of the past year.

Sure enough, and right on cue, as if to follow the predetermined script of a stage play, early the following year Hisamitsu was offered what he viewed as the opportunity of a lifetime. Four of his trusted friends in Los Angeles had agreed to pool their resources and buy out an established soda water business. They invited Hisamitsu to join them. The five of them would own and operate the facility themselves, catering mainly to the Japanese markets and restaurants in Los Angeles and neighboring communities. Four would tend to production and delivery while one, an experienced accountant, would handle the business management. It was called the Sunrise Soda Water Company, located in Little Tokyo, Los Angeles.[10] The possibilities seemed endless.

Hisamitsu and Hana found a small wooden bungalow nearby and moved their scant belongings into it. The American dream seemed about to become a reality. Two years later, with the business flourishing, they were blessed with a daughter, Yaeno.

Fate would rear its ugly head again. In late 1919, an influenza epidemic swept through much of the country, and in early 1920, six-and-a-half-month-old Yaeno fell victim. One minute, Hana had a feverish, distressed infant about to be examined by a harried, overworked doctor. The next minute, on viewing her, he merely shook his head and placed the now lifeless body into a black leather satchel and carried it out the door. Moments later, as Hisamitsu came through the same door with Hiroshi in hand, he discovered Hana standing as if in a trance, staring blankly at an empty crib. A familiar pain overcame both of them. This time it was a sorrow undiluted by suppressed guilt. It was truly *shikataganai*. Yaeno was buried in a tiny casket at the Evergreen Cemetery in Boyle Heights.

Due largely to the diligence of the partners, the soda works enterprise continued to prosper. They hired additional help on the production line in response to the burgeoning demands. Meanwhile, Hana presented Hisamitsu with another child on January 1, 1921, a daughter whom they named Kazumi.

This was indeed the American dream, they thought. After so much grief, disillusionment, and self-reproach (but never blame toward others), Hana and Hisamitsu were finally but cautiously daring to enjoy the rewards of their

FIGURE 1.2. Sunrise Soda Water Company, 325 E. Commercial Street, Los Angeles. Hisamitsu at far right, ca. 1920 (Kuromiya Family Collection).

perseverance. They bought their first car, a Ford Model T ragtop touring sedan. It was black, as were most cars of that era, and an item of pride as many people still lacked a motorized vehicle in those days.

As the business expanded, however, Hisamitsu had a disturbing feeling that all was not right. Somehow their net profits seemed to fall short of the increase in production. Perhaps his expectations were unrealistic, he mused, but the feeling that something was amiss persisted. He wondered if his partners sensed the imbalance, but they seemed unaware of anything wrong. So he kept his concerns to himself. Just to satisfy his curiosity, he kept careful count of the crates in each delivery and compared it to the figures that were logged into the ledger. He hated the sneakiness he had to resort to and the mistrust of his partners it implied, but he had to know the truth. He was appalled to discover in one case the figures were totally misleading and unaccountable. Could it be his trusted friend was cheating? He knew the friend bore a streak of vanity and tended at times to live beyond his means, even before they had formed their partnership. But to cheat his friends?

There must be some simple explanation, thought Hisamitsu. Perhaps he had some personal temporary financial setbacks such as gambling debts that he was too proud to admit, and perhaps he had every intention of replacing the funds when he was able to do so. Hisamitsu found himself in a moral dilemma. Should he confront the friend and risk humiliating him? Should he alert the other partners? After all, it was their problem too. But why should he bear the disgrace of being a snitch?

Hisamitsu confided his findings to no one except Hana, who had sensed his agitation earlier and who had finally demanded an explanation. Her response was an emphatic, "Reveal all!" It was not his responsibility to protect the reputation of an embezzler, especially when he (and she) were the victims. She never trusted the person nor his wife anyway. They were snobs, she declared, and deserved to be exposed.

But for Hisamitsu it wasn't that simple. Certainly, he was outraged at being duped, especially by a trusted friend, but the issue was neither about the friend nor even the money. It was about honor. It was about the age-old tradition of a samurai and his sense of honor—or, if you will, his own conscience and personal integrity. His, not theirs.

The following day, to everyone's astonishment, Hisamitsu announced his resignation from the partnership. He gave no explanation and demanded no compensation for his substantial investment in the company. As he quietly gathered his personal possessions, each person approached him with a puzzled expression and offered a hearty handshake. No one demanded an explanation. Only one could not look him in the eye. That person's eyes were blinded with tears and he kept his head bowed. Hisamitsu's suspicions had been confirmed.

In the following months the ledger would show a miraculous upswing, but there was no celebration. Nothing more was ever said about it—at least, not to Hisamitsu.

Hisamitsu and Hana moved back to Sierra Madre where they had many friends. They rented an unused storage room with a small kitchen and bath in the old *gakuen* (Japanese language school) as their temporary home. Hisamitsu performed gardening and other odd jobs to tide them over while they contemplated their next move. Hana gave birth to two more children, Yoshito, a boy, in 1923, with whom she was already pregnant when the "eruption" occurred in Los Angeles, and Kimiye, a girl, in 1924. They were both born with the help of a midwife in the well-known Japanese edifice on Grove Street. The night Kimiye was born a fire raged in the nearby mountains of Sierra Madre. Hisamitsu had volunteered with other local Issei (immigrant, or first-generation Japanese) to fight the fire, so could not be present at Kimiye's birth. With four children now, they needed to find a more permanent dwelling, and for Hisamitsu a more substantial occupation.

They located a small but comfortable bungalow in Pasadena in a neighborhood which included several other Japanese families. The old Japanese Union Presbyterian Church nearby conducted many social events they could attend, even though they were Buddhists by faith. Hisamitsu eventually acquired several gardening accounts in the wealthier neighborhoods of Pasadena. Although the work was much more labor-intensive and lacked the sophisticated image of a corporate businessman, he enjoyed the luxury of exercising his own high standards, both in the performance of his work and in matters of personal integrity. His once-shiny new car, however, took quite a beating transporting his equipment from job to job.

Hana also helped with the family income by taking in laundry. In the morning, after sending the two older children off to school, she picked up the soiled laundry of her accounts in the neighborhood, loaded them into the baby buggy alongside baby Kimiye, and with Yoshito in tow, pushed the buggy a few blocks to home. Yoshito, however, habitually ran off in the wrong direction, making the journey twice as long. In the late afternoon she would return the now clean laundry in the buggy with the baby, but leave Yoshito at home with the older children to watch him.

Thus, Hisamitsu and Hana managed for a few years until the next crisis was thrust upon them.[1]

---

1. The foregoing is a fictionalized version of actual events based on the recollections of my mother (Hana), as related to me in her dying months. Of course, in the earlier episodes, I was yet unborn, so I cannot attest to the accuracy of her memory, and know of no one who could at this late date. In the interest of keeping the story line more readable, if not entertaining, I have taken liberties in filling in the gaps with my own imagination. In order to avoid unintentional embarrassment, the names and identities of those not directly related to the family have been masked or omitted.

2

CHILDHOOD

As the third son (if one is to count Masami, who was stillborn as the first) and the fifth child to be born to Hisamitsu and Hana Kuromiya, there was little if any burden placed on me to preserve family traditions or ethical values, as is often imposed on a firstborn son in a Japanese family. My brother, Hiroshi, seemed to have inherited that questionable honor. I was free to make my own decisions relatively unfettered by family commitments, real or assumed. Hiroshi, on the other hand, was under the watchful eyes of our parents. This was understandable in view of the still strong influence of the rigid traditions and archaic judgments of ancient Japan—a samurai-idolizing Japan. But this was America! Only one question remained: Were we Americans?

Thus, if my brother Hiroshi had written this story, it would have been a totally different story. The events, though we may have experienced many of them together, would no doubt evoke different, even contradictory, responses. We saw the world through different eyes, but I was somehow unaware of this phenomenon until quite late in life, after his death.

While primarily intended as a tribute to my parents, Hisamitsu and Hana Kuromiya, who were extraordinary individuals in their own right in the difficult era into which they were born, this story may also be regarded as a pledge of atonement from number three son, for the additional trials and tribulations he may have contributed to their already harried lives.

https://doi.org/10.5876/9781646421848.c002

FIGURE 2.1. Family portrait, ca. 1927. *From left*: Hiroshi, Kimiye, Mama, Yoshito, Papa, and Kazumi. (Ninomiya Studio).

The earliest recollection I have as a baby is the warmth and security I felt sleeping between Papa and Mama in their bed. This, I realized later, was only to conserve space in the extremely small house we lived in and had nothing to do with either favoritism or entitlement. Upon the birth of my sister Kimiye, I was moved to a crib in a remote corner of the same room. I distinctly recall feeling abandoned and betrayed. I know I raised quite a fuss, but after a few days I must have gotten over it. *Shikataganai?*

Baby Kimiye was later moved into the crib and I shared a bed with older sister Kazumi. We fought, as siblings often will, to lay claim on our territory. So, Mama rolled up a blanket to form a barrier between us. Eventually, Kim outgrew the crib and was placed between Kazumi and me with an additional blanket barrier. Indeed, good fences do make for good neighbors. Especially with the three of us lying crosswise in the double bed, at least one would invariably wet the bed (usually me). Kazumi was happy to be the farthest away from me.

Hiroshi, being four years older than Kazumi and six years older than me, had little to do with his siblings, and we with him. I do recall, however, as a child with very few friends, envying him because he had so many pals. On one occasion I tried to follow him and his gang of five or six and he threatened to chase me home. But I persisted, wondering why he wouldn't let me join them. I watched from a safe distance and followed them from one activity to the next, alone, but going through the same motions that they had with my imaginary friends. When they spotted me, they ran off to seek the next attraction.

To jar the memory of old-time Pasadenans, the sites I recall were: the sawdust pile outside the auto body factory on Colorado Boulevard near where the Norton Simon Museum of Art now sits; the playground south of the Green Hotel, specifically the spiral slide; and the train roundhouse, where the locomotives were reversed on a giant turntable so they could return to Los Angeles. None of these facilities exists today except the playground, but without the slide.

They finally succeeded in ditching me near the edge of the arroyo at the path to Brookside Park. It was quite a hike for a five-year-old trying to keep up with a gang of eleven-year-olds, which is probably why they didn't want me along in the first place. If Mama was worried about my long absence, she didn't show it. No doubt she had more important matters to attend to.

On occasion we would have friends visit us. Most were Japanese with children about the same age as my sisters and me. Long after the kids were worn out and fell asleep wherever they happened to drop, the parents, especially the fathers, enjoyed talking into the wee hours of the morning. My favorite spot was on Papa's back with my arms wrapped around his neck. They spoke in Japanese and I didn't understand a word, but the deep, muffled sound of Papa's voice resounding through his sinewy back was the most reassuring experience I can recall. Somehow, I knew he spoke the truth and his words were very wise. I would fall asleep and never remember being put to bed or being carried to the car if we happened to be the visitors.

This was the only physical contact I ever had with my father. No matter how angry he was with me, he never struck me or anyone else I know of, not even an animal. Mama, on the other hand, consistently slapped me (but never hard) when I got out of line (which was quite often). No doubt it was out of sheer frustration. Even when I got a nosebleed, which was quite often, she would slap me first before attending to my distress. Like a moth mesmerized by a flame, I would always run to Mama (never to Papa, who was seldom available anyway) knowing I would be rewarded with a slap. I don't remember my siblings receiving any slaps, but of course they always behaved, or were too smart to get caught. In any case, I survived by pretending they were nothing more than overly enthusiastic love taps.

Meanwhile, the economy was quite promising. It was the Roaring Twenties and my parents had managed to save enough so Mama could retire from her laundry work. They agreed it would be a great opportunity for her to visit her childhood home in Japan and for us kids to meet our grandparents.

(The following is a brief essay I wrote sometime in the 1990s of my memories of that trip.)

I was six years old. My mother took me, my older brother, and two sisters for a visit to Japan. It was summertime of 1929. My father couldn't join us because he had to tend his gardening route, but he did promise he would pick us up in a brand new car when we returned.

In Japan I recall it being important to me to determine what was real and what was not real in this new world. Since there were no other children my age and no toys, I was left to entertain myself in any way I could. They seemed to have forgotten I was from America.

Have you ever wet your finger and popped it through a paper shoji screen? I was fascinated with this strange sensation and had destroyed most of the screens in my grandparents' house before being told that that kind of behavior was unacceptable.

Among other experiments, I discovered a neat little sitting place, a little alcove just my size in the wall of the main room. I removed the fat statue and the smelly incense and I had a nice little space all to myself. I was sitting there with my arms and legs folded like the statue I had replaced when my grandmother shuffled into the room. She seemed horrified, muttered something harsh in Japanese, pulled me firmly but gently from my throne, and replaced the statue. No big deal, I thought.

Later that night after we were put to bed on the futon mats on the floor, I heard voices in the next room. I crawled out and peeked through a recently perforated screen to see my mother kneeling, her face almost touching the floor and my grandparents towering over her, all five feet of them, their faces red in righteous anger. They threatened to send us back to decadent America in disgrace—all because of me. Punishment came in strange ways, I discovered.

My brother was about twelve years old and was sent to school for the summer. They dressed him in an official-looking uniform, not unlike those worn by Japanese soldiers in my Japanese picture book. I thought they were sending him off to war. I was beginning to dislike Japan.

When it came time to return home there was much talk of leaving my brother there to continue his schooling. They didn't want me for obvious reasons, for which I was grateful. Whatever the previous plans had been, Mama apparently had a change of heart and decided we didn't need a *kamikaze* pilot in the family. Her parents seemed disappointed in her. I was proud of her. So it was back to decadent America for us.

We could hardly wait to see the new car Papa had promised us. When we finally docked in San Pedro Harbor there was all the excitement and clamor one would expect on such a special occasion. It was almost as exciting as when we left, except—no Papa. Gradually the crowd thinned out until finally there was only the five of us left sitting on our suitcases. There was one other person, a Mr. Matsumoto, a family friend who kept an eye on us during our trip back because my mother was traveling alone with four kids. He finally called a taxi and invited us to join him for lunch in Little Tokyo.

There we found Papa. He still had the old ragtop Model T Ford with creased fenders and torn seats, and the floorboards still littered with grass clippings. He couldn't make good his promise and felt so bad that he had gone on a drinking binge rather than face our disappointment. Not until years later did I understand any of this. It was, of course, the beginning of the Great Depression, and he had lost some of his best accounts.

But it didn't matter to me. I was happy to see him and to be back in the USA, where I thought I knew what the rules were. It would be another thirteen years before I would learn that things didn't always make much sense here either.

As a six-year-old kid when the Depression first hit, I have no personal recollection of its full impact. All I recall is that for a few years we wore cardboard in our shoes where the soles had worn through, which wasn't much help when it rained. We just went barefoot a lot. All my clothes were hand-me-downs and our dinners seemed to be skimpier with a lot of *ocha-zuke* (hot tea poured over steamed rice). Needless to say, we never got the new car. Papa just patched up the old jalopy, and we swallowed our pride—or walked. But everyone was in the same boat so it didn't seem so bad. It's only when you're singled out through no fault of your own and no one else has to suffer that it's especially hurtful.

I learned that some who were wealthy enough to have stock investments and were accustomed to a softer lifestyle were so devastated with their losses that they jumped out of eighth-story windows. I couldn't understand how that would help. What about the kids who lost their papas on top of everything else? Perhaps we were fortunate that we didn't have that much to lose and we still had our Mama and Papa.

Papa in his infinite wisdom decided he couldn't risk the welfare of his family by being in a business that catered to the whims of others, especially when no one knew how long the Depression would last. He must find a niche somewhere in the food chain, he decided. Everyone has to eat. Therefore, he sought some business selling produce that would require a minimum initial investment. He heard from friends of a man who was about to retire from his house-to-house vegetable peddling route in the neighboring town of Monrovia. Upon inquiry, the cost for the business including the truck and inventory sounded reasonable. So off we went to Monrovia on yet another new venture. We found a house to rent in a fairly nice neighborhood, just in time for Hiroshi, Kazumi, and me to be registered for

FIGURE 2.2. Mama with Yoshito, Kazumi, Hiroshi, and Kimiye, ca. 1930. (Kuromiya Family Collection)

school for the fall term. I would be just starting first grade. We thought it rather strange that we were sent to a school at the extreme south end of town when there was one just a few blocks from us. It turned out that the school nearest us was an all-white school. The one we were enrolled in was racially mixed, and there was yet another one which was entirely black. It seems we had unwittingly moved into a racist town. But at six years old I was still too young to realize how seriously this would impact my life and my views on American justice. The few other Japanese families in town didn't seem to mind. *Shikataganai*!

(The following three short essays depict some of my childhood experiences during this period. They were written in the 1990s, after my retirement.)

THE COLLECTION BASKET

After our move to the small town of Monrovia when I was six years old, I and my two sisters, one older and one younger than me, had a difficult time making new friends. Our brother, who was a few years older, had no trouble because there were many boys his age in the neighborhood, but he would have nothing to do with us. There were no other minorities in the immediate neighborhood, so we were stared at a lot and nobody seemed to smile. At least, not to us.

Every Sunday morning two spinster sisters (real sisters, not nuns), with pasty white faces and pasty white hair and a rather strange smell, insisted on taking us to a pasty white church two blocks away. We assured them we could walk these two blocks ourselves, and "Thank you, anyway." If we missed one week, they would be at our front door scolding Mama and leaving stacks of Jesus pamphlets. Once they dragged me out from under the house where I was hiding. I think Kazumi, my older sister, snitched on me. Kim would never betray me.

I really didn't mind Sunday school that much. I enjoyed the Bible stories, but could do without the sermons. And I hated dressing up in starchy clothes.

Mama gave us each a nickel and three pennies: the nickel for the "correction" basket, as she pronounced it, and three cents for penny candies at the mom-and-pop store just across the street from the church. Candy selection was an art. If you didn't make wise choices you could end up with not-so-tasty candy that nobody else wanted. But if it was tasty or wouldn't keep well, like meltable chocolates, you could run out while the others were still enjoying theirs. The trick was selecting the tastiest, longest-lasting candy.

So one Sunday I waited for my two sisters to make their purchases and then ran a long list of my choices to the pathetically patient but kindly store owner. I quickly plunked down my nickel and grabbed my loot. Both girls gave me a startled look, but didn't say anything. Somebody snitched, because the next week I only got six cents to see if I would dare to put a measly penny in the collection basket. I did. The following week, I only got a nickel. No candy.

I think Mama was smarter than all the churches in Monrovia—and she was right! It was a "correction" basket.

TRICK OR TREAT

I must have been about nine years old. It was just before Halloween and a few of us kids were playing in our neighbor's backyard. His parents and older sisters were entertaining guests in the house. The mother called us to the back door and invited us to join them in an apple-dunking contest. It was one of the grander houses in our neighborhood, so we were careful to wipe our shoes on the doormat. I was the last in line and when I reached for the screen door, it was locked. I guessed that they didn't see me in the growing darkness. I knocked and waited, and waited—and waited. Surely my friends would realize I was missing and come after me. After several minutes it dawned on me. Maybe I wasn't wanted there. Could it be, this white family would be uncomfortable with my presence among their white guests? But they always seemed like such nice people! Bewildered, I finally went home and sat in a closet to think things over. I was too embarrassed to tell anyone.

In another ten years I would not only be banned from my friend's house, but evicted from my own house as well. In fact, I would be banned from the entire West Coast! What on earth were they afraid of?

MAIDEN FLIGHT

One afternoon after school my friend and I, also ten years old, decided to ride our bikes out to the edge of town and watch some planes take off and land at the small private airfield. When we got there, it turned out to be a slow day and all the planes had already been put away in the hangars. The lone attendant saw the disappointment in our faces and offered us a free ride if we would hoe out the weeds behind the hangars.

We had only worked about a half-hour when he wanted to close up shop, but would give us our rides. We could finish up the weeds some other day. Thrilled, we clambered into the two-seater open cockpit of the WWI relic, the only plane that was on the field, while he spun the single propeller and removed the wheel blocks. We bounced along the pitted asphalt runway, engine screaming and the propeller throwing dust and bits of debris in our faces. Thank God we were supplied with oversized goggles and leather helmets. Even then we could barely see over the edge of the cockpit and weren't sure we were off the ground yet. I didn't think the wings were supposed to flap, but the pilot didn't seem to mind, so I kept quiet. Then, all of a sudden, things got much quieter and instead of the tops of trees we saw silver clouds floating all around us. The engine didn't sound quite as desperate anymore. It was quite peaceful up there. We flew over our small hometown and I thought I recognized our house and Mama watering her perpetual flower garden. We motioned for the pilot to do some loops or other tricks, but he just nodded "No" and smiled. But he did make some erratic moves just to scare us.

That evening at the dinner table I was about to announce my exciting afternoon when Mama cut in and complained there was some crazy *bakatare* [foolish] pilot trying to crash a plane while she was watering her garden.

I decided not to mention our adventure.

Papa's business went fairly well, but proved to involve much more time and work than he had anticipated. He went into the wholesale produce market in Los Angeles at 2:00 a.m. about three times a week so his products would be relatively fresh. The Model T touring car was hardly capable of handling the load, so he bought a Chevrolet pickup truck that was barely adequate. The peddling truck finally fell apart, so he had to replace that with a much more substantial vehicle. He taught Mama to drive him to the wholesale market, which gave him about an hour of sleep each way. But no sooner did they arrive home than they had to unload the wares and set them up to display on the peddling truck. Hiroshi, by then in high school, was of great help but wasn't always available. The rest of us were of very little help and ate all the grapes and cherries.

One spring our elderly neighbors, a seemingly nice couple, were moving out of state, so they put their house up for sale. Apparently, a few of the prospective buyers were quite interested, but weren't sure about the "Japs" living next door. I'm not sure if our landlord refused to evict us because we were good tenants, but our neighbors went directly to the city council to have us evicted under the Jim Crow ordinance that forbade minority races to reside in a white neighborhood. There was quite a political brouhaha and we were not only bodily evicted, but humiliated. *Shikataganai!*

Papa, however, was not one to give up easily. I'm not sure how it came about, but he located a duplex on the famous Highway 66, which ran through Monrovia. It had an adjoining vacant lot which also fronted on the highway. The owners, a very kindly elderly couple, lived directly across the street. Thus, we became neighbors as well as friends. Their son owned a publishing company in Hawai'i that employed several Japanese, so they were quite familiar with the ethnic idiosyncrasies of our culture (our parents, not necessarily us kids). So when Papa wanted to build a produce stand on the vacant lot on the busy highway, they had no objections provided he bore all the initial costs.

As a family project we started out slowly and cautiously, just a couple of tables of strawberries and melons protected from the hot sun with beach umbrellas. After Hiroshi graduated from the local high school, Papa was able to give up his peddling route and concentrate on the fruit stand, which by then had gained many local "regulars" and was no longer dependent on transient highway traffic. We built a barn-like shack to house the produce. It served for a few years until the local merchants complained of unfair competition because of *their* higher overhead expenses. The building department for the city levied code restrictions upon us and we were forced to rebuild to a stricter structural criterion. But Papa took it all in stride because he had reached his goal as a successful businessman with a substantial enterprise, employing well-educated young Japanese Americans who could not find jobs in their specialized fields because of racial prejudice. It was now more than a strictly family enterprise. Things were looking good—too good, we would discover.

The year was 1941, a historic turning point for all of America, but an unimaginable crisis for all Japanese residents, citizens and aliens alike, especially those who lived on the West Coast.

3

RUDE AWAKENING

I recall the events of December 7, 1941, quite vividly. My brother, Hiro, and I were searching the used car lots along Colorado Boulevard in Pasadena for a car for him since he was about to be married. I believe the wedding plans were to be announced at a family party that very evening. It was quite rare that he and I ever did things together except while working in the store, where it was more a matter of each avoiding the heavier tasks at the expense of the other. Therefore, it was quite special for him to show respect for my knowledge of cars by asking for my help in finding one. We visited perhaps three or four lots without finding anything reasonably priced. I sensed it may have had something to do with our being Japanese and not noted for quibbling about price. It was about 10:00 or 11:00 a.m. as we approached the next lot. A burly, red-faced man came storming out of his trailer/office, shaking his fist at us and demanding we get off his lot. "We don't sell to sneaky Japs," he screamed. The only thing missing, I thought, was a shotgun.

As we got back into our car wondering what was eating him, we heard over the radio of the Japanese attack at Pearl Harbor. We were flabbergasted. We went straight home to alert our parents that the whole country had gone crazy. I knew exactly what was happening in Hawai'i, but was amazed that Japan would make such a suicidal move. It wasn't a "sneak attack," as propagandists encouraged radio and newspaper reporters to claim, but we were being blamed for it. America was righteously outraged. I had been keeping a daily account through the news reports over a crystal radio set I had assembled myself. It only got a single station (KFI)

https://doi.org/10.5876/9781646421848.c003

and only when the radio waves were just right. But it served to keep me informed during that critical period.

For quite some time, British Prime Minister Winston Churchill had been pleading with US President Franklin Delano Roosevelt to officially join in the battle against the onslaught of Nazi Germany. Roosevelt, ruefully aware of his campaign promise to the American people to remain neutral in the war raging in Europe, was caught in a political dilemma. Japan, of which he was never particularly fond, would provide the answer if she could somehow be provoked into striking the first blow. Thus, an oil embargo that would cut off all supplies to Japan was imposed. It would not only put an end to Japan's military dominance in the Pacific, but would also threaten her domestic survival as well. The US government and the military, at least to some extent, knew Japan *had* to retaliate in order to survive as she lacked natural resources for her industries. The question was just how, where, and when. World War II for America had already started, but the American public was not aware of it. Only FDR knew.

Meantime, two Japanese diplomats, Ambassador Kichisaburo Nomura and Special Envoy Saburo Kurusu, were kept waiting for several hours for a last-ditch conference with FDR to seek a peaceable resolution to Japan's embargo crisis. Were they knowingly or unknowingly set up by the Japanese government to act as decoys to lull America into a false sense of security while their carrier ships bearing lethal kamikaze pilots were rapidly approaching our unsuspecting fleet, basking in the calm waters of Pearl Harbor? Or were Kurusu and Nomura truly and desperately trying to deter their country from entering into a conflict they couldn't possibly win? The order to attack had already been made. US military intelligence agencies, having previously broken Japan's secret code, were aware that an attack was imminent. Yet the fleet in Pearl Harbor was not properly notified. Why? As far as our military personnel in Pearl Harbor and the American public were concerned, it may indeed have been a sneak attack. But who was the culprit? This question and others have long-awaited answers. (Many of the questions are answered in the well-researched yet still controversial book *Day of Deceit* by Robert B. Stinnett and published in New York City by Simon & Schuster in the year 2000.[11]) Of course, I only learned belatedly of the details through the dedicated research of others, but at that time, I suspected something was afoot when FDR so arrogantly rejected all possibility of peaceful resolution of the oil embargo crisis by humiliating the Japanese diplomats. To further ensure his warmongering strategy, FDR used known racist bigots and organizations, mostly on the West Coast, to fan the flames of war hysteria through racist propaganda, all the while assuring America, "The only thing we have to fear is fear itself."

Hiroshi and Emiko did get married. They also found a car to their liking. They rented a small one-bedroom bungalow behind our duplex. Everything on the home front seemed to be going well. Even our business seemed unaffected by any acts of hostility. Indeed, some customers assured us everything would be fine. And why not, I thought, we had nothing to do with the bombing in Pearl Harbor.

However, at Pasadena Junior College,[12] where I was attending school, a classmate, a Japanese American girl from Brawley, California, didn't return after Christmas vacation. She never said anything about quitting school, so I wondered what had become of her. Later I read in the papers that a crazed man upset with the war in the Philippines had knocked on a door of a farmhouse in Brawley. When the father and mother came to the door, he shot them both, point-blank. The names of the victims were the same as my friend's. I would never hear from her again. Immediately after the bombing at Pearl Harbor, the FBI increased their sweeps of potential saboteur suspects targeting Issei men (first-generation, non-US citizens) and Kibei men (second-generation US citizens educated in Japan), despite no evidence of culpability. Most were held without trial or any formal charges, and in some cases their whereabouts were undisclosed to their families for several months. Since many of Papa's friends had already been picked up, his traveling bag stood prepared and waiting at the front door. Luckily, he was never taken.

Many of the names of these suspects were provided to the FBI by the Japanese American Citizens League (JACL),[13] which, spearheaded by older Nisei (second-generation US citizens), apparently regarded the need to prove *their* loyalty to the US as a higher priority than the defense of the constitutional and human rights of their own people. It was all in the interest of national security, or so they claimed.

It became quite evident to me at this point that the JACL could not be trusted to represent the interests of Japanese Americans. Constitutional principles seemed to be too easily set aside when they were confronted with issues of political expedience. With our former community leaders, most of whom were Issei, now under government custody, the Japanese American community was left virtually leaderless. The JACL filled that void and appointed themselves spokesmen for all of Japanese America. They promoted cooperation with government edicts, no matter how unjust, as the safest course for Japanese American survival. Thus, the US Constitution was abandoned. Future events would more than confirm my suspicions of their basically self-serving political aspirations.

A curfew was imposed on us, just us and no one else I knew of on the West Coast. We couldn't travel more than five miles from home without special permission, and had to be home between the hours of eight in the evening and six in the morning. This certainly must have imposed many hardships on the stereotypical law-abiding Japanese. But I thought it was absurd and ignored it. I got stopped once when I drove my sister Kim and a friend to spend the afternoon roller-skating at the Shrine skating rink in Los Angeles, about twenty-five miles from home. We teenagers have a lousy sense of time, so I'm sure it was after eight. Suddenly an unmarked car flashed a red light on us. I pulled over to the curb thinking I was going to get another speeding ticket. Two plainclothes men shined flashlights into our faces and asked for identification. They seemed disappointed that we were just a bunch of Nisei kids and told us to go home and stop wasting their time. I was glad my parents weren't with us. It's a good thing they never learned how to skate or we would have all been in trouble.

But more serious matters were afoot. Rumor had it that we would be placed in "relocation camps" as a national security measure. Other versions had it that it would be for our own safety to protect us from the bigots. Well, thanks, but no thanks. I thought surely such a program would be on a voluntary basis and apply perhaps to our noncitizen parents. But could it possibly apply to us too, in spite of our US citizenship?

As if in answer to my question, on February 19, 1942, President Roosevelt signed Executive Order 9066,[14] which banned all Japanese, US citizens as well as "enemy aliens," from the three West Coast states of Washington, Oregon, and California, plus a portion of Arizona. I was astounded. Later I was outraged to hear that the JACL as our self-appointed representative had committed us all to cooperate in this super-patriotic effort to secure our country.[15] *Shikataganai! Gambare!*

4

POMONA ASSEMBLY CENTER

Since the Santa Anita Race Track was only a few miles from our home, we used to pass by it quite often. We noticed that the perimeter chain-link fence had been heightened with strands of barbed wire, and army-type barracks had been constructed in the huge parking lot. Then one day there were people there. They looked just like us. Many were idly clinging to the fence watching traffic go by. I must have been gawking because one kid stuck his tongue out at me.

Just as we began to think it wouldn't happen to us, we got a notice to appear at the Pomona Fair Grounds, located approximately twenty miles from the Santa Anita Assembly Center, in three weeks with only what we could carry. We had to sell off our inventory in the store for whatever we could get for it, as well as our furniture and appliances. I had to sell my hot-rod roadster (which was only lukewarm at best, but my pride and joy nonetheless). Fortunately, our kindly landlord offered to let us store whatever we couldn't sell in one of the rooms rent-free and assured us that we would always have a place to come back to. Of course, neither party suspected we would be gone almost four years (*over* four years for me).

Although we were warned to take only what we could carry, we took a little more on the truck we drove ourselves in. On reaching the gate, however, they told us to take only what we could carry off the truck and leave the key in the ignition. The truck sat in a fenced-off compound for a few weeks along with several other trucks and sedans, all partially loaded, until one morning they all disappeared.

 https://doi.org/10.5876/9781646421848.c004

I don't know if Papa was ever reimbursed for the truck and contents, but I don't think so. After all, we had been warned.

After standing in line for over an hour we were given cursory physical exams and shots, men and women separately. We then received large cotton bags to fill with hay for our mattresses and were assigned a single room as a family. Hiro and Em failed to register as a separate family so we all got jammed into one room. I think they went to the office to apply for a separate room but had to wait a few days for it because of all the confusion with the volunteer help, long lines, and poor instructions. Meanwhile Mama, Papa, my two sisters, and I started for the mess hall. There were long lines everywhere, so someone had to find the front of the line to make sure there was still a mess hall there and not a bathroom. Some people with crying babies almost reached the front of the line before realizing they were in the wrong line. It was long after dark when we finally reached the mess hall and there were only a few scraps left by then. I don't think Hiro and Em had dinner at all that night. I know they didn't have sex.

The following day was a kind of orientation adventure. We were amazed to see so many Japanese faces in one place. I recognized many, perhaps most, as from the San Gabriel Valley. I waved to a few whom I thought I recognized, but couldn't remember their names. Others appeared to be ashamed to be seen there and turned away. The Ferris wheel and the rides were missing, of course, but it was still the fairgrounds and the crowds were there, albeit we were prisoners—and for questionable reasons. I thought: "Once they do the necessary investigations and realize Mama isn't about to blow up the Sawpit Dam and flood all of Monrovia, they'll let us go home and maybe even return our truck. In the meantime, this has got to be costing the taxpayers a lot of money and no one seems to be enjoying it. What a shame!"

Word was that every able-bodied adult was expected to work to help maintain the camp [officially named the Pomona Assembly Center[16]]. My body was probably able, but my mind definitely was not. As a result, I was one of the last to apply for a job and was thus assigned to one of the most degrading available—the trash pickup crew. It wasn't too bad. At least it enabled me to discover areas in the camp I never would have thought to explore. In the maintenance area there was a sign shop tucked away in a far corner where directional and identification signs were hand painted. I inquired about a job there based on my previous graphics experience. One fellow who appeared to be the manager or foreman said he could use some additional help and would submit my name. In two short days I was transformed from a trash collector to a trash creator. Had I not been on the lowly trash crew I would never have discovered the sign shop.

About three months after entering the Pomona Fair Grounds we were informed that our stay there was just a temporary one and our real "relocation camp" was now ready for us somewhere in Wyoming. I guess we were still too close to the

Sawpit Dam, and they couldn't trust Mama. So again, we stood in line to exit the very same gate we had entered three months earlier. The kid in uniform about my age, still guarding the gate, didn't seem quite as nervous this time. At least the gleaming bayonet on the end of his rifle didn't glitter in the sun quite as much as before. He appeared kind of sad to see us leave.

The old coach car we boarded must have been a relic from WWI. It had a distinct mothball smell to it. It may even have been the same coach that brought Papa and Mama down from Oakland in 1916. We had to keep the shades down all the while and were sidetracked repeatedly as our trip conflicted with regular train schedules. We were traveling eastward. Everyone else seemed to be going west where all the action was. Sometime after nightfall we had an unusually long stop. We were again warned not to open the shades. There seemed to be a lot of activity outside so I peeked when the guard wasn't looking. My view through the narrow slit was down the center of a major boulevard with multicolored neon signs along both sides. This must be Las Vegas, Nevada, I guessed. I had never been there before, but had seen many pictures and movies of it. However, I was never a serious gambler and didn't have any quarters in my pocket anyhow, so it was nothing to get excited about.

Soon we were moving again and, as daylight broke, we were allowed to raise the shades and enjoy the scenery. Other than the trip to Japan that Mama had taken us on when I was six years old, I had never been outside of Southern California, so I was quite impressed with how beautiful America actually was—at least the land. For this I had the American Indians to thank, who helped keep it that way.

As we approached the Great Salt Lake, we passed a truck farm on the outskirts of what might have been Provo, Utah. There were a dozen laborers picking the crops by hand. They appeared to be Japanese, but were too far away to be sure. A few stood up to watch our train pass through their fields. I wondered if they realized we were Japanese, too, and some of us had been peacefully farming a few months ago, but our circumstances through no fault of our own were totally different.

But the real excitement of the trip was yet to come. After traversing a large part of Idaho, we approached the base of the Rocky Mountain Range and, in order to surmount the Continental Divide, they added two or three additional locomotives. As we chugged up the steep incline along the precipitous rock face, we could see the tips of 200-foot-tall trees far below us and the locomotives in the front and at the rear at the same time on the switchback turns. It made me feel very special. You can see it from the air, to be sure, but you can only *feel* it on the ground. I wondered how many Chinese laborers gave up their lives for the lack of safety measures in the laying of those tracks. Perhaps we will never know.[17]

After traveling eastward in Montana for a few hours, we headed south into Wyoming. The landscape became more dismal the farther we went. We finally stopped at a rickety old wannabe depot in the middle of nowhere.

"Nowhere" happened to be Heart Mountain, our destination and "home" for the duration. That is, for most of us. All the passengers grabbed their belongings grumbling about traveling so far only to be left in the desert. Everyone including women wore black mustaches under their noses from the locomotive smoke, which would soon turn white as a result of the dust storm that greeted us as we alit from the train. Thus was our "aloha" to Heart Mountain Relocation Center[18] in Wyoming, USA.

5

HEART MOUNTAIN

As we disembarked from the train, we were led to a registration barrack and there assigned family quarters according to our family number, ours being No. 5445. This was assigned to us when registering at the Pomona Assembly Center. Hiro made sure he and Em got themselves their own room this time, based on a different family number. We boarded a truck that already had our possessions on it, along with a few other families with their luggage. Thanks to Sears Roebuck and Montgomery Ward, all of our possessions had increased fourfold. Due to the wind and dust there was little conversation, but the looks on people's faces said it all: the doom and gloom of prisoners condemned to the gallows. *Shikataganai.*

During the brief time we were on the truck with about four toddlers, it struck me that it was the innocence and naïveté of the children, always seeking new adventures, that kept up the spirits of the more sophisticated elders. The popular saying *Kodomo-no-tame-ni* (for the sake of the children) seems to imply a need to sacrifice and endure for our children's welfare when in fact it may have been the children themselves in their innocence that bolstered the spirits of the elders. Perhaps we adults in our arrogance take more credit than we deserve.

A bumpy, dusty road took us up a bluff to a broad, flat plateau where we got our first glimpse of over 400 tarpapered barracks (perhaps 500, counting mess halls, latrines, and recreation halls) that would be our new home, and Wyoming's third largest suburbia. The truck pulled up to our barrack room, 14-4-E, and the muscular young volunteers tossed off our belongings. It was baggage car door to

 https://doi.org/10.5876/9781646421848.c005

FIGURE 5.1. Heart Mountain.

barrack door service and no tip expected, just a few *arigatos* [thank-yous] and obligatory bows. Everything was much better organized, as the volunteers had learned from the chaotic Pomona experience. The barracks, however, were not yet finished, at least ours wasn't. The Celotex panels inside the outer walls and those forming a ceiling had not yet been installed, so we had very little protection from outside elements. Without a ceiling there was a continuous open space above the room partitions that ran the full length of the barrack. A loud fart at one end of the barrack could be heard at the other end in the quiet of the night. Most people pretended not to hear it, but the kids would invariably scream in unison, "Who did that?" Within a few weeks, however, with a new shipment of Celotex the problem was resolved, much to the relief of all, especially the parents of the kids.

Each block of twenty-four residential barracks had two sectors, A and B. Each sector had one mess hall, one latrine (men's and women's) combined with a laundry room, and a coal-burning boiler room to provide hot water. The cooking stoves in the mess hall were also coal-burning as were the potbellied stoves in each room of the barrack. Coal was delivered on a regular basis and dumped in a huge pile just outside the boiler room. Everyone would run with coal bucket in hand to get a share, the spirit of *enryo* (reserve) temporarily set aside, until Mr. Ishigo, the boiler-keeper (husband of artist Estelle Ishigo), chased us off with his coal shovel. The kitchen stoves and the boiler heater had top priority, and he was in charge. We peons had to scramble for whatever was left over. *Enryo* could cost one some very cold nights. There was also one barrack in each sector reserved for general community services, such as special classrooms, recreation programs, church services, commissary, movie theater, barbershop, beauty shop, and meeting halls.

The administration buildings and hospital facilities were in a separate area at the far north-central section of the camp. The motor pool where they kept all the trucks and other vehicles and the facilities for servicing and repairing them was in the general area of the railroad depot where we first arrived. There was also a fire station and a police station, probably in the vicinity of the administration area, but I'm not sure. A high school would be constructed later in a large open area at the very center of the camp. Thus, our white captors could teach our children the beauty of our United States Constitution while in captivity.

All of this was surrounded by a barbed-wire fence with wooden guard towers at crucial intervals as was typical of the nine other "relocation centers" scattered throughout the badlands of America, symbols of hate, bigotry, ignorance, and fear.

Most accounts given by the erstwhile victims of this injustice seem to describe the camps in terms of the obvious physical discomforts, such as the incessant wind and dust storms and the extreme weather conditions to which most were not accustomed, having come from the milder climate of the West Coast. The lack of privacy was a common complaint but some measures had been taken to mitigate it, both by the administration and the inmates themselves. No doubt the complaints about these conditions, generally common to all the camps, were regarded as less volatile and therefore safer to express than the real causes for our distress—the inhumanity and the injustice of being persecuted in the first place. Why were we unable to express that which was already brewing in our minds and in our hearts?

Due to my previous employment in the sign shop in Pomona, I was automatically assigned to the poster shop in Heart Mountain. The poster shop was considerably more sophisticated than at Pomona, with facilities and personnel capable of a broader range of art and graphics work to serve the community. Some of the fellows were highly trained commercial artists. The primary media was silkscreen printing, which I became acquainted with for the first time. The regular crew consisted of seven men and five women. On occasion we would recruit high school students as temporary help, such as when we were requested (ordered) by the government to produce several hundred conservation posters for the military. Working there was quite enjoyable. It had a casual atmosphere, an aspect seemingly frowned upon by some of the more serious professionals. Well, I suppose we were getting top wages as professionals (nineteen dollars per month), so we should have acted a little more mature. But I do value the time I spent there and appreciate the training I received from the pros. I only regret not saying good-bye to all my friends there when I was compelled to leave camp abruptly and without warning.

I also attended the Art Students League, organized by Benji Okubo (brother of the noted artist Miné Okubo, who authored *Citizen 13660*).[19] Benji taught fine arts classes and we remained friends for several years after the camp closed until his death. He inspired me to spend many hours sketching aspects of the camp and the

FIGURE 5.2. Poster shop guys, ca. 1943. Yoshito in center of front row (Library of Congress National Archives).

FIGURE 5.3. Yoshito at drafting table working on government conservation poster, 1943 (Library of Congress National Archives).

mountain ranges around it. My favorite subject was Heart Mountain itself, which was the most prominent natural geologic formation in the area.[20]

In the year 2000, after hiking to the top of Heart Mountain, I wrote an essay on my thoughts during the period I was in camp.

THE WINTERS OF HEART MOUNTAIN

The winters were cold at Heart Mountain. As a native Southern Californian, I was ill-equipped to deal with the biting winds, sub-zero temperatures, and knee-deep snows. The snow did not fall gently at Heart Mountain. It came horizontally, like icy spears across the barren plains, to crash into the tarpaper barrack walls, as if to obliterate this abomination (euphemistically called a "relocation center")[21] at the foot of the majestic mountain after which it was named. The wind was incessant. Even in the heat of summer, dust storms coated our faces and hair with a fine white powder, as if to make us look more like our oppressors, a vain attempt to mask the damning evidence of our ethnicity, the apparent root of our woes and persecution.

FIGURE 5.4. Block 14 barracks and neighbor kids. Pencil sketch by author, 1943 (Division of Political and Military History, National Museum of American History, Smithsonian Institution).

The mountain took little note of the insanity occurring at its feet. It had, no doubt, witnessed in passed eras the massacre of others of dark skin, brutally stripped of their land, their culture, their livelihood, and their power of self-determination. It had, no doubt, witnessed the butchering of herds of buffalo for their hides and horns, leaving bloody naked carcasses to bake and rot under the blazing desert sun while calves stood bewildered and abandoned. So when the caravan of trucks came with loads of lumber, tarpaper, and spools of barbed wire, perhaps the mountain "sighed" and thought to itself, "Not again?"

But that was over fifty-seven years ago. Parts of the dry, desolate prairie have long since been converted to verdant, productive farmland, thanks in part to the labor and ingenuity of the inhabitants of the former prison camp who built life-giving canals from a nearby river. The camp itself no longer exists. A single tall, brick chimney at the far corner of what was formerly "home" for ten thousand wartime hostages stands starkly like a sentinel guarding three ancient abandoned barracks—a grim reminder of what occurred there many years ago. It is a memory which is visited rarely by those who by chance of ethnicity were imprisoned there, a memory even obliterated by others who feel overwhelmed by the pain and self-imposed shame for allowing themselves to be victimized. Indeed, some have created illogical myths based on the rationale of desperate survival expediency and devoid of all restraints of ethics and principle. They sought personal salvation by accommodating government actions regardless of how brazenly the government defied the founding principles of our country. They claimed this constituted undeniable proof of unwavering loyalty. Loyalty to what?

Though the camp no longer exists, the controversy simmers on. But it is no longer a question of the resisters versus the JACL, or the "No-No's" versus the

FIGURE 5.5. Block 14 mess hall. Pencil sketch by author, 1943 (Division of Political and Military History, National Museum of American History, Smithsonian Institution).

veterans, or even the government versus an ethnic minority. The inescapable issue is (and always has been), *what is the citizen's rightful response to constitutional transgressions?* What indeed is a citizen's responsibility when racially based civil rights restrictions are imposed by an errant government? Japanese America has evaded this essential question, using various distractions and excuses too long. Even the glorious sacrifices of our fighting men, painfully reminiscent of ancient, ritualistic human sacrifices to appease the white gods of antiquity, seem only to confuse the issue further.

Heart Mountain still stands, proud and unbowed, like the memory of our Issei parents who endured a lifetime of senseless humiliation, sometimes from their own offspring (whose integrity for the most part remained intact and their dignity resolute).

The undulating hills at the foot of the mountain play a fanciful game of tag with the shadows of wind-blown clouds dancing over them when viewed from atop the venerable old mountain, a good half-day hike. The ever-changing shadows flit over barren hills, plains, and the more recently cultivated patchwork of farms, unmindful of the changing character of the once desolate landscape. The clouds bring to all equally sprinkles or deluge, and even horrendous floods when nature's laws are ignored. A continuous circle of mountain ranges forms the far, far horizon. The range to the west, the Rockies and Yellowstone Park, are the nearest and most dramatic. Heart Mountain sits isolated in this great basin like an off-center hub of a lopsided wagon wheel, but seems to find dignity in its solitude, like the chimney at the former camp site, silent witnesses of eras gone by. The winters are still cold at Heart Mountain—but not as cold as the winters in the hearts of men.

FIGURE 5.6. Mama and Papa in front of our barrack, ca. 1944 (Kuromiya Family Collection).

My parents seemed to be adjusting surprisingly well to the unjust treatment to which we were subjected. I worried about Papa, in particular, who was so adamantly sensitive about matters of ethics and principle, even to the point of

FIGURE 5.7. My sister Kim (Kimiye), winter of 1944 (Kuromiya Family Collection).

martyrdom. I knew Mama to be a survivor, but she, too, thanks to her exposure to Papa and his costly ethics, was painfully aware of what was really happening and that it wasn't right. But I needn't have worried, and would not have been surprised had I paid more attention to them and their tragic history of shattered dreams and the resultant inner strength and resiliency they had developed to survive thus far. Indeed, it was they who were worried about their number three son and the mess into which he was about to get himself.

Papa was, in fact, enjoying himself washing the pots and pans in the mess hall kitchen and playing *goh* with the neighbors the rest of the time. True, there were times he came "home" in a full rage because "the idiots in the mess hall were doing things all wrong." To which Mama would say, "That's interesting. When did they make you into the boss?" I don't recall Mama ever having a job. I believe she just picked up where she left off as a teenager, knitting afghans and gossiping with the neighbors. I don't think she even missed her identity as mistress of the house

FIGURE 5.8. Block 14, laundry room and latrine. Watercolor by author, 1943 (Division of Political and Military History, National Museum of American History, Smithsonian Institution).

and ruler of the kitchen. They knew how to roll with the punches, and this was just a rest period between bouts. The government had met its match.

It is interesting to note that many of the prominent prewar leaders of the Japanese American community became the primary targets of the Nisei-constituted Japanese American Citizens League (JACL) in its battle to wrest control as representatives of our community from the mostly noncitizen Issei. By casting suspicion on the Issei and Kibei as potential betrayers of our national interests, the JACL pandered for favors from government agencies by agreeing to act as spies and informers, ostensibly in the interest of national security, thereby also enhancing their own images as loyal citizens worthy of the government's trust. Therefore, most of the victims of the witch-hunt conducted by the JACL, or at least with their avid cooperation, were the very people who were most highly respected in our community. The JACL also targeted those who were the most outspoken about the betrayals of the JACL, as well as those who questioned the constitutionality of the government's actions. In short, the JACL became undercover agents for the government—not representatives of the Japanese American people, as they claimed.

In the wake of these machinations by the JACL, there developed a subgroup of victims of governmental human rights violations who seem to have eluded the attention of even the most astute of Japanese American history writers: the wives of the Issei and Kibei "suspects" who were incarcerated immediately after Pearl Harbor. Many had toddlers and preteen children; some were pregnant when their husbands were picked up. Most were denied knowledge of where their husbands had been taken and the nature of the charges that were being made against them. The suspects were denied legal representation and were not allowed to communicate with their families.[22] With the advent of the "evacuation" orders, most wives were faced with major decisions with which they were ill-equipped to deal. Most had relatives, perhaps, but they were burdened with their own unanticipated dilemmas. It was a chaotic time for all Japanese Americans on the West Coast, but these wives and mothers were by far the most heart-wrenching victims of all those who were targeted by governmental indiscretions. *Shikataganai*, in their case, was hardly an adequate palliative.

Many were eventually reunited with their husbands (none of whom were ever formally charged or convicted of any acts of sabotage), but were compelled to remain incarcerated in Tule Lake[23] or Crystal City,[24] both of which were "segregated" camps, and where they were vulnerable to deportation as hostages for prisoner exchange with Japan. Regardless of the final outcome of their individual circumstances, it is inconceivable that these wives and mothers escaped without deep emotional and psychic scars, typically suffered in silence.

It is this subgroup of victims of the government's human rights violations[25] I regard as the *true* unsung heroes of the Japanese American wartime experience. And it didn't happen on the battlefields of Europe. It happened right here in the United States of America!

6

FAIR PLAY COMMITTEE

Generally, each inmate was assigned to the mess hall in which his or her barrack was located. Where the distance to one's workplace made it impractical to eat at that inmate's own mess hall, such as for lunch, the necessary adjustments could be arranged. Thus, the food served would always be in balance with the supplies delivered to each mess hall. On occasion, when someone was tempted to eat at an unauthorized mess hall because there was an expert chef there or perhaps prettier servers, that person would soon earn the hostile glares of the regulars upon proceeding to eat someone else's dinner. The threat of public humiliation was found to be an effective deterrent and behavior modifier in this artificially contrived community.

Because of its spaciousness and relative accessibility (bypassing formal permits from white administrators and dealing directly with the more sympathetic "internee"[26] managers), the mess hall became the logical site for spontaneous meetings and other inmate activities. Almost every family had a member or relative on the kitchen crew, so it became an unofficial secondary communications center via the grapevine—especially since the camp newspaper, the *Heart Mountain Sentinel*,[27] was known to be heavily pro-administration and not necessarily sympathetic to inmate interests. It is not surprising then that the mess halls would become the birthplace of the Fair Play Committee (FPC).[28]

In early 1943 the government distributed a questionnaire ostensibly to determine one's loyalties to Japan or the United States.[29] It was an extremely clumsily

https://doi.org/10.5876/9781646421848.c006

written, confusing, ineffective, and misleading document, which would become the single most polarizing instrument in the government/prisoner relationship, and a very divisive element within the prison community itself. While failing to protect our country from any *real* threat, if in fact there ever was one, it undermined any remnant of trust in our government that may have been held by the victims of the unjustified persecution. In essence, it compelled the accused to prove innocence, instead of the accuser having to prove guilt, contrary to democratic principles and fundamental judicial procedures.

In February of 1943 a group known as the Heart Mountain Congress of American Citizens[30] was formed, led by Frank Inouye,[31] Kiyoshi Okamoto,[32] and Paul Nakadate.[33] This later evolved in early 1944 into the Heart Mountain Fair Play Committee (FPC), with Okamoto as chairman and Nakadate as secretary. By this time, Inouye, I believe, had left the camp for personal reasons. In any event, the Congress attempted to get clarification from the camp administration on the questionnaire, but received none. Apparently, everyone was told to "just follow orders." Even the government agents who distributed and monitored the questionnaires seemed uninformed, or at least would divulge no further information. The Congress warned the community that the questionnaire could very well be a prelude to imposing the military draft in the camps. A simple "yes" on question 27 could be interpreted as a willingness to enlist into the armed forces and be deployed wherever ordered.

The two crucial questions that were posed in the questionnaire were:

27. Are you willing to serve in the armed forces of the United States on combat duty wherever ordered?
28. Will you swear unqualified allegiance to the United States of America and faithfully defend the United States from any or all attacks by foreign or domestic forces, and forswear any form of allegiance or obedience to the Japanese emperor, or any other foreign government, power, or organization?

Depending solely on the answers to the questionnaire as evidence of one's loyalty or disloyalty, it was arbitrarily determined that a "no" to both questions 27 and 28 constituted disloyalty to the US and cause for segregation and possible deportation. A "yes" to both questions constituted "proof" of one's loyalty. A combination of yes and no would require assessment of how the rest of the questions were answered to determine one's loyalty. Failure to respond to any question was regarded as a no. Reasons or conditions attached to a response would be disregarded; only a simple yes or no was acceptable.[34]

I suspected the entire process was an attempt by the government to justify the existence of the camps. The questionnaire was essentially a witch-hunt to reveal (through self-incrimination) that there were in fact "disloyal" persons within the camps. On the other hand, the yes-yes responses would hasten the closing of the camps, which were rapidly becoming a political embarrassment to the government. Thus, it was designed to be a win-win situation for the government.

It was often referred to as the loyalty questionnaire. How could one's loyalty to our country be determined by a question which requires a simple yes or no answer? And just who is to make that determination and what would be their qualifications? Would it even be legally sustainable? The government agencies apparently found nothing unreasonable with the procedure. And surprisingly much of Japanese America, especially the JACL, used it as undeniable proof to justify their accommodationist policy by stigmatizing those whom they deemed disloyal based on such arbitrary evidence.

The questionnaire was, in fact, nothing more than a citizen's waiver of any claims against the government of civil rights infringements and a vow to obey governmental dictates no matter how unreasonable.[35] As James Omura, the pre-war editor of *Current Life*, a magazine of arts, letters and public affairs, had earlier suggested at the Tolan Committee hearings,[36] the Gestapo had come to America.[37]

I finally heeded the mimeographed warnings posted by Frank Emi[38] [destined to be a prominent FPC leader along with Okamoto and Nakadate] and answered with a conditional yes to question 27 (the condition being that I first be accorded equal constitutional rights as Caucasian American citizens) and a yes to question 28 (although I had never sworn allegiance to the emperor in the first place).

The Congress was right, of course. Early in 1944, without further hearings or explanations, my draft classification was changed from 4-C (enemy alien), to 1-A (eligible for conscription). It was a relief to know I was no longer considered sinister, but the condition of the reinstatement of my civil rights seemed to have been ignored.

I was quite determined that I could not in good conscience bear arms under the existing conditions, but I also had trepidations about protesting alone. What good would it do? I decided to attend a meeting of the newly formed FPC. These were becoming quite frequent as some registrants were already getting their pre-induction draft notices.

As I approached the mess hall building, I noticed the absence of the usual clatter of dishes, pots, and pans. There were neither the familiar shrieks of children nor the incessant chatter of gossip. Also missing was the pungent aroma of steaming rice, homemade *takuan* [pickled daikon radish], and not-so-fresh fish, which would normally escape every time someone opened a door to enter or leave. There was only the deep rumbling of subdued voices, interrupted occasionally by the squeal of a table or bench dragging on the concrete floor. I entered the smoke-filled room, searching for familiar faces. Not finding any, I settled into an open space between two strangers on a hard wooden bench near the back of the room. I noticed my glasses didn't fog up as they usually did when entering the steamy mess hall on cold evenings. All the important players were sitting at two ten-foot-long tables abutted end to end at the front of the room where the serving counter acted as a barrier between the kitchen and the larger dining area. Papers were being shuffled back and forth among those at the front table. Sitting so far back and with all the smoke in the room, I couldn't see very well but I didn't mind. I was there primarily to hear, not see. Besides, close access to the rear door was reassuring in case I didn't like what I was to hear.

Suddenly, a middle-aged man (everyone seems to be middle-aged or elderly when you're twenty), rather slight of build, but with a voice of one twice his size, stood and announced in no uncertain terms the start of the meeting. This put an abrupt and permanent end to many unfinished sentences in the now-crowded room. Perhaps I exaggerate a bit in describing Kiyoshi Okamoto, but he was so atypical of the quiet, contained Japanese image. I was immediately captivated by his demeanor, directness, and (I hoped) his sincerity. His language was brutally crude, sprinkled generously with four-letter expletives, but the content was essentially an articulation of my own deeper thoughts and feelings. Further, he seemed to have an impressive knowledge of constitutional law, indispensable in any civil-rights forum. Other speakers followed, but I don't recall much of what was said. I was busy in my own head, separating the seed from the chaff, wondering if I had heard correctly.

I attended other meetings. I paid a two-dollar fee and was placed on the growing membership roster. The meetings were held in various mess halls whose managers were amenable to our cause (not all were). Each time I sat a little closer to the front table. I grew to respect all the male leaders (the steering committee) as principled individuals who knowingly jeopardized their own and their families' welfare in an effort to regain dignity, if not justice, for all inmates. Most were too old for the draft or had dependents, which would get them easy deferments. One [Guntaro Kubota[39]] wasn't even a US citizen, but he was concerned about the plight of those who were.

On about March 16, 1944, I received my notice to report for a physical exam prior to induction. Many thoughts ran through my head. I regarded the notice as yet another insult, the first being the curfew which now seemed so long ago. How could I continue to go along with this morally corrupt charade? I was being asked not to serve in defense of my country, but in a war of aggression in foreign lands for principles I was denied here at home. Further, it was presented as an opportunity to "prove my loyalty." Apparently, my guilt of disloyalty was assumed and I should welcome this opportunity to prove otherwise. Something was seriously amiss.

What of my family, still detained in this infernal prison camp? What of our suspended constitutional rights? What of our past cooperation with the government in surrendering those rights in the name of "national security"? What of the democratic principles which had been denied us—the very principles we were now asked to defend on foreign soil?

NO! This is *my* country! This is *my* Constitution! This is *my* Bill of Rights! I am here finally to defend them. I regret that I had surrendered my freedom. I shall not continue to surrender my dignity nor the dignity of the US Constitution!

Thus, after receiving the notice to report for the pre-induction exams, *I refused to comply!* Had the mainland United States been threatened with invasion, I would not have taken this stand. But to join in the killing and maiming in foreign lands, not because they were the enemy, but in order to prove my loyalty to a government that imprisoned me and my family without hearings or charges, I felt would be self-serving, irresponsible, and totally without conscience. Indeed, the real threat to our democracy was at my very doorstep.

At the next FPC meeting I sat at a front table, next to that of the steering committee. It was at a previous meeting that it was suggested there had been enough rhetoric and it was time to take a stand. The vote was almost unanimous, that a test case be initiated to determine the status of our citizenship and clarify our rights and obligations. The group had escalated from a passive protest forum to one of active resistance. The crowd at this point was well over the fire-restriction capacity for the building, perhaps by as much as 50 percent. They were mostly young Nisei men with a scattering of Issei parents and a few women of both generations.

In the course of the meeting they called for a show of hands of those who had received their pre-induction notices since the last meeting. Several, perhaps a dozen including myself, raised our hands. They asked me, perhaps because I was at the closest table, what I intended to do about it. I stood up and explained I was instructed to be on the bus to Powell on the morning of the twenty-third. Then I found myself declaring I would *not* be on that bus. There was a sudden cheer that rattled the windows and startled me. I felt a million eyes on me, and as exhilarating as it was, my knees began to buckle. I was thankful to sit down. There were others who stood and declared their intent to resist, but also a few who had not decided. I wondered how many who had received their notices were reluctant to even raise their hands.

As for me, I had passed the point of no return. It was now cast in stone. There would be no turning back.

7

RESISTANCE

The following day I told my parents what had occurred the prior evening at the meeting. They were already aware of my inner conflicts about the inherent dishonesty of using the military as a means of demonstrating one's loyalty and thereby attaining acceptance by the government and the American public. Such acceptance was not my primary goal. My loyalty was never the issue. I did nothing to justify anyone's questioning my loyalty. Indeed, the issue is and always has been the unresolved misdeeds of the government in placing the fundamental principles of our country in jeopardy. The existence of the concentration camps and the circumstances surrounding them does indeed constitute a threat to those principles. I felt it a duty as a concerned citizen to take this first opportunity (which might be my last) to demand resolution of the inequity before submitting to military conscription.

I don't think Mama grasped the idea. She seemed only concerned that I might very well end up in prison (conveniently overlooking the fact that we were already in prison). She suggested I just go along like the other fellows and not make such a fuss. Maybe I might flunk the physical anyway. At any rate, *shikataganai!* Papa didn't argue with her or with me. I firmly believe he understood my position and might well have done the same had it been him. Kazumi had already left the camp to stay with friends in Chicago.[40] I don't think she would have agreed with me, for she seldom did. Kim, on the other hand, I could always rely on, whether I was right or wrong, which made it even more important to me that it was right, in

https://doi.org/10.5876/9781646421848.c007

order to justify her faith in me. In reality, there was no right or wrong. Under the circumstances, it was merely a matter of one's priorities. The divisiveness of public reaction was the problem, not the issue itself.

A few days later, I encountered Em, my sister-in-law. It was just outside our barrack and her ten-month-old son, Kiyoshi, was crawling in the dirt at our feet. Em was very upset about my decision and accused me of being selfish and a coward. I had condemned her baby Kiyoshi to having a "draft dodger" for an uncle. She claimed that, if she had known I was such a coward, she never would have married my brother. Needless to say, I was taken aback by her outburst. But knowing she worked on the *Sentinel* staff under Bill Hosokawa, an avid JACLer, it was naïve of me to have been caught off guard. This single incident haunted me for several years, but was eventually ameliorated twenty years later when Kiyoshi became a civil rights activist and a close family friend of Martin Luther King Jr. He also became a leading political force in the gay rights movement.[41] Apparently, Em has gained new insights contrary to her wartime camp mindset of JACL dogma. She now claims she had always supported my resistance and denies any memory of her outburst in front of our barrack. It seems my brother, Hiro, had always disagreed with my actions, but we never discussed it, so I was never sure. I always thought he avoided discussing it because he didn't want to upset Em. Apparently, they both disagreed with my stand. And perhaps they disagreed with Kiyoshi when he showed an interest in civil rights activism. Perhaps that is why Kiyoshi opted to remain in Philadelphia, even after finishing school [the University of Pennsylvania] there, so as not to embarrass his parents by contradicting their JACL-contrived Model Minority image.

Kiyoshi sensed that the West Coast, in spite of its cosmopolitan racial composition, was not a wholesome, humane environment for progressive thinking and spiritual growth. Perhaps there were too many skeletons in the closets of West Coast history. After all, he had been exiled from California to be born in a Wyoming concentration camp. He confided to me what he could not express to his own parents. After Hiro's death in 1982, Em came out openly in support of Kiyoshi's humanitarian stance and mine as well. As I observed earlier, we elders have much to learn from our offspring. Wisdom does not automatically blossom with age. Many of my generation are a grim example of that.

One morning, as anticipated, a black limousine came right to the door of our barrack and a US marshal and an FBI agent asked for me. I recall telling them it was about time and I had thought they had forgotten about me (silly boy!). I asked if I could go to the bathroom first and they said, "Okay, but don't take too long" (silly them). I ran in through the laundry room door and out the boiler room door to say good-bye to my girlfriend Michi, whose barrack was close by, then back again knowing they would be getting nervous, which they were. It was Mama who seemed the most worried, convinced that I had run off (stupid me).

By then, a small group of neighbors had gathered, whispering and pointing. I felt bad that Mama and Papa were subjected to this humiliation on my account, but said quick good-byes to my family and a few close friends I recognized in the group. There were five other fellows already in the car, none of whom I knew. By the time we reached the highway, I realized I really should have gone to the bathroom. *Gambare*!

Fortunately, we stopped in Cody, Wyoming, a scant twelve miles from the camp, where we were fingerprinted and had mug shots taken—the kind we used to see in post offices, with numbers across the chest. I don't think we had any numbers, though. I was allowed to use the bathroom.

Our "tour" took us through the Wyoming town of Thermopolis, where we may have stopped for lunch. I do recall driving through what the US marshal said was the Wind River Canyon. It was an awe-inspiring deep gorge through the mountains, created by eons of wind and water erosion of the Bighorn River. Sheer walls of granite rose above us from the riverbed and highway for a few hundred feet (or so it seemed to this creature of the flatlands). Mother Nature's artwork puts man's meager efforts to shame. For the moment I had forgotten where our scenic tour was actually taking us.

Ike Matsumoto, who sat in the front seat between the marshal and the FBI agent, was in a nervous sweat since Thermopolis. Someone's pistol had slipped out of its holster and kept poking him in the butt, no matter how much he squirmed. I don't know why he didn't speak up. Maybe it was placed there purposely as a test and only held blanks. He told me about this later when I asked him why he was sweating so much.

We traveled the rest of the day and arrived at Rawlins, a small town outside of Cheyenne. Apparently, we resisters were scattered throughout southeast Wyoming because the Cheyenne County Jail couldn't accommodate us all.

Since there were no other sinister patrons in the small but clean jail, we six were allowed free access to much of the second-floor facility. This isn't going to be so bad after all, we thought. We even got home-prepared dinners brought to us by the jailer's very pleasant wife, an excellent cook. One barred window was located directly over the main entrance to the city hall below. I spotted a twenty-ish Nisei girl with her middle-aged mother, local residents no doubt, emerge from this door. I called the others over. We whistled and made catcalls to get their attention. They both looked up, whereupon the girl whispered something to her mother and hurriedly dragged her along. The mother, still with the look of pleasant surprise, kept waving and attempted to come closer. Her daughter, embarrassed at seeing Japanese faces behind bars, impatiently pulled her away.

In a few days we were transported to Cheyenne. The jail building was old, dark, and dismal. The soot-coated windows along one wall faced the blank wall of the neighboring building, against which sunlight reflected for a few short hours each day. Meager as it was, it was a welcome supplement to the three or four yellowed light bulbs hanging high above us from the murky ceiling, which was long ago painted in some obscure muddy tone. I could almost imagine it to be a starless, moonless night sky, between my bouts with depression and anxiety (which I carefully concealed from the others). The ancient mattress and threadbare blanket reeked of urine and vomit, so I took care not to roll my face into them when trying to sleep. We were to be kept there for two and a half months, after which the grand jury would convene. Camp life was beginning to seem like a long-lost paradise. I missed my family the most.

I didn't know anyone in the group except one whom I had met briefly as a member of the Arts Students League that I had attended in camp. I was surprised and somewhat uplifted to see him there. Nonetheless, I felt pretty much an outsider and did not participate much in the conversations or limited activities. I was vaguely aware there were some communications going on with the camp, but never bothered to get involved. My isolation was self-imposed.

Every Sunday morning a small group of five or six missionaries came to visit us, sing a hymn, and read from the Bible. I noticed the word "sin" kept popping up quite often. We were politely attentive at first, even the Buddhists among us, but later we felt it was an imposition on a "captive" audience and many ignored them. A few even sat on the toilet in full view in hopes they would get *our* message. But, of course, they were doing God's work, so they persisted in trying to "save" us. A few of us were civil enough to thank them, but failed to convince them that we were the victims and they should be preaching to the perpetrators, not us. Each time after they left, my artist friend would mimic them by waving an open palm over our heads while intoning words from the gospel. Thereafter, he was dubbed by our group as "Father Imai." That name would stick throughout our ordeal in Cheyenne and subsequent prison term at McNeil Island.

One evening, two representatives from the JACL came to interview us separately and privately, Joe Grant Masaoka[42] (whom I viewed with suspicion and distrust) and Minoru Yasui.[43] Earlier, Yasui had challenged the curfew order by deliberately violating it. He had gained the respect of many of us by affirming principles not unlike our own. Yet, here he was espousing the JACL accommodationist policy. It was rather confusing. They asked what my reasons were for resisting the draft and what I hoped to gain by it. They sympathized with my motivation and commended me for my ideals and courage to act on them. They did not question my sincerity, but they scoffed at my expectations and dismissed them as unrealistic and naïve. They proclaimed: "This is not the time to quibble about personal freedoms and constitutional principles. More is at stake. The entire Japanese American future, our very survival, depends on assuring white America that we are trustworthy and loyal in spite of the fact that we look like the enemy." They asserted that we "draft dodgers" were tarnishing the extremely precarious image of Japanese Americans and were doing our people a great disservice.

They then proceeded to question me about the Fair Play Committee. Did anyone, Kiyoshi Okamoto, for instance, suggest to me that breaking a law wasn't a criminal act if I didn't agree with the law? Had I heard of James Omura, English editor of the *Rocky Shimpo*? How often did I read Omura's editorials? Did his editorials or any of the FPC leaders influence me in any way to "evade the draft?"

I assured them that my sense of outrage and feelings of political impotence preceded any knowledge of the FPC or the reinstitution of the draft. These events merely provided a long-awaited opportunity to publicly air my grievances. "It's not too late," they persisted, ignoring my remarks. If I would sign a statement and name names, they promised they would do everything in their power to plead my case, to have the draft violation dismissed, and give me a second opportunity to prove my loyalty by enlisting in the army. Otherwise, they said, I would face rejection by our community for marring their image as loyal citizens. *They* would personally see to that!

A few months later, seven leaders of the Fair Play Committee and editor James Omura would be indicted on charges of "conspiracy to violate and counseling others to violate the Selective Service Act."[44] The *real* purpose of Masaoka and Yasui's visit to the Cheyenne County Jail became quite clear.

Interestingly, the two representatives of the JACL were allowed access to us by the district attorney without the presence of our attorney, whereas previous requests for visits by family or friends had been and continued to be denied.

8

THE CIRCUS

One might suggest that the spirit of the Heart Mountain resistance movement was rooted in the ancient samurai tradition of honor, commitment, and perseverance. Whereas in Japan these attributes were directed toward the welfare of a sovereign state or lord, here in America it is the Constitution and Bill of Rights that must be honored, committed to, and preserved. I prefer to characterize the resistance movement as following in the spirit of the authors of the Declaration of Independence. That is, that of taking personal responsibility for one's liberty or lack thereof, and actively protesting governmental oppression in whatever form available, not necessarily to attain tangible goals, but in defense of the involved principles. I believed this to be what inspired the birth of the Heart Mountain Fair Play Committee.

I recall thinking it was a rather silly name for a group professing such lofty ideals. It sounded more like a Little League baseball commission or a recreational mediation board. But there was nothing silly about the issues it would soon challenge, or the compelling principles it would invoke to jar the conscience of all who believed in the sanctity of citizens' rights. It was, in every sense of the word, a bona fide civil rights entity a decade before Rosa Parks and Martin Luther King Jr. But certain segments of Japanese America would not recognize it as such. They would only see it as a threat to their well-groomed image of compliance and subservience, and proceed to bury it along with their guilt of complicity in the most blatant civil rights violation in our country's recent history.

https://doi.org/10.5876/9781646421848.c008

My initial purpose in attending the FPC meeting was to elicit information about the moral and legal justification for our continued detention without hearings or trial. I was also seeking what recourse we might have when, while still under such duress, we were ordered to fulfill the same military obligations as citizens enjoying the freedoms denied us. The Fair Play Committee began as a grassroots forum to discuss these matters so pertinent to our citizenship status and our rights and obligations therein. It was after the War Relocation Authority[45] provided no answers and would only remind us of the dire consequences of disobeying government orders that we as a group voted to individually ignore the notices to report for pre-induction exams in order to contest the issue in a court of law.

I don't know how many members received their draft notices subsequent to this proclamation, but I would guess a few decided to comply with the orders rather than risk a term in prison. Sixty-three, including myself, did resist, however, and we had our test case—one which would be the largest such case in Wyoming history. The trial would not take place until mid-June, about two and a half months away. Heart Mountain Director Guy Robertson, fearing that our presence in camp during this period might disrupt the ongoing induction effort, requested that we *not* be returned there. We couldn't afford the $2,000 per head bail, anyway. Also, paying bail for the privilege of awaiting trial in a concentration camp seemed rather absurd. Thus, as noted earlier, because the Cheyenne County Jail could not accommodate us all, we were scattered in small local jails all over Wyoming.

Meanwhile, in camp the *Heart Mountain Sentinel*, the pro-administration and pro-JACL newspaper, was especially vicious in its editorial attacks, accusing the FPC leaders of treason against our country and betraying our people. It characterized the members (me) as deluded, dim-witted cowards, allowing ourselves to be manipulated by the trouble-making leaders to fulfill their sinister agenda to obstruct the war effort and detract from the heroic sacrifices of our fighting men.

When the trial date approached, all those held in outlying jails were transported to the Cheyenne County Jail, conveniently located about a block from the courthouse. I had been there for most of the two and a half months, so luckily had my own bunk. The newcomers had to throw their sleeping mats onto the floor in whatever space they could find, and thereby risk getting stepped on during the night. It was very crowded. Because of the lack of space, I suspect, a few drunks and petty thieves were left on the streets of Cheyenne during our trial. Indeed, the circus had come to town and this was just the beginning.

The stage was pretty well set on the very first day of our trial when Judge T. Blake Kennedy[46] addressed the sixty-three of us as "You Jap boys—." We all looked at each other and didn't know whether to laugh or cry. We knew then that things would not go well for us. Earlier, we had waived our right to a jury trial, reasoning that although we were entitled to a jury of our peers, our peers and potential jurors were behind barbed wire. In their stead we would most likely be stuck with twelve

FIGURE 8.1. The trial of "The 63" in the Cheyenne courtroom. Yoshito (obscured) at far right, second row (Densho).

locals who would view us as the enemy and would be happy to rid their great state of Wyoming of this scourge the federal government had foisted on them by sending us to a prison in some other state. Much wiser, we thought, to plead our case to a professional, someone experienced in the art of jurisprudence and familiar with the intricacies of constitutional law. To our dismay, we got T. Blake Kennedy, a self-professed racist who would be more than happy to use his noble bench to rid his great state of Wyoming of this scourge by catapulting us into the prisons of some other state, preferably somewhere back on the West Coast.

The second clue that things would not go well for us came when our attorney, Samuel Menin,[47] during one of his rare visits to the Cheyenne jail, suggested we all crew-cut our heads *bozu* style, so as to thwart identification. Of course, all of us "Japs" looked alike to the cowboys anyhow, but without individual identification in the courtroom, he thought he might be able to get us off on a technicality. He seemed oblivious to the fact that *we* had initiated the trial to plead our grievances and were seeking judicial relief from our own and our families' unjustified incarceration *before* joining the military. Unfortunately, several of the fellows in youthful defiance went along with this transparent ploy. Predictably, the prosecution submitted our previous fingerprint records and mug shots as proof of our identity. Mr. Menin was chastised for wasting the court's valuable time. We defendants suffered a serious blow to our credibility. I am reminded of this unfortunate and costly charade every time I view the now famous courtroom photograph with the many defendants sporting identical crew cuts.[48]

The trial itself was a travesty of justice. It was yet another blow to our now fragile hope of ever establishing credibility in the idea that the Constitution and the Bill of Rights are the supreme laws of the land, and that not even the US Congress or the US president himself could abridge them. When the justice system bends to the whims of political expediency, where do we turn? At times it appeared our case might be settled by fisticuffs in the back alleys of Cheyenne when the two attorneys got into a particularly heated argument, took off their coats, and challenged each other to settle matters the old-fashioned way. It was high noon in Judge Kennedy's courtroom.

Toward the end of the trial, prosecutor Carl Sackett,[49] apparently feeling quite smug in successfully countering defense counsel's attempts to introduce the loss of civil liberties as reasonable grounds for civil disobedience, was rocking back in his chair with his hands confidently clasped behind his head. Suddenly, with a loud bang, he disappeared behind the heavy table at which he was seated. Startled, but thankful for the break in the tensions that had pervaded the now stuffy courtroom, we all laughed. That is, all but Judge Kennedy, who was madly pounding his gavel like a lion tamer, having lost control of his performers. Mr. Sackett reappeared, red-faced over the indignity he had brought upon himself, brushed off his coat, and angrily righted his recalcitrant chair. He then pointed a shaky finger at us and declared, "You guys won't be laughing when you hear the verdict!" It was as if he and Judge Kennedy had already conferred on the matter.

He was right, of course. We didn't laugh. The circus was over and nobody cheered as we were quietly led back to our cages.

We sixty-three were deemed guilty of violating the Selective Service Act and sentenced to three years in a federal prison. As we suspected, the lower courts could not, or would not, rule on constitutional matters, especially during wartime. An appeal to a higher court would be our only recourse.

In spite of our convictions, a second group of twenty-two from Heart Mountain followed in our footsteps in the ensuing months. They had no hopes of winning, of course, but acted on principle and as a symbolic gesture of unity in defiance of Judge Kennedy's court as an insult to the US Constitution.

As we were marched back to the jailhouse, a block away behind the courthouse, no one said a word. Even though we thought we were prepared for setbacks, especially in the early stages of our battle, I don't think we were emotionally prepared to accept the notion that today we had technically become convicts, felons, the bad guys, a threat to society, social outcasts. "But how can that be?" I asked myself. "I don't feel any different than I did when I woke up this morning. But maybe tomorrow I will. At any rate, I'd better enjoy the sunlight and fresh air while I can. The jailhouse is going to be even gloomier than usual tomorrow."

As soon as we arrived at our second-story "apartment," my first thought was to write to Mama and Papa via my sister Kim: "No doubt the *Sentinel* will have quite a field day with their 'I told you so's.' I know Papa won't be surprised, but Mama and Kim may not understand. I want them to know I am fine and not to worry. It seems I'll be going on a short vacation and at least I'll know why, unlike while in the camps. I must write to Michi, but it'll have to wait as we're only allowed one letter per week."

Meanwhile, the discussion within the group that evening centered mostly on our appeal and about pursuing the matter even further if necessary. But we were confident the FPC was handling that and all we could do was to wait and see. I only hoped they would find a better lawyer for our appeal than the yo-yo we had for our trial. I suspected he was only showboating for publicity at our expense since finding a self-respecting lawyer to take a case such as ours during wartime was almost impossible. We might have to wait until after the war, but a precedent had to be established no matter how long it took or at what cost. Too much was at stake if, in fact, the constitutional integrity of our case was our ultimate goal.

The sixty-three of us were divided into two groups to serve our sentences. The older group of thirty was to be sent to a high-security prison in Leavenworth, Kansas. The younger group of thirty-three, of which I was one, was scheduled for a minimum-security prison on McNeil Island in Puget Sound of Washington State, near Tacoma.[50] It is interesting to note that this was in the "restricted zone" on the West Coast where all Japanese American residents had been forcibly evicted two years earlier. A few of those same former residents were in our group. I believe we were among the first Japanese Americans to be allowed back to the West Coast—over six months before the restrictions were officially lifted. Even the JACL, in spite of their pandering ways, never had that privilege.

In my letter to Michi I described briefly the shameful court proceedings of that final day. Then I explained that three years was a little more than I had expected, and we shouldn't hold each other to our previous hopes and plans. I couldn't even assure her I'd be the same person after three years in prison. So if she chose not to respond to the letter, I would be okay, I would understand. Not very romantic, to be sure, but at this point I didn't feel I had the right to make any demands or have any expectations. But in truth, I did need a friend, terribly.

With that taken care of, I tried to become more attentive to my cellmates and got into pointless conversations that I knew would go nowhere. I think the others were trying to escape their anxieties also. Somehow we all managed to survive our disappointment and maybe even bonded more tightly than in the previous two and a half months we were forced to tolerate each other's presence. And we did respect one another's privacy, knowing it was a difficult time for all of us even though some pretended it was no big deal. After all, weren't we all warned that the constitutional issues that were key to our case probably could not be determined in the lower courts?

Michi did respond to my letter. She expressed dismay that I would give up on our relationship so easily. (It wasn't easy.) Soon after I was arrested, she had left the camp to work in a town not far from Cheyenne. Shortly after our conviction, she joined a few of her workmates seeking job prospects in the Salt Lake City area. Was she unaware that Salt Lake City was a hotbed of JACL activity? She continued to write each week. Then the letters became less and less frequent until eventually came the dreaded "Dear John."

Strangely, she didn't say she no longer loved me. She just remarked that her "friends" had convinced her that what I was doing was wrong, that our actions were a discredit to our people, and she shouldn't write to me any longer. She asked that I return all the photos and letters she had been sending me. As devastated as I was, I didn't argue. I lied and told her I understood.

Her sudden change of attitude about the civil rights protest puzzled me the most. Why had she felt it necessary to discredit an issue she knew I was already committed to? Why were her newfound friends' values suddenly more virtuous than what we both had agreed was the only conscionable course? If she had had second thoughts about having to wait longer than expected for my release, it would be understandable, and I could accept that, even if reluctantly.

I recalled the parting remarks made by Yasui and Masaoka at the end of their failed interrogation at the Cheyenne County Jail earlier. "This is not the end," they had threatened. They would personally see to it that we resisters would be discredited in our community for our "ill-advised" actions and we would eventually regret rejecting their well-intended efforts to salvage our futures (or something to that effect).

So could this have been the first round of the retribution they had promised? I, no doubt, was the target, but why did they have to involve Michi? It didn't make much sense.

Later, I would learn of the constant harassment James Omura, the journalist, was subjected to by the JACL leadership. He had been falsely accused, along with the Fair Play Committee leaders, of aiding and abetting the draft resisters. He, presumably, was cleared of all charges under the "freedom of the press" clause pertaining to journalists,[51] but the legal fees had bankrupted his meager savings. He lost his editorship of Denver's *Rocky Shimpo* under pressure by the JACL. All attempts to find and hold employment within the Japanese community ended in failure as the people to whom he had formerly donated much aid and encouragement inexplicably turned their backs on him. Further, his marriage to his wife and soulmate ended in divorce. She could no longer tolerate the unending, senseless JACL harassment.

My ordeal suddenly seemed rather petty. Why did they even bother?

I often wondered if the Fair Play Committee leaders and some of the more outspoken resisters had experienced similar harassment. Perhaps they did, but regarded it a personal matter and chose not to discuss it. How much of the pathos of Japanese American history lies deeply hidden in the culturally conditioned silence of a people not known to advertise their deepest suffering? I am reminded of the beautifully written story by the noted author Wakako Yamauchi,[52] "And the Soul Shall Dance," which reflects similar sentiments.

In spite of the forewarning that the constitutional basis of our case would most likely have to be determined in a higher court rather than at the district court level at which we were tried, our disappointment at the loss was quite obvious. We were puzzled, however, on receiving reports from our families in camp that many (but not all) who showed support for us prior to the trial seemed to have turned against us. To me it was apparent that those who gave up so easily were never truly committed to the principles of our cause. Perhaps they never understood, but saw it as an opportunity to vent their anger against the unfair authoritarian persecution to which they were subjected. Small wonder it could be so easily withdrawn and remained so for decades later—long after the camps were closed.

Largely due to the JACL influence over the Japanese American media, the resistance effort was virtually omitted from our wartime history, except in discrediting terms. A few historians, however, were not so easily intimidated but were either unaware of the unique implications of the resistance as a grassroots civil protest or failed to gain the cooperation of the former resisters themselves because of *their* reluctance to speak out. In any case, it was generally regarded in the ethnic Japanese American community as an issue too "controversial" in its quest for an image of unquestionable loyalty. Also, during the resettlement period after WWII and the retraction of Executive Order 9066, our overwhelming needs were to seek sustainable income and reasonable family housing, so for this reason the rehashing of camp debates on what constituted loyalty or disloyalty served very little purpose.

It wouldn't be until the seventies, eighties, and nineties, after the civil rights movement and our own redress movement, that the Sansei generation became mature enough to inquire why they were robbed of their rightful historic legacy. Their query was essentially, "Why was there so little protest? Why the silence? Were we ashamed of who we were?"

9

MCNEIL ISLAND

In a few days, we who were bound for McNeil Island gathered our scant belongings and were marched to the train station a few blocks away. I think the Leavenworth bunch had left several days earlier. A handful of spectators, caught in the middle of their morning errands, stood gawking at us, more out of curiosity than hostility. Some even appeared sympathetic but were hesitant to approach us. I realized then that we may have misjudged the citizens of Cheyenne when we opted for a court trial instead of a jury trial. The end result might have been the same, but my respect for our justice system would not have been as devastated. Fortunately, we were not bound in chains or even handcuffs. Our average age was perhaps twenty-one or twenty-two, and being Japanese and generally looking younger, we probably appeared to be a high school soccer team—far from convicted felons under guard.

The train was already waiting for us. We boarded a special car not unlike the one that had brought us to Heart Mountain almost two years earlier, with bars in the windows instead of shades. Then I heard the train whistle, the same wailing whistle I had heard each night from our cell, except louder this time. I'd often wondered from whence it came and where it was headed; now I would find out. We headed westward, roughly following the highway that had brought us from Rawlins to Cheyenne. When we passed through Rawlins, I tried to spot the jailhouse/city hall building we had stayed in for a few days. I visualized the girl and her sweet mother who tried to communicate with us. I also recalled the jailer's wife who cooked such wonderful meals for us and brought them to our cells. But

 https://doi.org/10.5876/9781646421848.c009

FIGURE 9.1. Aerial view of McNeil Island (Department of Corrections, McNeil Island Corrections Center Photo Collection, 1855-2010, WA State Archives, Digital Archives).

from the railroad car I didn't recognize a thing. Perhaps I was sitting on the wrong side of the car.

We continued westward into Utah and Idaho, all of which was very scenic. I wondered if this was how a condemned man felt having his final meal on the eve of his execution, but ours was a last view of "freedom" before a temporary confinement. It was not a very reasonable comparison. I suddenly realized I had been confined for economic reasons for most of my life in Southern California anyway, until the "evacuation" released me. Still, that didn't make it right.

I was beginning to feel queasy and noticed that the guard who sat at the front of the car facing us was smoking a cigar. The wind current was carrying the stench through his open window and back into mine, so I closed my window. It helped a little, but not much. The rest of the trip was quite miserable. Jim Sako noticed I was turning green and tried to distract me by telling amusing stories. I couldn't laugh, but will forever be indebted to him for his efforts. I noticed everyone was starting to grow mustaches under their noses again from the locomotive smoke coming in through the open windows.

Once we neared Portland, Oregon, the air was cooler and less oppressive. It was nice to see and feel the Pacific Ocean again. We traveled northward toward Tacoma, Washington, but stopped at the small port town of Steilacoom, where we disembarked. We were on the shores of Puget Sound and could see our future temporary "home" across the calm waters. It appeared more like a vacation island than a prison. It was about four miles long, and the only substantial structure in view was the concrete prison building tucked along a hillside at the nearest edge of the shore. All else seemed to be covered with fir trees, alders, and a scattering of fruit orchards. There were some areas that had been cleared for various human activities, but in all it appeared a serene, pastoral setting, typical of all the smaller islands in the sound. I believe it had been primarily private homesteads before the federal government bought it for a prison site.

We were led from the train directly to a waiting ferry, which would traverse the short distance, perhaps four miles at the most, to the pier at the island, just below the concrete building that we could now see. It was about five stories tall and appeared much more foreboding than when we had first seen it from the train depot. The building was out of view as we disembarked and were led up a steep concrete ramp cut into the face of a cliff at the water's edge. As we emerged at the top of the ramp, the building suddenly loomed at our right. There was a wide concrete walk about 150 feet long to the main entrance of the building. But what caught my attention, being one of the first in line, was a little old Japanese man about my father's age, with a pair of hedge shears in his hands trimming the low myrtle hedge that flanked the walkway. Upon spotting us, his jaw dropped open and he rubbed his eyes in disbelief. He must have thought we were Japanese prisoners of war. As we marched past him, waving and smiling, he kept bowing and saluting. He may have dropped his shears and hurt his foot, but I had already passed him by then.

Later we discovered that he had been there for forty years (from 1904?) with a life sentence for a murder in Alaska. His name was Mikami, which we later shortened to "Mickey."

After we were checked in, identified, and processed, we underwent medical, physical, and psychological exams, and were held in the quarantine ward for several days until all medical reports were cleared. During this interval, we were assigned to individual cells that were immaculate but deathly quiet, with no communication allowed with neighboring cells. We were allowed reading material, however. A library cart managed by a trustee (a prisoner who had earned the trust of the guards) would come by on a regular basis. We could reserve what we wanted from a list of books and magazines. It was all quite civil and well regulated.

It wasn't until we had passed our exams and were released from the quarantine ward that we discovered that life in the "Big House" was very much as it is depicted in the movies. We were led down a long corridor that connected the lesser buildings to the Big House (the main prison). At the end of the corridor we waited for the gate guard to check our papers and unlock the gate. On entry into the huge concrete shell of a building, we were confronted by five tiers of steel cages within the shell. Each tier was at least eight feet high so the total height of the cages including the flooring was perhaps forty-five feet. It would require a building at least fifty feet high to encase all of that.

At any rate, we were led in groups of six or seven to whatever tier we were assigned. The gatekeeper would electronically release each cell gate in sequence as we approached that particular cell which had a vacancy. I was placed in a cell already occupied by four white men and three black men (or was it four black men and three white?). They pointed to an upper bunk next to the toilet, and no one said a word. We had an hour a day for recreation, but other than that there was little mingling within our group. There was only one fellow I became friends with during this time. Lucky Stokes was a young black kid who was court-martialed by the navy for impersonating an officer. He was the lightweight boxing champ on their battleship and while at McNeil too, I believe. He offered, "If any white dude gives you a bad time, let me know. I have connections." I was touched by his attempt at reassurance. But what if it was a black guy, I wondered, but was afraid to ask. It was quite scary in there. Fortunately, we were there for only a few weeks and were scheduled to be transferred to the minimum security "farm," which was a whole different environment.

As in the camps, transportation was in the back of trucks, unless you happened to be an official. Then you were chauffeured in a car. For a *special* official it would be a *big* car, even a limousine. I don't think there were many of those on the island, neither special officials nor limousines. So we were loaded onto the back of trucks for the two-mile drive to the farm. As we crested a gentle hill, there it was, in a large clearing at approximately the center of the island. It was a two-story masonry building, a simple large rectangular structure with the main entrance and stairwell in the center, flanked on both sides by dormitory wings. Architecturally unimpressive, it was nonetheless adequate for the purpose it was to serve. There was only room for a few of us initially, and the rest of us were housed in a wooden barracks just outside and to the right of the main building to wait our turn. The barracks were similar to the ones at Heart Mountain, except that the doors were at each end and there were no partitions; it was just one big open space with army cots along each side. A section was partitioned off at the far end to form a communal toilet and washroom. Dining facilities and showers were in the basement of the main building.

Within a few weeks we (our group) were all in the dormitories of the main building. Since its inhabitants were mostly short-termers—those who had completed most of their sentence and posed very little likelihood of escaping—turnover was quite rapid at the farm. I think we qualified because none of the officials regarded us as violent criminals. In fact, after they learned of our case, some of the guards implied that they would have done the same had they been treated as we were.

There were neither enclosing walls nor fences at the farm, except perhaps at the animal pens, but I don't recall where they were. I know there was a chicken pen, but not a single strand of barbed wire. I don't recall the guards being armed either, but I'm sure there were arms locked away somewhere, perhaps in the warden's office. In any case, nothing exciting enough to require guns occurred during the time we were there, except one morning when the warden arrived to find a large banner strung across the second-story dorm windows which read, "If Warden Stevens had a conscience, he would be a CO" (conscientious objector).[53] He immediately ordered the confinement to the dorms of all the COs, which was about one-fourth of our population. He questioned them individually. One CO told us later that he had asked the warden why he was accusing only the COs. The warden retorted angrily, "You're the only bastards on this island who know how to spell 'conscience'!"

A few months after we were transferred to the farm, we were joined by the group of twenty-two draft resisters from Heart Mountain who had been tried and convicted soon after us. There were also two Nisei students from the University of Washington and Gordon Hirabayashi[54] [a former student at that same university], all of whom were conscientious objectors. There were as well several Nisei from the Minidoka[55] and Topaz[56] "relocation centers" still in the Big House, who would be sent to the farm after we left. No wonder Mickey Mikami thought it was a Japanese invasion the first time he saw us at the entryway to the Big House. Imagine forty years of not seeing a Japanese face, and then, all of a sudden, a horde of the "yellow peril" thrust on him, and he having only a pair of hedge clippers with which to defend himself. Thank Buddha for the white guard with his trusty rifle.

The farm was composed mainly of war-related violators, conscientious objectors, Jehovah's Witnesses, camp resisters, and miscellaneous offenders such as ration cheaters, military frauds, all minor and nonviolent, but federal offenses nonetheless.

One morning we woke to the news that Mickey had been brought there on the previous evening. The Nisei all gathered around to greet him, which caused all kinds of delays in the morning's schedule. The work crew trucks were left waiting outside with only half a crew. Shy little Mickey was suddenly a celebrity. He always was our mascot, unbeknownst to him. He didn't know what to make of it. I think to us, collectively, he symbolized our parents, which many of us were separated from for the first time in our lives. Perhaps to him we represented the sons he would never have. He seemed wary of becoming too attached to us, however, knowing we would someday abandon him as everyone else had. He was later assigned as chief caretaker of the chicken coops. Some of us were honored to find a freshly laid egg on our pillow when we returned from work. He denied knowing anything about it when we tried to thank him. I think the guards knew also, but why should they spoil an old man's fun when he had nothing else to share? Everyone liked Mickey. He was the gentlest person I ever knew. Yet, as a twenty-year-old in a fit of passion, he had killed. An all-white jury and a white judge sent him to a white prison where he was virtually alone for forty years. He had created his own prison within a prison. So why should the prison guards bicker over a few eggs?

Like most of the newcomers my first job was in the vegetable fields—stoop labor, that is. By request I was transferred to the wood-chopping crew. They were clearing a swath through dense brush, fir, and alder forests to move existing farmhouses to a site closer to the Big House to be remodeled for prison personnel housing. I don't know why they couldn't use existing roads, but they needed firewood for the boiler room anyway. So maybe it was to make work for the inmates, provide firewood, and afford a shortcut in their house-moving project. In any case, it all seemed unnecessarily destructive, so I applied for a job salvaging some old weed-infested fruit orchards adjacent to some of the soon-to-be-moved houses. They gave me a very small army surplus caterpillar tractor to disc out the weeds, which were almost as tall as the stunted, abandoned trees. Since most of the terrain was hilly, it was tricky getting the cultivator to follow the tractor and not slide down slope, wiping out fruit trees. As a city boy, I realized a farm boy (as most in our group were) should be doing this, not me. I was more destructive with this machine than I was with the axe. But I wasn't about to give up the solitude and independence I had found, even if I had to decapitate a few desperate fruit trees that I was supposed to save from the threatening weeds. Just before sundown the crew-truck would honk its horn and I would throw a tarp over the killing machine and head for "home." Did I just hear the trees sigh?

Meanwhile, back in Wyoming steps were already underway to ensure that the military induction program would suffer no further delays. Little did we suspect—we who had insisted on the primacy of our appeal—that all our projections were for naught. Not only did we not get the wholehearted support of our own group of thirty-three at McNeil, but efforts by the government to render the FPC ineffective had already been initiated. The seven most visible leaders of the FPC, including two who were earlier consigned to Tule Lake Segregation Center as "troublemakers," were indicted in the Cheyenne District Court for "conspiring to violate and counseling others to violate the Selective Service Act." Understandably, all FPC resources were temporarily diverted to the defense of the seven leaders. This was at the expense of the resisters' test case which, to my knowledge, was never again submitted after the initial rejection by the court of appeals.[57]

For the FPC conspiracy trial they succeeded in acquiring the noted civil rights attorney A. L. Wirin.[58] They were convicted in the district courthouse, the same one that had tried "the sixty-three," but the convictions were later reversed by the court of appeals on grounds that the jury was not properly instructed by the court that one who feels a law is unjust has a right to publicly express that opinion.[59]

They had spent eighteen months in Leavenworth Prison, along with thirty of the sixty-three resisters from our case who were already there.

When the FPC leaders were released, the camps had by then been closed, so they were truly free and now had access to the appropriate facilities to pursue our appeal. But no appeal was attempted.[60] Did the FPC and the thirty resisters at Leavenworth decide not to pursue the appeal? I don't recall being consulted on the matter at McNeil, but if such was the case, wouldn't it appear that the unspoken motive behind our resistance was, in fact, to evade the draft, and now that the war was over, we had accomplished our goal? Or was it possibly because there were no longer any funds after the FPC trial and subsequent appeal, and no easy way to raise the funds without donors conveniently confined at a single site?

In any case, again, I don't recall those of us at McNeil being consulted. It would seem the only justification for the FPC appeal to take precedence over the appeal of the original "test case" of the sixty-three would be to help implement the latter appeal. But, apparently, I was wrong.

The success of the Mitsuye Endo Supreme Court case[61] had established in December of 1944 that it was unlawful to detain a loyal citizen in a concentration camp without formal charges. This claim was also one of the key reasons for non-compliance with the Selective Service Act in the trial of the sixty-three. An appeal based on this precedent certainly seemed justified, if not morally mandatory in view of our previously claimed constitutional commitment. I inquired on several occasions what the meaning was of the oft-repeated FPC motto "One for all, and all for one." I never received an explanation.[62]

Indeed, it does lead one to wonder what precisely was the legacy of the Heart Mountain Fair Play Committee (all of whose leaders are now deceased) to the Japanese American community. Little wonder there is so much confusion about the integrity of the draft resistance movement, with many resisters even at this late date preferring not to publicize their former association with it.

10

THE FARM

As the first anniversary of our sentence approached, some in our group began speculating on the possibility of parole. We were still banned from the West Coast (unless we were confined in a prison), and most of us had no one we knew who would sponsor us anywhere else. I didn't think they would accept us back in the Heart Mountain camp after all the grief we had caused. Sure enough, two of the fellows who worked in the warden's office retrieved copies of letters from the War Relocation Authority requesting the parole board *not* release us back to the camp as it would work counter to their efforts to close the camp (and, no doubt, disrupt the military induction program).

I wasn't particularly disappointed and held no grudge against the parole board. I hoped this would be the last time I would have to deal with the sneaky WRA. I had much more respect for the federal penal system than the WRA, and certainly more than for the US justice system—or even the US presidency itself. I discovered more humanity at McNeil Island Federal Penitentiary than in all the government agencies I had encountered since E.O. 9066! Since I had nowhere else to go, I was glad to remain at McNeil until my time was up.

Meantime, I sure missed my family. We resisters from the camp were probably the only prisoners who never had a visitor—and that wasn't the warden's fault. I was almost sorry the COs had made so much fun of him. But at least he had a family to go home to at night. On weekends and holidays baseball was the favorite sport on "campus," weather permitting. There were several teams among

https://doi.org/10.5876/9781646421848.c010

the inmates, at least two among the resisters and at least one each of the COs and Jehovah's, and one or more of "mixed breed." The resisters probably had a distinct advantage as their teams were offshoots of teams from the camp and were somewhat better organized. I don't think the others were aware of that fact. Indoors, however, on evenings and rainy weekends, which were quite common in the Northwest, there were always bridge games and chess matches going on simultaneously. Conventional playing cards were not allowed in prison so the inmates modified dominoes, the dots representing the numbers and the color of the dots designating the four suits. The banning of playing cards was intended to discourage gambling, but there were some poker games on the sly anyway, using dominoes. Clever, these cons (and they were just the ones that got caught). There were various other solitary activities the inmates occupied themselves with such as artsy-craftsy projects using donated heaps of industrial scraps in the workshops (a real challenge to one's imagination), or body-builders' pumping irons with makeshift steel bars and weights, wannabe writers lamenting the lousy hand they were dealt from the deck of fate, or the perpetual dreamer who was studying stacks of law books so he could outfox the system the next time around. It is fascinating what mischief men can get themselves into without the distraction of women—or were they merely exploring their inherent natural creativity that emerged somewhat distorted because of years of suppression? Perhaps the answers lie somewhere in the Book of Genesis with Adam and Eve and an apple or a pear, or something. But I can't remember that far back.

Much more serious matters were occurring in the insane world we had somehow managed to escape (for the time being):

- July of 1944, shortly after we arrived at McNeil, D Day in Europe marked the decisive point when the Allies were no longer on the defensive, but took the offensive.
- November of 1944, President F. D. Roosevelt was reelected for a landmark fourth term.
- December of 1944, the Mitsuye Endo Supreme Court decision established the illegality of confining loyal citizens without charges.
- January of 1945, the prohibition on the West Coast to Japanese Americans was lifted, but few were psychologically or financially prepared to return there.
- April of 1945, FDR dies and is replaced by Harry S. Truman.
- May of 1945, the war in Europe ends with Hitler's defeat.
- August of 1945, Hiroshima and Nagasaki are subjected to inhumane nuclear bombing as a demonstration to the rest of the world of the military prowess of the United States, an obscene display of overkill! Later that same month, Japan would surrender.

Many celebrated the victory, and while they regretted the horrendous loss of human lives, they nonetheless referred to it as "The Good War." They chose to ignore the fact that somehow, while focused on the tangible aspects of "fighting for freedom," America had sacrificed its moral fidelity and through various acts of moral turpitude had become an insensitive international bully, a fact our offspring and following generations would be keenly aware of (the more astute among them, that is) and collectively rebel against. The universal uprising would not be limited to just the war, but to the general lack of moral guidelines worldwide, where America had become part of the problem and not a part of the solution in spite of the lofty aspirations of the founders of our country. Then again, it may have been evidence of the approach of the "Age of Aquarius," which had been predestined, according to some, as the advent of a new consciousness. The evil dragon would finally be slain—almost.

At McNeil we could only wait and see. It was a strange kind of luxury. As a group, of course, we never truly felt as alone as perhaps Mickey did. We never suffered from any sense of guilt. We were convinced we were there for a just cause and there was a sense of camaraderie in that cause. We were fed, clothed, and boarded, and even had our health needs tended to, all free of charge. We even had free movies on occasion. But most important, there was an underlying sense of mutual respect at the farm between the prisoners and guards. Only occasionally would there be personality conflicts, which I suppose was inevitable as there had to be certain personal frustrations in all of us from time to time.

Speaking of time, we were allowed "good time" for good behavior. We got one day off our sentence for every three days we stayed out of trouble. Thus, for most of those in our group the three-year sentence would be reduced by a whole year. I had preconditioned myself to look forward to the early release, yet I had mixed feelings about leaving the island—or was it just the farm? I don't know how the others felt, but I found the farm much more humane and civilized than any other situation I had experienced thus far. It was certainly better than the WRA camp with its oppressive bigotry, deceptions, ignorance, and ineptitude. Here the prison personnel were hired by the government to tend to our needs. As long as they acknowledged our humanity, we acknowledged theirs. The benefits were mutual. We were there for totally different reasons, of course, but we would be leaving long before they did. Who, then, were the keepers?

Meantime, efforts to close the camps had started in earnest. The government realized by then the horrendous mistake the entire displacement program had been. Still, President Roosevelt deliberately delayed the return of the Japanese Americans to the West Coast until his reelection was assured. He wanted to delay the ire of the West Coast bigots by not releasing the returnees until after the 1944 election. Even the landmark decision of the Supreme Court's Endo case, which would force the closing of the camps, was not announced publicly until after the election in November.

Papa was determined to be the last to leave Heart Mountain. He claimed the government had put him there illegally, so now they were stuck with him. They would have to come pick him up bodily. Mama pleaded with him, but to no avail. When they shut down the mess hall and turned off the water to the latrine, things became pretty nasty. He finally relented. It was a short-lived, solitary, fruitless resistance. He did get the last word, however, when boarding the train which would take them back to California. He threw the fifty-dollar travel allowance (twenty-five dollars each) back in their faces, much to Mama's dismay. Such is the madness of a stubborn if honorable man. It was all a matter of principle, or so he said.

Kim must have left camp earlier once she was reassured Mama and Papa were already packed and could handle matters themselves. Perhaps she made the trip back to Monrovia to make sure our former landlady, Mrs. Showers, had indeed saved our house and belongings so we had a place to come back to. She had! She had rented the house in our absence during the housing shortage and regretted that some of our possessions might have been stolen, but assured us that the place would be available, true to her promise. So fortunately they had a familiar place to come back to, unlike many returnees who had difficulties resettling, as housing and jobs were almost nonexistent. I, of course, still in prison, was of no help at all.

I wondered if Mama and Papa on their trip back to California reminisced about their initial train trip twenty-nine years before as newlyweds. All their hopes and dreams of life in a Free and Just America now lay shattered. All their labor, conceding their pride to stoop to demeaning tasks with faith that somehow it would all be rewarded, came to naught. A concentration camp turned out to be their reward! Or was it? Perhaps the reward was the discovery that good people like Nettie Showers would recognize good people like Mama and Papa, and be there when they were needed. Perhaps nature's subtle sense of justice is far superior to that of man's, but being men, our egos would never allow us to believe that. We who were sent to the McNeil Island farm might well consider our good fortune as a taste of nature's justice. It certainly could have been much worse. I felt bad for those who were sent to Leavenworth.

As fate would have it, a few days before our release date, a horrendous accident occurred, overshadowing any sense of gaiety for our upcoming day of release.

Fred Iriye, whom I regarded as one of the more intelligent and sincere among us, and who was in charge of the entire electrical power system on the farm, a highly technical responsibility, was training an inmate who would be taking over those responsibilities after Fred's release. They were in the central power station when Fred casually flipped a heretofore disconnected switch just to demonstrate how it worked. There was a sudden blast and smoke filled the small one-room building. For some reason unbeknownst to Fred, the circuit had been energized and he was instantly electrocuted. His shoe print was etched into the concrete floor and would remain there for decades.

FIGURE 10.1. Day of release, July 14, 1946. Yoshito in back row, second from left (Kuromiya Family Collection).

I don't recall any investigation being conducted regarding Fred's "accident," or the FPC leaders even making any inquiries since they had been freed earlier. I don't recall any of them attending his funeral, which was held in the old Union Church in Little Tokyo in Los Angeles,[63] but I may be mistaken and can't recall clearly due to the emotional trauma I was undergoing.

Needless to say, the day of our release was not the joyous event we had long anticipated. All the inmates as well as the guards and other personnel joined us in our grief, and I'm sure even in the Big House word had gotten around of the tragedy. Fred was highly respected by all who knew him. Mickey was especially sympathetic with our loss and found himself the giver of solace rather than the recipient, a rare experience for him, no doubt. We, on the other hand, were sorry to leave him behind when it was time for us to go. His other "sons" would take care of him for the short time they would still be there—then what? Perhaps his chickens would become his family.

Even on the train trip from Washington State to Southern California, as our group got smaller and smaller—especially in San Jose where most of our friends got off—we who were left remained quietly introspective. We were trying to fathom a possible deeper meaning than just an "unfortunate accident." Was it some sort of *bachi* [retribution]? Was it instead punishment for self-righteous arrogance? Why Fred? He certainly wasn't guilty of arrogance. And if not Fred, then who? Maybe all of us—and Fred paid the price. Yet why should we be punished for what our conscience demanded of us as the only honorable choice, given the circumstances? And where indeed is the arrogance in defending the constitutional principles we swore to uphold? Were we merely reacting to the fear that we might be held responsible for Fred's demise—a fear of what others might think? In essence, it was the same fear of public censure that led many of our friends in camp to die on the battlefields of Europe "to prove their loyalty." How ironic!

On arriving at the Los Angeles Union train station (or was it the [South] Pasadena train station?), Mama, Papa, and Kim were there to greet me.[64] We were all happy to see each other, but they detected right away that I was in no mood to celebrate. I think Mama drove, as she had become accustomed to doing most of the driving from before camp when Papa was too overworked and we kids were too young to be trusted. She did not honk the horn as we left the parking lot as the circumstances at that time made it prudent to maintain a low profile. Once on the highway, I explained what had happened just before we left McNeil. No one said a word, but they understood my lack of enthusiasm. I was relieved that they didn't question me further.

When we got back to Monrovia, I gave a sigh of relief that we were home again at last. Everything was pretty much as we had left it, just a bit tired looking, nothing that a little sprucing up couldn't solve. I discovered that Hiro and Em, now with two kids, had earlier resettled in Minneapolis, Minnesota, to escape camp and had returned a few weeks ago now that Mama, Papa, and Kim had taken the risk of possible racist reprisals and it was relatively safe to return. The fact that Hiro hadn't bothered to pick me up at the train depot seemed to indicate that he did, indeed, disagree with my decision to challenge the draft. But I still didn't get the message through my thick skull—not until after his death thirty-six years later when Em would set me straight. It is strange how we cling to our childhood naïveté and remain blind to all evidence of its unreality.

II

THE RETURN

Before our forced removal, the six of us in the family had shared both units of the duplex. Currently one unit was still occupied, so all eight of us, including Hiro's family, were crammed into a one-bedroom, one-bath unit. Fortunately, the kitchen and dining room were fairly roomy and would serve as a second bedroom for Hiro and Em. Kazumi, who had adopted the name Corki and had left camp earlier, was still in Chicago and apparently preferred to remain there. Being the last to arrive back, I had to settle for a tight corner on the porch with all the luggage and unpacked crates. The porch was enclosed by a wire screen, otherwise open to the outdoors, but the weather was still warm and, fortunately, this arrangement would be temporary.

My sister Kim had been dating Ted Furuya, Em's brother, since she had returned to California. He had served in the famous 442 Combat Unit.[65] I was already uncomfortable with Em since her sudden outburst in camp (which was never mentioned again, to my knowledge), but now her brother was about to woo my favorite sister away from me. In a few months they would marry. I was terribly disappointed in Kim's choice, but vowed not to interfere with her happiness. I felt she had always supported me (not necessarily my choices—I suspected she didn't always understand them), just because I was me. Now it was my turn, but Ted would not make it easy for me.

It wasn't until years later that I realized it wasn't Ted who was the culprit. It was the person I had feared he had become, the symbol that Japanese America had

https://doi.org/10.5876/9781646421848.c011   89

FIGURE 11.1. Family reunion after WWII, 1946. *Back row, left to right*: Hiroshi, Kazumi, Kimiye, Yoshito. *Front row, left to right*: Emiko, Meri Jane, Kiyoshi, Papa, Mama (Miyatake Studio).

created to validate our right to live in America. It was the arrogance of all symbols and images that exploit our inner fears of inadequacy and rejection, images invented by the people who ultimately enslaved us to them. Ted had become a victim, as many in his situation were, of our collective need as a community for a positive symbol. We were all suffering for lack of demonstrable validation, even to the extent of creating false idols. The emperor, indeed, had no clothes! And we who had the temerity to say so became instant pariahs in our respective communities. Ted and those of his ilk had become willing symbols of the hypocrisy. They, in their naïve vanity, had been and continued to be exploited. Those who never returned from the battlefields had paid the price. The JACL and its Model Minority image would reap the benefits.

Papa and Hiro were gardening, as were many of the returnees. Gardening seemed an appropriate occupation as it required a minimum of initial investment for equipment, offered a degree of independence, satisfied many returnees' natural affinity for plants and the soil, and perhaps most importantly it provided relative freedom from the government agencies they had learned to distrust. I was seeking something more in the line of graphic arts or illustration where I could get on-the-job training, as further scholastic pursuits seemed very unlikely.

One day I happened to be in Little Tokyo. It might have been to make my monthly report to my parole agent, Mr. Hirohata, an insurance agent and family friend who was kind enough to vouch for me during my parole period. I unexpectedly ran into Albert Dohi, one of the "pros" I had worked with in the camp poster shop and for whom I had great respect. After chatting awhile, as I hadn't seen him since the day before I was so rudely nabbed by the FBI, he asked if I was working. He said that he was managing a silk-screen print shop on Fourth Street and could use some experienced help if I was available. I wasn't sure about the daily commute from Monrovia to Los Angeles, but I certainly welcomed the opportunity to work with Al. It would be like old times. I agreed to give it a try if he could arrange it with the owner of the business.

I took the Red Car (streetcar) that ran from Monrovia right into Little Tokyo and walked only a few blocks at each end of the line, but with so many stops along the way it took well over an hour, sometimes two hours, each way. Besides, I didn't like the stuffy, dismal old warehouse in which the shop was located. The lack of adequate ventilation made it quite oppressive. The downstairs office, however, was nicely decorated. The owner/boss dressed nattily in a suit and tie and he drove a fancy car. We peons were grossly underpaid. It was virtually a sweatshop. Al had a family to support and couldn't be choosy, but I felt we were being ripped off. Al and I had worked together in camp and the boss knew about the camps and how submissive some of us were. I believed he was exploiting us, much like Mexican illegals are today. I told the boss (I don't remember his name) I would have to quit because the commuting was killing me. He offered a raise to help offset the travel cost and offered a raise for Al, too. I made sure Al would get his raise, but quit anyway because I had lost all respect for the boss. I suspect the time I spent at McNeil, instead of rehabilitating me, had spoiled me beyond all repair. Mama was sure of it.

I tried a few freelance odd jobs in graphics design that I found to be uninspiring. Mrs. Nettie Showers, our kindly landlady, allowed me to use a vacant upstairs attic room in her large Craftsman-style, shingle-clad house just across the street from us as a studio. As I recall, the windows to the room were two dormer types that when viewed from outside appeared as two sad eyes peeking from behind a mop of green hair, which was the vine-covered roof. The room was cozy, comfortable, and bright, no doubt a room in which one of her children was raised. But I knew I couldn't impose on her generosity if I had no work.

One day I got a rather strange telephone call from Hawai'i, someone claiming he was Nettie Showers's son (or maybe nephew) asking if I would be interested in a job on his newspaper. It was all so sudden I didn't even ask what the job would be. He must have thought I was some kind of idiot. He assured me he had several Japanese on his staff and knew I would be comfortable there and gave me his number in case I decided to give it a try. I sat for a while in a daze wondering what that was all about. Then I remembered. When I was still in high school and was appointed art editor for the school newspaper, Mama had proudly showed my work in the paper to Nettie. Nettie had remembered. And someone in her family did indeed manage a newspaper in Honolulu. Good fortune had finally come my way!

But I wasn't ready. After pondering it for a few days I called, thanking him for his thoughtfulness, explaining that my parole conditions wouldn't allow me to travel that far. I might try again after the restrictions were lifted, if the position was still available then. In reality I knew I wasn't ready for new challenges. There had been too many disappointments. I had been away too long. I had missed my family and the sense of home, such as it was, too long. I had been shunted senselessly from place to place by inept authorities for too long. There was no pot of gold at the end of the rainbow. It was, rather, a steaming cauldron, a melting pot where cultural diversity was regarded as a liability and the goal was to erase one's cultural identity and become part of a mindless nonentity—or so it seemed.

But neither was it time to surrender. My first priority was stability, and stability meant relying on one's own resources, not the generosity of others. Stability meant building a firm foundation below the earth in order to rise above it. The Issei such as Papa had it right. Gardening wasn't just a safety net in a tough job market. It was symbolic of starting at the beginning, or starting anew; it meant going back to Mother Earth and establishing new roots or reviving old roots. I would work with Papa, an old-time gardener, who could teach me the fundamentals, and then I would be on my own, wherever it took me. Thus would I join the army of returnees who, aware or not, were doing exactly what nature was calling for in a world gone insane.[66] I would later understand the profound significance of the rock gardens of Manzanar[67] as symbols of stability and sanity in the midst of human callousness and despair.

Meantime, the postwar economic boom was just beginning (not to be confused with the artificial wartime boom on the West Coast). The property that our rental sat on, having major highway frontage, was in high demand. The local Chevrolet dealership had made a handsome offer for it. Mrs. Showers said nothing to us about it, but Papa knew she couldn't hold out much longer. Even her own house was up for grabs by the greedy entrepreneurs. The property taxes were threatening to double.

So Mama and Papa started looking for a house to buy. I was surprised they had enough saved to even consider a purchase, aware that the loss of income during the war and the donations Papa had certainly made to the FPC for our trial and the appeal that never occurred must have virtually devastated them financially.[68] But I also knew they could be quite frugal (except in matters of principle, such as Papa rejecting the WRA travel money).

We were not surprised to discover that we had no bargaining power, and were relieved each time the door wasn't slammed in our faces. We couldn't find a real estate agent to represent us, so we checked the newspaper ads and looked for "For Sale" signs in not-so-upscale neighborhoods, preferably where some Nihonjins [people of Japanese ancestry] had already settled. We focused mainly in Pasadena,[69] where Mama and Papa felt the most comfortable, having lived there before.

After several weeks, we found a fairly decent clapboard house with a stone foundation and handsome stone front porch of mid-twenties vintage. It had two bedrooms and one bath, all quite roomy, with hardwood floors throughout. The interior décor was typical Craftsman-style with built-in cabinets of varnished wood and glass doors. Our heavy, round, solid oak dining table would finally find a space worthy of its classic character. The property was actually a lot and a half. At the far rear of the adjacent half-lot sat a tired, easily overlooked wooden house with a sagging roof; a turn-of-the-century single-bedroom relic which was origin-ally supplied with gas light, it had since been wired for electricity. The small bathroom had a toilet with a wooden tank up by the ceiling with a brass pull chain. The cast-iron bathtub was supported by four cast-iron lion's claws. The linoleum-covered floor sagged conveniently to one corner where someone had drilled a hole for easy drainage. It was a priceless museum piece if one could hold it together long enough to move it. All the space in front of the bungalow would become Mama's garden.

We may have paid a bit more than market value for it, but Mama and Papa felt comfortable there. We were not too far from where we had lived before moving to Monrovia.[70] Soon after we moved in, the whole white neighborhood seemed to flee in panic and many Nihonjin were able to join us. Imagine Mama, the notori-ous blockbuster.

Hiro and Em stayed in the duplex a bit longer as the kids had started school, but later would buy a house at the edge of town near the town of Bradbury. Em would get a job at a hi-tech electronics firm just across the street from their house so she could be close to home for the kids if needed. Hiro would eventually give up gar-dening when offered a job with Von's produce transporting department, the kind of work with which he was familiar. Kim and Ted lived with his parents just a few blocks away from the house that Mama and Papa had just purchased. Kim became quite a frequent visitor as she and Mama had always been very close.

Once we were settled in Pasadena, I started my own gardening route. Papa had given me a couple of his accounts to start with and said, "Good riddance!"

Mama said, "Who would want you for a gardener?"

It's nice to have fans supporting you on your maiden voyage. We lived under the same roof (theirs), but after Mama fixed our breakfast and bagged our lunches, Papa and I went on our separate routes.

Papa was slowing down. After all, he was over sixty years old. When I kidded him about it, he retorted that I was always in such a hurry it made him nervous. I suddenly realized that our roles had reversed. When we started, even when working in the store before the war, *he* was always pushing *me*. Now he wanted to pace himself and enjoy his old age with the least amount of stress. For me, it was now a challenge to push my limits even higher, which to him translated into money and greed. He called me a mercenary (whatever that translated to in Japanese). I called him a hypocrite for calling me a mercenary when he was well aware how he had almost killed himself striving to make the store succeed until E.O. 9066 came to his rescue. Who, indeed, was the mercenary?

I kept up my pace. Papa sat back and laughed. Mama said it was all so stupid and disgusting, two hardheads arguing about whose head was the hardest. Mama was in no way responsible for Papa being born under the zodiac sign of a stubborn Taurus, but she was at least partially responsible for my being one. Everything was back to normal. It felt good!

On weekends some of the fellows from McNeil and I would get together in Los Angeles. We spent most of our time at the bowling alley and movies or at the beach in summer. We drove up to San Jose, California, on a couple of occasions to reunite with the fellows up there. We all seemed to be in a state of limbo. Soon the group dissipated as some got married or moved to other areas, or both. I met Haru about that time, who happened to be staying with her aunt just around the corner from us, on the same block. Here I had been looking all over the countryside—in all the wrong places. Kim was a close friend of Marge and insisted I meet her niece, Haru. We took an immediate, if cautious, liking to each other and eventually decided to get married. We would move into the old relic behind Mama and Papa's house until we could afford something nicer.

In late summer 1948, we were married in a private chapel in Pasadena. It was a very hot day as I recall, and Reverend Glen Smiley, a conscientious objector whom I had befriended while at McNeil, married us. I was so nervous I don't recall much of what transpired. Perhaps, like Mama at her wedding, I was feeling more like a spectator than (in my case) the instigator. It must have gone okay though. Before I realized it, we were husband and wife.

Not only did the bedsprings creak that night, but so did the floorboards of that rickety old house. I was afraid the sagging roof would collapse at any time. At about two or three the next morning we were rudely awakened by the clanging of an alarm clock. We didn't own an alarm clock. We finally located it wired under the mattress slats. Who would do such a nasty thing? Haru blamed it on my friends, I blamed it on hers. Later that morning we were off to Yosemite Valley on our honeymoon, somewhat bleary-eyed but happy.

The trip would prove to be a test of our patience. About a week earlier, I had noticed clouds of blue smoke coming out of the tailpipe of my old Ford coupe. Ted offered to overhaul the engine as a wedding present. I would help him, of course. Apparently, one week was not long enough to break in the new rings and

FIGURE 11.2. Yoshito and Haru as newlyweds, 1948 (Kuromiya Family Collection).

rod bearings that we had installed. As Haru and I encountered the steep grades of the Grapevine (which was still a two- or three-lane, two-way highway at that time), the engine would steam up and we were constantly stopping to refill the radiator. It became particularly exasperating as well as dangerous when we got stuck behind a large truck and didn't have the power to pass. What if a hose should burst? We would be stuck in the middle of nowhere without a cell phone (which hadn't been invented yet). We somehow made it over the Grapevine and it was less stressful for us and the car on the level Highway 99 through Bakersfield, California. Also, the sun was setting so it was beginning to get cooler. We stopped at a motel somewhere near Tulare, California, I believe, hoping the car would start in the morning. Thankfully, it did.

It wasn't until we came to the mountainous roads beyond Fresno, California, that we had to start praying again. It seemed to take forever to reach the Yosemite Park entrance, which turned out to be only half the distance between Fresno and the mouth of Yosemite Valley itself. When we arrived at a tunnel, we sensed that we were very close. Upon emerging from the far end of the tunnel, all of a sudden there it was! The full splendor of Mother Nature's handiwork at sunset, the grand finale when the sun's rays from behind us spotlighted each distant waterfall for a final encore before the curtains of darkness fell. Even the faint rainbows embracing the mist created by the falls would gradually fade. The sheer rock faces reflecting the golden hues of the setting sun would slowly sink into darkness in the valley. Thanks to our ailing car, our timing couldn't have been better. It was pitch dark with only a few campfires and kerosene lanterns to guide us by the time we located our accommodation: a tent on a wooden platform, which was all that old moneybags could afford, even for a honeymoon. Haru never complained.

During the following days we hiked up many trails, each culminating at a waterfall or two. On one occasion we drove to Mirror Lake. In those days we could drive all over the valley on our own, even if our car steamed up occasionally. We parked at an almost empty lot and took a short hike to the edge of the pristine lake. It was a windless day so the reflection of distant mountains in the lake was almost as clear as the mountains themselves. No wonder so many artists are inspired to paint it. On returning to the car we noticed a small group of hikers gathered there. A bear cub had gotten into our open-windowed car and was helping himself to cookies and potato chips. Fortunately, Mama Bear wasn't around. We opened the doors and shooed the cub away, hoping Mama Bear wouldn't show up. We found crumbs in the seams of the seats for several days after, no matter how much we vacuumed. Why couldn't he have just taken the bags and eaten somewhere else? Why couldn't we have just rolled up the windows? So much for our brief encounter with the wildlife of Yosemite.

The morning after we came home, the car wouldn't start. The engine was frozen up tight. It refused to budge. I would have to get a new rebuilt engine. Little did I realize I couldn't even afford the tent we had rented at Yosemite.

12

BACK TO BASICS

In spite of the lofty ideas about gardening being basic to man's nature and digging deep into Mother Earth to establish firm roots for whatever it might be we aspired to in reaching for the skies, I found gardening, at least our commercial adaptation of it, to be damned hard work! Not only do you have to sweat it out on sweltering days, there is also the humiliation one must endure when the owner, or even a casual passerby, holds his nose after you finish broadcasting cow manure over a client's lawn. Often the owner and even his kids expect you to gather the droppings of their pet hound while the mutt keeps snapping at your heels. Needless to say, they're the first to get dropped [as customers] when a better offer comes along.

I had a retired doctor client in San Marino who had the nerve to ask me to crawl under his house to check for termites. He even instructed me on what to look for. I detected signs of exactly what he feared, but told him everything was fine. He thanked me and gave me five dollars. I quit the job before his house collapsed.

It's a shame someone didn't collect old gardeners' stories told while waiting for our mowers to be serviced at the lawnmower shop. I say "old" because it was mostly the Issei and Kibei who spoke in Japanese who related them. Somehow concepts, images, and the words themselves that animate them could be hilarious when expressed in Japanese, but would be downright vulgar and tasteless if expressed in English. I often wondered about this phenomenon and suspected it might have something to do with the distorting effects of the Victorian era of western culture, or the dualism of western thinking; i.e., good and bad, virtue versus evil, our ever-present need for judgment. I wondered if somehow this related to our having been targeted during WWII for mass removal, while the Germans and Italians were not. But I will have to defer to greater minds to make these connections, if in fact there were any. After all, I was just a simple, smelly gardener.

In any case, I thoroughly enjoyed the raunchy, risqué stories of the Issei with all their obvious exaggerations, but could never repeat them to my friends in English. Somehow, it never came out funny—just dirty. Such a collection would, of course, have to be written in Japanese. I don't know if such a collection exists or not.

Gardening in those days was quite different from what it is today. Everything involved a much more direct physical contact with the soil or plants or chemicals with which one was dealing. And we didn't have to lock up every piece of equipment lest it be stolen. Today even your lunch bag could disappear if left on the seat of your truck—if, in fact, your truck is still there.

Actually, it was a transition period where even the power lawnmower had become a must-have. Today many chores are mechanized and cover a larger area in less time. Some future day perhaps the gentleman gardener will just sit in a lawn chair and push buttons on his computer. I'm afraid that day would herald the death knell for professional gardening as we know it. As with all other pursuits, it seems man is obsessed with rendering himself obsolete.

In the faint hope that I might still be fortunate enough to find a niche in the graphic arts, I enrolled in night school classes at Pasadena City College in architectural design and general drafting. At the same time, my gardening work continued to attract new clients, making it possible to consolidate my jobs to specific neighborhoods each day, eliminating the waste of time and energy loading and unloading my equipment and traveling from place to place. I could cover two or three or more jobs simultaneously with maximum efficiency.

The year after we were married and moved into the rickety old shack behind Mama and Papa's house, Haru and I had a baby girl. We named her Susan (Suzi, as she prefers now). This was the postwar era where we Japanese Americans were still overreacting to the pain of being regarded as "non-aliens," so Suzi was denied a Japanese name.

I realized I had to take my work more seriously now that we were a family and budgetary problems would soon catch up to us in spite of my work being more lucrative than expected. I would have to abandon any dreams of pursuing a career in the arts. Further, in two years we would have a second child, another girl, whom we named Sharon. It became imperative that we find larger quarters.

Fortunately, we found a nice two-bedroom bungalow in a quiet neighborhood in the northern section of Pasadena. Apparently, we caught the crest of "white flight," as did many Nisei and Kibei of that era who were just starting to raise families and were seeking permanent homes in the general Los Angeles area, and perhaps all along the West Coast. Many of those moving into the neighborhood were novice gardeners just like me. Their children would become the playmates and schoolmates of our kids, some even lifelong friends.

The irony of white flight was not lost on me. Many of these people who smugly stood by while we were unfairly demonized and removed from their communities were now in a panic to escape the horde of "non-aliens" invading their neighborhoods—victims of their own fears and bigotry. I was amused to watch them run.[71] Nature does indeed have her own system of justice.

Mama and Papa insisted on making the down payment on our new/old house. I thanked them for the offer but I assured them I could handle it myself. I knew they must have donated substantially for our trial and subsequent appeal while in camp without the benefit of any income. I could not in good conscience impose on them further. They insisted that the camp situation was different and they were treating each sibling equally and helping each on our first home. Knowing it was fruitless to argue with Papa, Haru and I devised a budget wherein we would pay back whatever we could each month on the same day we made our mortgage payments, until we were square. They didn't insist we pay interest if it was, in fact, a loan and not a gift. That part I regarded as the gift.

Before moving in, we painted the entire house inside and out. Just as I thought I had made the final touches on the picture window frame in the living room, I turned around to discover the large wall behind me, which had been painted earlier, scribbled with multicolored crayons for its full length to a height of about three feet. Two-year-old Suzi had decided it might be nice to have a mural there. She would grow up to be quite an artist, but her voluntary initial creative endeavor unfortunately had to be painted over.

On another occasion, I believe it was a Sunday, after working on the house all day, we were relieved to finally clean ourselves up and head for home. We were halfway home when we sensed something was missing, or maybe it was Suzi who asked why we had left Sharon at the house. Baby Sharon was fine in the darkness, blanketed in a small washtub in the middle of the living room floor, probably wondering why it had suddenly become so quiet.

It was about this time that a gardener friend congratulated me on the presidential pardon. What pardon? I didn't know what he was talking about. So later he produced a news clipping he had saved for some reason. It was the *Los Angeles Times*, dated December 1947. It indicated that almost three years previously President Truman had granted a special pardon to all WWII violators of the Selective Service Law. The article listed all the names of Japanese Americans who resisted the draft while being confined in the camps, 282 in all, including me. I was astounded! I don't know if any of the other resisters were notified by mail, but I certainly was not. It seemed strange that we weren't even notified that such amnesty was being applied for by the Fair Play Committee without our consent.[72] I have no objection to the spirit of the amnesty, but it did preclude any chances for a reversal in a court of appeal of our case to establish a legal precedent for future cases of government malfeasance—the originally stated goal of the FPC protest. I felt betrayed. Unwittingly perhaps, but nevertheless the FPC leadership had failed all of Japanese America *and* our US Constitution.[73]

On a lighter note, but no less disturbing (to me at least), was the news that Mickey was being released from McNeil, only to be deported to Japan. This, I thought, has to be a cruel joke. How would he survive in a land devastated by a war that should never have happened? Or did he choose to go there, perhaps to die in the land he probably should never have left. In any case, we in Los Angeles got together with others in San Jose to gather care packages for his send-off. We wrote letters wishing him well, but had no idea of his personal connections in Japan as he never shared any of his personal life with anyone. It was rather awkward, but we hoped he got the feeling he wasn't totally alone. I don't know if any of the others got a response. I didn't. It would be the last I heard about Mickey.

I made a renewed commitment to my work, mostly out of necessity. How on earth was I going to pay for all of this? I quit the drafting class and transferred to a home gardening class. (I was getting tired of having my clients tell me how I should care for their gardens.) The class also catered to professional nurserymen and landscape contractors. It was taught by Homer Pownall, a landscape architect and, I would discover later, a member of the super-patriotic Native Sons of the Golden West—one of the most bigoted, racist organizations to lobby our government for the permanent removal of all Japanese from the West Coast.[74] Mr. Pownall and I got along quite well, however, as neither of us wanted to mention the past. We both had too much at stake. It would be especially fortuitous for me not to have reacted. Mother Nature's unfailing justice would cross my path yet again.

I hungrily absorbed the treasure trove of information Homer had to offer. He was quite well versed in all facets of horticultural science, or so it seemed to me. He brought several samples of plants to the class and would explain their environmental needs and other characteristics, especially those which were reasonably adaptable to the Southwest area. I recognized many of them as rather common to the gardens on my route. So the next time Mrs. Know-It-All advised me on how to care for her favorite shrub, I would rattle off the botanical name of the plant and the fact that she was slowly killing it by overwatering. When I asked for a raise to help cover the cost of the new truck I had just bought, nobody argued. Just a little bit of knowledge could indeed be dangerous—for the other person. Papa was right. I was a mercenary.

As time went on, some of my gardener friends with entrepreneurial skills were doing so well they did exactly what any smart businessman would do (me not being one of them). One particular gardener friend hired inexperienced help, trained them with minimum wages while working with them, only to discover that they would eventually buy their own equipment (or borrow some of his) and start their own business on the side. They sometimes borrowed my friend's clients as well by underbidding him. After years of honest labor in a field in which it was easy to get started, that very characteristic could become its downfall when competition claimed its share. Also, with the proliferation of toxic chemicals and greater technology in the equipment, a degree of education and regulation seemed reasonable for public safety and the safety of the gardener himself. This, of course, would require a reasonable criterion of minimum standards for state licensure for the professional gardener, as is quite normal for most other occupations dealing with the public.

We in Pasadena, as the Crown City Gardeners Association,[75] in the interest of protecting our livelihood as well as for public safety, spearheaded a proposal which we felt would bring credibility to a too-long overlooked and often disparaged occupation. The overwhelmingly negative response caught us by surprise. It came mainly from the Japanese communities that were still wary of any governmental intrusion. It was like E.O. 9066 all over again. Many communities formed their own gardener associations, which later would unite and become the [Southern California] Gardeners' Federation[76] (ironically using a term often associated with the government they couldn't trust). We approached some of these groups assuring them that they, as established gardeners, would automatically qualify under a grandfather clause which would protect their status and not jeopardize their source of income. It would only apply to the newcomers. Our efforts were to no avail. In the minds of non-English-speaking Japanese, the distrust spawned by E.O. 9066 was still their reality and would probably remain so for the remainder of their lives. Sadly, gardening as a respectable, proud, and dedicated profession would be nipped in the bud and become the notorious mow, blow, and go maintenance operation we find today, with few exceptions.

One positive result, however, was the establishment of the widespread [Southern California] Gardeners' Federation, which gave a voice to the Japanese gardener, such as it was. It provided educational information for its membership and political empowerment when needed. It established financial aid programs and other community contributions. It provided camaraderie and entertainment. It could not, however, provide the necessary incentives for younger generations to follow in our footsteps.

Within four or five years after we moved into our new house, we had paid off the loan from Mama and Papa. All the while they insisted it wasn't necessary, ignoring the fact that it was important to me. I believe it was the only argument with Papa I ever won.

In 1954 we had another child—yet another daughter, in fact. We named her Gail, but still no Japanese name. We seemed to be in a rut. We treasured all of them, each with their distinctly unique personalities while sharing a common interest in creative pursuits, in music, in literature, and mainly in the graphic arts.

FIGURE 12.1. Suzi, five; Sharon, three; and Gail, seven months, 1954 (courtesy, Haru Kuromiya).

As children the two older ones would sometimes take advantage of the newcomer. Perhaps it was a test of their newfound sense of power. Gail once joined them for a walk, but as they approached a blind corner they dashed ahead and hid behind a hedge. By the time Gail reached the corner, they had completely disappeared. Gail came home in tears. I had been mowing the front lawn and witnessed it all. Just a childish prank? Perhaps, but it also might contain an important message that parents often overlook. The younger, sometimes cuter ones get all the attention at the expense of the older. Unfortunately, as parents, not only do we often fail to hear our children, but fail to understand or to even remember when we do hear. Parents too often make lousy students. We were so busy trying to "teach" our children, forgetting that we too were learning to be parents.

Meanwhile, back at the night school horticulture class, Homer Pownall, "The Bigot," would prove to be the key in the turning point for the career aspirations of Yosh, "The Sneaky Jap." One evening after class he took me aside and suggested I look into the landscape design course offered at the California Polytechnic College in Pomona.

What, me? I'm thirty-five years old and have a family to support. I can't afford to sit in a classroom all day like a teenager while my family starves. What would the neighbors think? He explained it wasn't the lessons that I needed. I already had all the qualifications, such as my knowledge of plants, their needs and characteristics, an awareness of environmental factors, a familiarity with architectural processes, and the graphic skills to illustrate and communicate concepts in visual terms. Being a landscape architect himself, he recognized these qualities after the first month I had enrolled in his class. Cal Poly would just be a formality to get me on the right track. Here I was looking in all the wrong places again. The gardening efforts to provide for the immediate needs of the family and the lifelong dream of expressing in the creative arts were different facets of the same goal. They were and always had been one and the same. Was it I who was blind and not the one I had thought to be a "bigot"?

13

CROSSROADS

While still not ready to admit my blindness to what was right in front of me all those years, I drove out to Cal Poly between two of my jobs to try to enroll for the fall semester. Although I signed up for only two classes, I was surprised when they accepted me, no questions asked. School would start in a few weeks so I had to re-arrange my route schedule. I realized the daylight hours would be getting shorter so I might be working by flashlight in the dead of winter, or maybe have to work on Sundays with the Presbyterians scowling their disapproval of me. But I managed somehow, even if I had to spend endless hours on weekly design assignments on a makeshift drawing board on the dining room table or in the bedroom to escape the distraction of three kids. More than a few times I worked throughout the night. One of the girls, I can't recall which, asked her mother, "Who is that man?" It was a rough period for all of us, mostly because I refused to give up any of my gardening jobs. I was so sure the bubble would burst and I would be back to square one.

During my second year at Cal Poly, we had our annual Open House program, where the students' work was on display for public viewing. A substantial number of the spectators were practicing landscape architects who were seeking new prospects for their offices. After viewing the display, a prominent landscape architect, Raymond Page,[77] approached me and offered me a job—not just as a draftsman, as is usually the case with neophytes, but as chief designer! Who, me? I was astounded, but thought I'd better grab it before he came to his senses. He wanted

 https://doi.org/10.5876/9781646421848.c013

me to start immediately, but I explained I would have to find a replacement for my gardening route first. He thought I was kidding, but I assured him I wasn't. He was hiring a gardener to run his profession—that is, if the offer was still open. Apparently, he was desperate enough to give me a try, wondering what the hell I was doing behind a lawnmower. I'm just trying to make an honest living, sir.

Fortunately, I found a young Kibei fellow who had a family and was willing to take over the route. I introduced him to all my clients. (Since he didn't speak much English, it was a bit awkward.) Most of the clients expressed regret that I was leaving but wished me well. A few may have been disappointed that my replacement seemed to know so little about gardening and would be difficult to communicate with, but I assured them he was very intelligent and honest and would learn quickly. I never heard from him again, but am confident he survived (even if I had to lie for him).

Raymond Page and Associates turned out to be a second-story office suite in the middle of Beverly Hills, California, near the now famous Rodeo Drive shopping district. I guess I was the "associate" as there didn't seem to be anybody else around except an old codger at a drafting table in the far corner of the studio. Ray explained that this was an architect of a bygone era who shared the space, but he had nothing to do with our office. I was to be the chief designer as was promised, but also the entire drafting crew and the chief coffee-maker as well. It seems his former design crew had gradually dropped out one by one for some reason and Ray, being quite a promoter but not a designer, had been stranded with several unfinished projects. No wonder he was so desperate.

His clientele consisted of many notables connected with the film industry, including several stars (or has-beens). I never met any face-to-face, only their agents, who took care of such mundane matters. It didn't matter to me; they probably thought I was their gardener anyway.

The old man in the corner (I believe his name was Herb Alden, or something like that) didn't seem to have any good words for anyone. Everyone was cordial to him, but they generally seemed to avoid him. He would often mutter racist remarks when the news program on his radio reported a tragedy in Africa, Asia, or the Middle East, even in my presence (or maybe because of it). However, when no one else was around, he would wander to my corner and look over my shoulder and give me valuable pointers on architectural techniques and design tips. His style may have been of a past era, but his attention to detail and obvious eagerness to be of help to me were sincere. In viewing some of his work, which he usually kept hidden, I realized his architectural renderings were masterpieces of art. But his work went beyond skillful training and dedication to his trade. I sensed an element of a basic integrity about the person himself, who refused to compromise his design ideals. So how did this relate to his outward bitterness against all of humanity? I knew that sensitivity often turns to cynicism when one discovers that he alone cannot change the world. Was his voluntary isolation a means of retaliating against a world that failed to recognize his genius? Later, when others were hired into the office, he seldom came to our section of the studio and we could all hear him mutter under his breath about the "yellow peril" overrunning *our* country.

The work, or at least the pressure of the backlog, proved to be overwhelming. Despite my efforts, we seemed to be falling further behind. I don't recall whether Ray made the call or I did, but we managed to get a couple of my former classmates, just-graduated Sansei from Cal Poly, to join us at least on a temporary basis. Somehow, as a classic case of the blind leading the blind, we managed to clear up the backlog without any serious mishaps. Even old Herb, who did help us with a few time-saving tips along the way, thawed out long enough to join in the celebration. I think we all realized he was just a harmless, embittered, tired old man who had sadly missed his calling—and nobody seemed to care.

After my first year with the office, Ray suggested I apply for a state license to become a certified landscape architect; in fact, he insisted on it. After all, he was on the California State Licensing Board and it didn't seem right that his associate was not certified. I reminded him that I didn't have the necessary academic credits (thanks to him), or even the minimum training period required to apply for the exam. I happened to know that Raymond Page, as a founding member of that board, had set up the minimum requirements himself when the California law was enacted a few years before. It was at the same time we were pushing for licensing gardeners. Which reminds me: it's probably just as well in my case the gardener's certification hadn't passed, since if it had, I might have felt committed to remain a gardener for the rest of my life.

At any rate he said, "Never mind that." He was still a member of that board and would attest to my qualifications. Two weeks later I received an invitation to take the test, with all minimum requirements waived and signed by each board member.

The exam turned out to be not as difficult as I had feared. The first day consisted of a written test—questions regarding the technical, legal, theoretical, and ethical aspects of the profession. There also may have been a short essay required on the subject. The second day we were given a plot map of several acres on a gentle hillside slope and a floor plan of a single-story school building which was to be sited on the plot with the various outdoor activity areas that an elementary school would require. We had to provide:

1. A schematic plan that depicted relationships between the different activities and general traffic patterns such as pedestrian, vehicular, etc.
2. A general grading plan showing drainage patterns and steps and ramps as required for the handicapped and for maintenance access.

3. A schematic sprinkler plan.
4. A general planting plan.

Due to time restrictions all drawings were in rough schematic form, but the intent had to be made clear.

No doubt the test criteria have since been upgraded and refined, as this was still in the early years of the state licensure process. In any case, I needn't have worried so much, as I would learn from Ray later that I had scored second-highest in the entire state of California for that year. The person scoring the highest had a degree from the University of California, Berkeley, and would later become a partner in an internationally recognized firm with which I would also become associated.

As time went on, the daily commute from Pasadena to Beverly Hills began to take its toll on me, not just the physical aspects, which were bad enough, but the inherent waste and inefficiency of time and energy it represented. We tried a four-day week of ten hours a day, which seemed to work slightly better on paper, but not so well in practice as long as the rest of the world was on an eight-hour workday schedule. I was there sometimes when I was not needed and not there when, sure enough, a crisis would arise. Another option, of course, would have been to move closer to work, but I didn't feel the necessary stability of the situation to justify disrupting the whole family for my own convenience.

Ray had long sensed my unrest and offered a raise to help compensate for the imbalance, but I assured him that that was not the issue. It was the waste and inefficiency about which I felt guilty, while at the same time crusading about it being at the root of many of our social ills. This, I felt, was basic to a landscape architect's responsibility to society, so we in particular were obliged not to allow waste and inefficiency to occur in our personal lives.

As if in answer to a prayer, I heard through the grapevine that a highly reputable office in South Pasadena was seeking replacements for two of their top designers who were resigning to start their own practice. The chief partner of this office was none other than the internationally acclaimed landscape architect Garrett Eckbo,[78] who authored a few books on the subject, one of which was the primary textbook at Cal Poly. I had admired him not only for his expertise as an environmental designer, but also as a humanitarian. I *had* to meet the man, whether I had the qualifications for the job or not. And it would certainly be conveniently close to home if I did succeed in getting a job there. I immediately made an appointment for an interview.

I grabbed everything I could find, rough sketches and detailed drawings, anything I thought might impress him, and stuffed them into a folder. I knew him to be a rather casual, unpretentious person, so I was careful not to overdress—just enough to show respect.

The office was one sector of a modern complex consisting of an architecture studio, a structural engineering studio, an urban planning studio, and the landscape architecture studio—all distinct facets of the environmental design disciplines. The entire complex was sheltered under a steel-vaulted overhead shade structure, imparting a sense of comfortable, casual, but professional interaction.

As I entered the front office I was met by a middle-aged receptionist who I was later to learn was Hana Moss. Hana, unlike my mother Hana, was not Japanese. Hana was of Jewish descent and was not a receptionist or a secretary, but the office manager, or in more realistic terms, the office warden. As it turned out, Hana was the unofficial backbone of the entire operation. Nobody, not even the bosses, messed with Hana. After a very brief chat, she led me into Garrett's office, which was a bit of a mess. I pretended not to notice the mess while she bade good-bye to both of us. She had only come in that Saturday to see what kind of idiot Garrett was about to hire this time. I think the fact that she was leaving indicated that I had passed her test. As Hana went out the door, Garrett chuckled a little as if he had just won an argument.

I started to open my folder, but he said it wouldn't be necessary since he was already familiar with my work, having viewed the design department's student display at Cal Poly. He must have recognized much of his own design style and philosophy in the examples, as he had inspired me while I was at Cal Poly. He was, in essence, admiring his own work. He said that he had inquired among his colleagues for likely prospects and my name kept popping up. He knew about the concentration camps and my civil rights stance and the consequences of my protest. He knew I was working for Ray Page, and therein might be a problem. He informed me of the ongoing political feud between him and Ray, and said that Ray would no doubt accuse him of pirating me. I assured Garrett that I would inform Ray that it was I who had approached him (Garrett) because the office was conveniently close, and that it had nothing to do with personal or political preferences. In fact, it was both a professional and a political preference, but I wouldn't mention that. Garrett asked me how soon I could start. I said I would notify Ray on Monday so it would be two weeks after that, unless Ray wanted to fire me earlier. I don't recall discussing what exactly my duties or my wages would be. I was so elated I would have done his gardening on the side, if he wished.

Garrett was right. Ray didn't take the news very well. I don't know what bothered him more, that I was leaving or that I was joining his archenemy. I was genuinely sorry to leave Ray after all he had done for me, and I thanked him for it, but I just couldn't handle the commute any longer and he knew it. Anyway, I was aware all the while that he had been grooming another designer to take my place. I spent the next two weeks training my replacement. It was difficult to say good-bye to old Herb. I had become more attached to the sour old recluse than I realized.

Dear reader, I must confess I haven't been totally honest with you or with Ray Page. Yes, the commute was beginning to wear on me in a very practical sense, but in truth it was the entire experience—the job, the place, and the apparent goals—that conflicted with my long-held belief in the principle of "doing more with less," the age-old economic survival dynamic basic to all of mankind. Beverly Hills and the adjoining Tinseltown glitz became to me, for whatever reason, symbolic of man's ultimate desecration of human as well as other natural resources in his mad dash to cater to the ego whims of a few (and the money it would attract). I know many would disagree with me, but I found the daily exposure to this pretense to be emotionally and spiritually draining. I don't believe the waste can be justified by the illusion of this being a "land of plenty." It merely raised the question: plenty of what? I found it to be a sickness I couldn't cure, but I certainly didn't have to remain a part of it either.

Previously, while attending Cal Poly, I was introduced to a concept I found to be intensely compelling. The title of a book written by Garrett Eckbo said it all: *Landscape for Living*.[79] It questioned the assumption that professionally designed gardens were essentially the exclusive right of the nobility, and to some extent the privilege of the rich and famous. Contrariwise, the author suggested that everyone has a birthright to a sensible, wholesome environment. That the goal the professional designer should be striving for is to make this knowledge reasonably accessible to the broader populace. Environmental consciousness is everyone's responsibility, and the landscape architect must play a pivotal role in bringing about that awareness through his work.

That is why I was elated with the opportunity to work with Garrett Eckbo, the humanitarian. But, of course, we cannot know what lies beyond until we scale the peak that lies immediately ahead of us.

14

TRANSITIONS

Meanwhile, on the home front the three children were growing up and becoming quite active, so it was getting a bit crowded again. We considered adding on a couple of rooms, but knew a freeway was coming through eventually, and our house was right in the path of the proposed route.

I asked a real estate agent friend to find us a place farther north nearer the foothills. He was a Nisei, a former gardener who had recently acquired his real estate license and was thus new to the profession. He said he would have to limit his search to the prescribed area for minorities as determined by the local real estate board. I had heard of such unethical gerrymandering and was disappointed that my friend would accede to such blatant racial manipulation.

So, in the course of searching on my own, I came upon a redwood-and-glass contemporary-style house built into a slope in a canyon covered with native oak trees, all of which intrigued me. It had been designed by an architect for his own family and the landscape was designed by the Eckbo office, the earmarks of which I recognized right away. It was being sold by the owner, so Haru and I asked to see the house. It wasn't much larger than what we already had, but could easily be added onto with an extra bedroom and bath and possibly even a studio over the existing carport. Haru wasn't particularly impressed, and would have preferred something more traditional, but I knew it had been built just for us.

I went to the real estate office of John Carr, the son of William Carr,[80] who had done so much for the Japanese Americans on our return to the West Coast

     https://doi.org/10.5876/9781646421848.c014

after the war. John had taken over his father's agency on his recent retirement. I retained John to negotiate with the seller on our behalf so we could acquire the house, which he did. Not only that, but his father offered to carry the mortgage for us at a very reasonable interest rate. Our faith in the basic goodness of humankind had again been confirmed.

Like a jigsaw puzzle, all the pieces seemed to be falling into place. If it was all a dream, I didn't want to wake up. I would be starting work at the Eckbo office in a few weeks, which to me symbolized a new awakening of environmental awareness. It also coincided with the political stirrings of a new generation of human rights consciousness which would sweep the country, upset the status quo, and challenge smug apathy. It was the prelude to the "Age of Aquarius" and a revolutionary transformation of man's collective consciousness. However, the transformation would prove to be a long, arduous one, covering several decades and involving many setbacks, but there would be no turning back.

Upon arriving at the office of Eckbo, Dean and Williams in South Pasadena[81] on a Monday morning, I found it still closed, as were all the other offices in the complex. It must have been about eight o'clock and I wondered if it might be a holiday. While gardening I was accustomed to being on the job before seven, and even when working for Ray, I started at seven in order to get in my ten-hour day. Therefore, I waited in the central patio which had a small pond with a half-dozen goldfish and a bubbling fountain. At about eight-thirty people began dribbling in complaining about the traffic or the lousy weekend they'd had. But it was all good-natured joking; they had little else to complain about in such a nice environment. The Eckbo crew turned out to be only four, of which two were regulars and two were temporary part-time trainees from Cal Poly. The two regulars were recent Cal Poly graduates and I remembered them from the design classes I had earlier attended. It was after nine o'clock by the time we had coffee and the donuts one of them had brought. They just sat there as if waiting for me to tell them what to do. I figured they were testing me and that they already knew exactly what had to be done. I asked when Garrett would arrive and they said, "Oh, didn't you know? He's in Japan on a lecture tour and won't be back for at least another week." I wondered, could it be they really didn't know what they should be doing? I asked where Hana was and was told, "Who knows? She just pops in and out whenever she wants and has very little to do with the design department unless a client gets upset about something. Then she will blame it on us!"

I wondered, why do I always seem to step into a mess?

I spent most of the week reviewing the status of all the current projects that were being processed to make sure they would meet their deadlines, and making corrections and adjustments where necessary. I had to read Garrett's mind to determine what his intentions were on each project to ensure its execution would be consistent with his design style and philosophy, which I assumed was what the client expected. This, without having met the client and speaking to Garrett only briefly. Fortunately, I had read his books, which had imparted a basic honesty about the man that I sensed I could rely on.

Hana confided to me that Garrett had debated canceling his lecture tour, which had been prearranged for some time, and that his two top designers knew it when they decided to quit on him to start their own practice. My request for an interview had come just in the nick of time. Garrett already knew about me, but was reluctant to arouse further animosity from Ray Page because of their political differences. He had asked Hana to apologize to me for his not being there when I started. I confessed to her that all this while I thought *he* was saving *me*. No wonder his office was such a mess that first day I met him and the projects were in such a state of disarray.

I approached Hana very cautiously, knowing that she was not one to be taken too lightly if I hoped to remain there for long. But in spite of her crusty outer shell, she proved to be a very sensitive, warm soul once I got to know her. She was an avid folk music aficionado and guitar instructor. She introduced me to the world of American folk music, the likes of Woody Guthrie, Joan Baez, and Peter, Paul and Mary. She tried to teach me to play the guitar, but I was a lousy student, and being left-handed made it even more awkward. Later, my daughters would discover the abandoned instrument and bring it to life. Hana remained a very dear friend of Haru's and mine through her husband's death and, later on, until her own. I often wondered what nature of persecution or injustice she or her family had suffered, but never felt the time was right to ask. Many victims of man's inhumanity try to conceal their emotional scars, but they can often be detected by other victims because we know they exist.

The four crew members and Hana had managed to keep matters somewhat under control before I arrived, so it was mostly a matter of bringing myself up to speed on a process already established, unlike the crisis at Ray's office where we had to start from scratch and reestablish a process before any production could occur. Accordingly, by the time Garrett returned, we could celebrate not only his return, but his fiftieth birthday as well and the fact that he still had an office to which to return. The birthday party must have been Hana's idea because she was the only one who knew his birthdate. She had brought her guitar along that day in order to entertain us with some of her favorite folk songs, thereby revealing a softer side of her character about which very few within the business world were aware.

I worked as closely with Garrett as opportunities would allow, hoping to gain what I had missed when I quit Cal Poly prematurely. On all major projects he would rough out a general scheme, which to most people might appear as a shapeless blob (sometimes, to me also). In any case, I would give it some semblance of structure as it related to other fixed elements within or near the general space it occupied, if for no other reason than to enable a contractor to build it. Sometimes I wondered whether he was testing me or teasing me, but I always followed through. I don't think I would have done so with anyone else.

On one occasion it was an outdoor plaza for a major corporation in the center of downtown Los Angeles. Amid the sophisticated geometry of the plaza, there suddenly appeared a shapeless blob like a giant pumpkin that fell out of a passing helicopter and splattered in the middle of a rather rigid geometric pattern. Like the pumpkin, I couldn't contain myself. I had to ask Garrett what this mess was supposed to be. I was prepared for some very esoteric scholarly rhetoric, but all he would say, in his unassuming way, was, "Well, I just thought it would be nice. Just make it work."

I had to think long and hard on that one. I knew he was serious, although he had chuckled a little when he said it. While visualizing myself in downtown Los Angeles, especially in the newer high-rise area, I was very aware that it was a man-made environment with rigid geometric forms, lending a sense of predictability and stability which was reasonable for a business center, but even the people were somewhat robotic in their behavior. Was this Garrett's way of protesting the take-over of our society by mega corporations? But the corporations themselves were essentially people—or were they? Were they, in fact, the original victims?

While acutely aware that we were in "enemy" territory and social change would be difficult without his cooperation, it would be unwise to announce our opposition prematurely such as those who take to the streets in a demonstration to gain public support. But to work undetected from within to bring about a change of consciousness in the oppressor would be our tactic, if only because we had the opportunity to do so. All of this without capitulating and becoming part of the problem, which is too often the unfortunate demise of many good intentions. So how did this relate to the space that corporate America had provided us? *Gardens Are for People,* Thomas Church's book, would provide the answer. A later book by Garrett Eckbo, *Urban Landscape Design,* deals with the issue more thoroughly.[82]

It would be an oasis where the human spirit could find a brief respite from the daily rat race that pitted it against its fellow man (or woman) while others raked in the profits. It must appear innocuous, of course, but carry a clear subconscious message regarding the evils of human exploitation, and indeed, of self-delusion. I no longer questioned Garrett's intentions, but focused on what he had left for me to decipher and "make it work." I was flattered that he would entrust such a challenge to me. Garrett Eckbo was a master of understatement. Planet Earth was his canvas and the sanctity of man's soul was his message.

That was almost fifty years ago as I write these words. Garrett's brainchild caught on briefly once corporate America realized that there were untold benefits to investing in the development of environmentally friendly spaces for people. But eventually the short-sighted money-changers challenged such "wasteful pursuits" and redirected the slush fund toward glamorizing the corporate image and filling the pockets of their CEOs. Garrett's garden no longer exists. It is difficult to place a dollar amount on the value of uplifting the human spirit in all our diverse environments, but the battle must go on if humankind is to maintain its sanity.

Indeed, the Eckbo, Dean and Williams corporation itself was undergoing some very serious transformations. The Seattle, Washington, office was discontinued, and Francis Dean, the principal there, would be joining us in South Pasadena. Garrett was offered a position as the dean of landscape architecture at the University of California, Berkeley, and would maintain limited involvement with the partnership through the San Francisco office. They also advanced Donald Austin, a former associate, to partner and manager of the office in Texas. It was now Eckbo, Dean, Austin and Williams, or EDAW.[83]

It was not the geographic shifting of the top brass that was the most disturbing. It was a more universal reorientation of the role the designer would play in an industrialized world that was being transformed by a rapidly changing technology. Television had just been developed, and computerization for the masses was just around the corner. The art of communication had come a long way since smoke signals and tom-tom drums, to pictographs and papyrus, from the early telephone to the wireless technology of fax and e-mail, and the trend is destined to continue. But, change itself was not the culprit. Indeed, the ability to adapt was one of man's primary characteristics. It accounts for his survival over the ages while other creatures become extinct. Further, it is man himself who was instigating these changes. It was the ever-increasing *rate* of change that now challenged man's innate ability to adapt.

Our generation, Garrett's and mine and others, would fall into that general category, and we would be particularly confounded by the increasingly confusing acceleration of change. Even younger generations would be somewhat at a loss as they would eventually find themselves without appropriate role models. The changes, which were basically technological, unfortunately omitted other important elements of man's identity, such as his spiritual, mental, emotional, moral, and, more generally, his non-finite nature. A clear danger lies in our apparent abandonment of the continuing development of this essential perception of man's true identity—that which Garrett, in his own way, was determined to preserve.

But alas, the corporate bulldozer would destroy Garrett's garden, a finite symbol of the infinite.

Garrett never confided in me, a mere associate, about any of this, but I sensed his uneasiness when we accepted a contract from the Jet Propulsion Laboratory (JPL) in Pasadena, a research and development laboratory which involved contracts with the military. Previously, we had discouraged contracts with agencies that dealt with the military, but pressure from the EDAW corporate body to modify this policy in order to compete with other leading design discipline offices on an open market was apparent. The battle between corporate greed and philosophical ethics had come knocking on our door.

Eventually Garrett would opt for the university position. Later, he would bow out of the partnership altogether and establish a small private office in San Francisco on his own terms, apparently weary of his solitary stand against the one-eyed corporate behemoth that he himself had created, with its seemingly self-serving goals. But that wouldn't occur until a few years after I had left the office myself.

I remained with the EDAW corporation for eight years and was grateful for the opportunity to be involved in many major projects throughout the western states, mostly university campuses and other community gathering facilities as well as a few private residences. The larger projects often required coordination with other design disciplines such as architects, engineers (both civil and mechanical), planners, environmentalists, and, of course, the money managers—plus the inevitable idiot who was totally insensitive to what our design goals were but had to be tolerated because he held the purse strings. I soon tired of the inflated egos of most designers and the political hypocrisy of the money managers. Design by committee to me was a total farce. I avoided those projects, especially the meetings, and preferred consulting with private homeowners on a one-on-one basis. I did enjoy working with Francis Dean,[84] who, like Garrett, was a dedicated humanitarian, but not a businessman at all.

Neither was I. I submitted my resignation in 1968, with no preparation whatsoever, catching everyone in the office by surprise and to some extent even myself, although I had been toying with the idea of starting my own practice for some time to escape the dehumanizing effects of the corporate scene. Francis's final words to me were, "The door will always be open to you if you ever change your mind." But I knew I didn't belong there any more than Garrett Eckbo or Francis Dean did. It was easy for me to leave, but for them it was a lifelong commitment, and their success had become their jailer. I had already done my prison time protesting social/political ills and wasn't about to volunteer for an additional stint, as enticing as the prospects may have seemed.

I5

LOYALTY TO WHAT?

The move to our new house eight years earlier, in 1960, to the canyon in Altadena, California, required the girls to change to new schools and to find new playmates in the neighborhood. What neighborhood? Being in an almost mountainous area the houses were rather sparse and somewhat remote compared with the tight-knit standard grid pattern of our former site. The kids could no longer run in and out of a neighbor's house and into another a few doors away and always be among friends and schoolmates. They had become accustomed to the convenience of being among others of their own ethnicity, age, and lifestyle, as if of one big family. Also, the parents of these children were those who had earlier experienced forced removal from their homesteads after the outbreak of war with Japan and who had been imprisoned in concentration camps just as we had been. With this common background there developed a sense of security and trust as "being among our own people," typical of many West Coast communities, where many former wartime prisoners had resettled after the war.

Although we enjoyed the closeness to nature our new home afforded us, with a natural forest of native oaks, a running stream in the canyon below, access to nearby hiking trails, and nightly visits by a family of raccoons, we did miss the sense of community the former neighborhood had given us. However, we were not as isolated from the Japanese American community as it initially appeared because soon the Union Presbyterian Church of Pasadena, the same one that was in my childhood neighborhood before we moved to Monrovia, would build a

 https://doi.org/10.5876/9781646421848.c015

modern structure, the renamed First Presbyterian Church of Altadena, less than a mile from us. It was designed by the noted architects Smith and Williams, of the design complex shared by EDAW. I was involved in the landscape design of the project, although I was never a member of the church, or any other church for that matter. Haru, however, was a volunteer Sunday school teacher for several years and taught many of the children of our former neighborhood.

Well, surprise, surprise! In 1962 we were blessed with the birth of yet another girl. It had been eight years since Gail was born and we weren't planning on any more, so it did come as something of a surprise. But, of course, one is never really surprised, as there are many physical clues for months ahead if one is paying any attention at all. On the other hand, paying too much attention could be a part of the problem in the first place.

At any rate, by the time Miya Robyn came along, we apparently felt comfortable enough with our ethnic identity to give her a Japanese name, a consideration we realized had been unfairly denied the three older siblings. We were no longer influenced, albeit unconsciously, by the subtle self-reproach engendered by the racial bigotry to which we had been subjected. It arose out of a debilitating sense of inadequacy that was reinforced by the JACL, which implied that our ethnic roots were a liability in our "assimilation" process in "becoming" true Americans. Haru and I had heretofore accepted our given Japanese names, but were hesitant to burden our children with what we had experienced as a handicap, but what in reality was nothing more than white man's lack of cultural enlightenment. As children, many Nisei were carelessly subjected to embarrassment or even humiliation by teachers who failed to pronounce our Japanese names correctly. Some students were arbitrarily given simple English names by the teacher for his/her own convenience, but not necessarily for the students themselves. Many Nisei may have welcomed it because it made them feel more "American." Some Issei parents gave their children English names, foreseeing the problems that could occur otherwise, and even adopted English names for themselves. Some children adopted English names on their own, with or without parental encouragement. Thus, quite innocently, adapting one's identity to accommodate the limitations of others implied a willingness to accept an inferior social status. That, in essence, is what many acceded to in order to avoid embarrassment.

However, our three older children, Suzi at thirteen, Sharon at eleven, and Gail at eight, in spite of the lack of Japanese names, were already showing a remarkable ability to incorporate the positive attributes of their ethnic heritage to enhance their identities in a predominantly western culture harmoniously, and without sacrificing the inherent attributes of either. They somehow seemed to have managed without much conscious effort from their parents. They appeared relatively free of the psychological scars their parents' generation had been forced to endure. They shared in common such traits as a natural creativity and a compassion for

FIGURE 15.1. Miya and Haru (courtesy, Sharon Kuromiya).

all living creatures. Their creativity was expressed through various channels at different times, through literature and music, but mostly through the graphic arts. They possessed individual styles, and one would not dare confuse the works of one with another. Even Miya developed her own individual style in the graphic arts, no doubt inspired by her older sisters.

While the girls were still quite young (even before Miya's birth), I explained to them about the camps during the war and about my stint in prison for refusing to be drafted. Perhaps they were too young to understand the gravity of my actions or the circumstances that brought them on, and were merely anxious to go out to play, but they assured me of their acceptance of my choice and its consequences. Well, that was easy, I thought, but expected the questions to come later. In a few days they presented me with a small (about three-inch-tall) comical doll in a convict's striped suit with a ball and chain attached to one ankle. I don't recall, but it may have been a Father's Day gift. That symbol, now faded and dusty, has hung from my desk lamp for almost fifty years and is my most prized possession,

FIGURE 15.2. Convict doll, a gift from the girls (courtesy, Suzi Kuromiya).

besides my four daughters, of course. They may question my reference to them as possessions, but they know what I mean.

In the meantime, they survived all the usual physical ailments of childhood, all the emotional trauma and melodrama of their teens, and have blossomed into the compassionate, creative, inquisitive, intelligent, entertaining, beautiful beings they were always destined to become. But I will always treasure their special childhood symbol of acceptance and reassurance that only a father can know through the unconditional love and innocence of children who know not of hate, fear, vengeance, and betrayal.

I firmly believe that most Issei immigrants, including my parents, had hoped to merge into the more humane democratic American mainstream, not solely for what they could gain from it, but also to contribute by sharing what they could of their eastern culture. Not all were determined to make a monetary killing in America to take back to Japan as so many stories imply. Many, I believe, were eager to introduce to America their rich heritage in the many arts—in literature, poetry, the theater, painting, etching, the symbolism of the tea ceremony, flower arranging, ceramics, garden design, and the martial arts, all of which had been refined and redefined throughout the centuries long before America even existed. Unfortunately, America was not ready for them. The immigrants were met with hostility, suspicion, and subjected to exploitation. Their offerings were regarded as sinister, deceptive diversions at worst and useless, quaint trinkets at best. The self-denial and industriousness of the immigrants were not respected as signs of remarkable self-discipline and character, but as unfair competitiveness in the industrial communities of America. Laws were enacted to avert what some feared would lead to their own economic disaster if not checked.

Perhaps the timing was not the best and much sacrifice was already destined to occur, but no one had much luxury of choice. In any case, the Issei immigrants would prevail, at great sacrifice to be sure, for themselves as well as their offspring, but they would indeed prevail.

For most, if not all, Nisei during our childhood and throughout the war years, to be American meant to think, behave, and adopt the general values we saw in our Caucasian counterparts. This often required us to abandon many things associated with our parents' Japanese culture. It was like "throwing the baby out with the bathwater."

This, unfortunately, was to a great degree the mindset of the Japanese American Citizens League, creating further stress in the generational gap within many families. In some cases, in their desire to be recognized as Americans, the Nisei began to view their Issei parents as liabilities. Could there possibly be a connection between this dilemma and oft-expressed need to "prove one's loyalty"?

The onset of WWII further exacerbated the crisis in the already tenuous identity of Japanese Americans caught in the crosscurrents of political turmoil. One's "loyalty" became synonymous with the ability to appear "American." Americanism itself became a matter of outward behavior, i.e., the willingness to accommodate the political interests of our government and not necessarily the constitutional principles it was meant to represent. One's ethics became a matter of political expedience rather than of personal integrity guided by one's conscience.

In the midst of wartime hysteria, the leadership of the JACL became agents for the government, voluntarily in the beginning, but eventually as official government spies to aid in the ferreting out of those whom *they* regarded as possible enemy spies within the Japanese American community. This shameful episode in our wartime history is best explained in the documentary evidence contained within *The Lim Report*.[85] It is a thoroughly researched account of the activities of JACL leadership before, during, and after WWII, compiled by attorney Deborah Lim at the request of a later generation of JACL members. Much of the data was derived from FBI files and the files of the JACL of that era. Obviously, the damning evidence revealed in the files would never have been exposed had the committee requesting the report been aware of the truth behind what was, until then, regarded as mere irresponsible rumors. Of all of those who were fingered by the JACL in their concerted witch-hunt of mostly Issei (and some Kibei), who were interned in Department of Justice camps, to my knowledge not a single soul was ever charged or convicted of any criminal acts of disloyalty.

Further, I know of no instance of any member of the JACL who had boasted of his participation in what amounted to a witch-hunt ever extending an apology to any of the victims who were wrongly accused. Nor did the national JACL render any statement of apology for their erroneous assumptions that brought so much undeserved grief and hardship to so many families. Perhaps a large part of the "No-No" stance of the Tule Lake Segregation Center and Department of Justice camps for so-called "disloyalty" was a direct result of this cowardly JACL betrayal, and had little to do with one's loyalty.

Indeed, the simplistic and arbitrary use of the terms "loyal" and "disloyal" as defined by the JACL rendered both terms meaningless. Those abiding by the government (and JACL) directives, no matter how unreasonable, were regarded as "loyal." Those resisting, or even questioning, the directives were regarded as "disloyal." Thus, the "No-Nos" at Tule Lake and the various DOJ camps were regarded as "disloyal" even though they were never convicted in a court of law of any act of disloyalty. The few who challenged the constitutionality of the government's actions were regarded by the JACL as "disloyal" except, of course, in the few cases where their court convictions were reversed. Then they became "civil rights leaders" and in some cases "national heroes" and were regarded as a credit to our community with the endorsement of the JACL. As absurd and transparent as this JACL criterion was and still is, most of Japanese America accepted it then and continue to abide by its absurdity.

Under such a pervasive atmosphere of the total breakdown of ethical standards, it is understandable if the average victims—unworldly, unsophisticated, mostly former inhabitants of isolated farms and small rural communities, and already laboring under a generational communication and cultural conflict among family members—would be overwhelmed by the confusing onslaught of unreasonable government directives, none of which held any reassurance of what was the right path. It is small wonder that many withdrew from reality under the guise of *shikataganai*, and for decades later refused to discuss the matter. *Shikataganai* literally means "it can't be helped," but to too many Japanese Americans it has become a debilitating Pandora's Box of unresolved emotional trauma. Even the highly touted "redress" movement[86] did little to rectify or to even acknowledge the existence of this personal hell.

My own direct confrontation with this phenomenon was when so many (most) of my fellow draft resisters were unwilling to publicize their wartime protest and the constitutional principles behind it. It wasn't that they feared reprisal for questionable loyalty or the simplistic accusations of cowardice. It was the realization that they had become pariahs within their own communities, communities that apparently had become convinced that a primary duty was to serve one's country regardless of the circumstances (an unquestionable obligation in Japan), and that the issue was one of proving one's loyalty, not a matter of constitutional fidelity. Further, almost every family had at least one relative who had fought in WWII, and they could hardly doubt the honor of their own kin, especially if he had paid with his life, as many did. The families of the resisters would be made to suffer for the resisters' "selfish" acts. Thus, many resisters felt it best to let sleeping dogs lie, and even suggested I not be so outspoken about civil justice, constitutional responsibilities, and matters of conscience. I was astounded! How ironic that circumstances would dictate the reasonableness of remaining silent about an issue to which we all had once felt so committed. Yet we recognized this as a personal issue and one we never anticipated. Each individual dealt with it in whatever manner was best for him, without judgment from the rest of us. Most decided to remain silent, not necessarily as an attempt to conceal, but simply as a personal prerogative, which I shall respect. Once again, I felt the sting of our failure to strive for the appeal of our convictions.[87] The dilemma we face today is a direct result of that failure.

On occasion we resisters have been questioned about why we hadn't protested our unjustified incarceration earlier. Why did we wait until the government regarded us as acceptable citizens and therefore qualified to fight for our country? A fair question. Government directives, although seemingly unfair and possibly unconstitutional, were tentatively accommodated on the questionable grounds of "military necessity" and as evidence of our basic loyalty. However, the resultant rewards of our established loyalty were not freedom and compensation for the false imprisonment and loss of property, as might be expected, but the opportunity, nay, the obligation to serve in the military to fight abroad for the very freedoms we had been denied by the government we were now expected to serve. This, while our families were still being held in concentration camps. If we were, in fact, loyal citizens, why were we being inducted into the military from a concentration camp? Why were we denied the choice of which branch of the military we would serve in as it was with other inductees? Why were we limited to a racially segregated combat unit?

Why, we are asked, did we protest when the Selective Service draft was upon us and not before? Because it was our last opportunity to protest as civilians. The violations to our civil rights had occurred while we were civilians. Rectification had to come through the civilian judicial system. Our protest against induction had to be addressed in civil court while we were still civilians (albeit prisoners), not after we became members of the military, at which time it would become a military issue. We did not determine when the protest would occur or if there would be a need for protest, as the initial question seems to suggest. The Selective Service Board inadvertently made that decision when they sent us the notice to prepare for military service in spite of the unresolved status of our citizenship.

I personally found it difficult to ignore the contradictions the government and the JACL leadership were asking me to abide by, contradictions I would eventually have to confront in inescapable human terms as I faced an enemy without benefit of reasonable cause to take his life or give up my own. I had to deal with that moral dilemma *beforehand*, not on the battlefield. Blood is blood; could I in good conscience stain my hands forever with the blood of a stranger and regard it as a noble deed? Perhaps under other circumstances, but under the unjustified, unreasonable conditions which had been forced upon me? Definitely not! To me, no amount of rationalization, patriotic proclamations, medals, memorials, or heroic sagas, real or contrived, would wipe that blood away.

So until someone can convince me otherwise, the little convict that hangs proudly from my desk lamp will remain my medal of honor. One's conscience, after all, is a very personal matter.

16

DEPARTURES

The 1960s and 1970s were a time of dramatic social change in the United States. The post-WWII baby boom generation, soon to reach adulthood, was fueled by a new consciousness, often referred to zodiacally as the "Age of Aquarius." It challenged many of the social/ethical assumptions held by the elder generations, considering them archaic, hypocritical, and confining. The resulting unrest would be expressed throughout the world, especially in the more technically advanced nations, through social, political, racial, economic, and cultural institutions.

We would experience the onslaught here in the United States through racial turmoil, peace marches, antiwar movements, and people-versus-the-government confrontations. It occurred to me that the citizens' rights issues that formed the basis of most of the controversy was similar to that which happened to Japanese Americans over twenty years before, during WWII, except that now it was on a broader, more universal scale. Could it be that the unresolved injustice of that period had returned to exact justice, which had been long withheld, through the social consciousness of a new generation?

In any case, few Nisei and Sansei chose to become involved. As before, most Nisei turned a deaf ear to efforts to rectify the injustices they and their families had suffered, relying on others to fight their battles for them. They chose to play it safe by striving to become a self-proclaimed "Model Minority," setting a sincere, if misguided, example of overcoming adversity for all downtrodden minorities through compromise rather than confrontation, conveniently ignoring the fact that many of our social virtues were the direct inheritance of our parents' culture, a culture that so many neo patriots had disavowed during WWII. After what we Nisei had experienced through the dogma of racist bigotry and at the hands of deceitful government agencies, it is puzzling that most Nisei chose to remain apathetic when civil rights were at the heart of most of the New Age protests.

However, the shake-up nationally did inspire a profound new awareness of long-held misperceptions of race relations and gender stereotyping. It also heralded a clearer appreciation of the delicate balance and interdependency within our natural environment, and the critical role that man, in this industrialized economy, must play in insuring his own survival. Unfortunately, it did little to transform man himself as a spiritual being with a conscience with which to monitor his ethical integrity, except in a few isolated cases. Indeed, technological advances would provide a multitude of opportunities to escape issues of human compassion (which the New Age protagonists proffered as an essential element in the transcendence of man into his higher beingness) and thereby continue to avoid encounters with one's conscience. Thus, it seems, man's persistent sense of enslavement was not due to the lack of freedoms, but due to the lack of understanding and control over his own greed and inflated ego. True honor resides not in clamorous grandeur but in quiet humility. Or so it always had been in Hisamitsu's world.

As previously mentioned, my work at the Eckbo office gradually became less exciting as we were increasingly subjected to the corporate dictates of the San Francisco office. We seemed to drift away from the original people-oriented ideology I had initially found so intriguing. I finally resigned in late 1968 to start a private practice on my own terms, even though it meant sacrificing the sophistication and worldly exposure I had enjoyed at the Eckbo office. I still felt, perhaps somewhat naïvely, that the client/consultant relationship on a one-on-one basis to be primary, and not to be compromised by corporate pressures. I found the task of representing a corporation to be rather cold, impersonal, artificial, and, at times, downright hypocritical.

I subleased a small one-room office space from a newly formed architectural firm in an old building in downtown Pasadena, not far from what would soon become known as Old Town Pasadena.[88] The studio was very limited but adequate, as I had no illusions of hiring a staff to do the design and production work (which I preferred doing myself) while I pounded the pavement promoting new projects (which I detested). I would depend on the integrity of my designs to attract new work. I had already contacted a few architects and landscape contractors as sources of future prospects. The only staff I needed was a part-time typist to handle formal written documents such as contractual agreements and proposals. It would be an experiment in "doing more with less," consistent with my general design philosophy. Thus, the operation itself would be an experiment in minimalism, in the elimination of unnecessary frills and distractions. I was starting on a shoestring and enjoying every minute of it. I was on my own again, but this time pushing a pencil instead of a lawnmower and in an air-conditioned office, not under the searing Southern California sun.

In 1969, as our nation landed the first man on the moon, Hisamitsu Kuromiya, after a brief illness, came to the end of his life-long, solitary struggle to set an example of the virtues of self-imposed moral integrity. I believe his real-life goal was to become, to his own satisfaction, the epitome of ethical fidelity during his stint of human incarnation on Mother Earth. He never spoke of this, however, as to do so would only raise questions of its credibility. He never preached virtue. He merely followed his conscience. His silence spoke volumes to those few who could "hear."

However, as commendable as it may have been for him to maintain his uncompromising dedication to his ideals, it was my mother Hana who, I suspect, paid the price for this indulgence. She, no doubt, had romantic dreams as a teenager coming to America, the land of plenty, only to discover she could only look but not touch. And it seemed largely because of Hisamitsu's rigid morality that her own dreams and yearnings would never be realized. Her official role in all their ventures may have been one of silent partner, but as with many immigrant mothers, she was in reality the mainstay of the family. She would often deny herself the simple luxury of a day's rest when running a high fever or giving childbirth. Of course, I was only a year old when Kimiye, her last child, was born, so I am merely surmising the latter.

This is not to suggest any comparison between my father and me, but merely to point out the coincidences of the events we encountered and the similarities of the end results. He was of a different generation and was raised in a totally different environment under cultural criteria difficult for me to imagine, much less abide by. He was the direct descendant of strict, sometimes unforgiving, traditions that few dared to challenge. Further, as the firstborn son, the responsibility for perpetuating the family's moral integrity fell heavily on him, especially being of the samurai class. His was not an easy childhood. Indeed, his intuitive decision to forego all the traditional social and political advantages of his inheritance in Japan in exchange for the unknown challenges of a foreign land, all for the slim possibility of realizing a vague sense of spiritual freedom, certainly required substantial courage and optimism. One of the freedoms he sacrificed so much for was the freedom of expression. But, alas, his concern for the feelings of others was so deeply ingrained in him that he often, if not always, declined to avail himself of even this to his own (and Mama's) eventual disadvantage. Such was the irony of his dedication.

This, then, is the legacy which he denied himself for fear of appearing too self-serving, but which I have been given and shall continue to utilize as my conscience dictates, as a means of raising the awareness of all who would listen: that of the immorality of the many deliberate deceptions of an era of Japanese American history that has become the questionable legacy we Nisei are passing on to subsequent generations, a history which has all but ignored the rich cultural heritage and moral integrity of our Issei forebears.

It is a shameful history in which our nation turned against a segment of its own citizenry as being subhuman and therefore unassimilable as "true" Americans. The rejection was further exacerbated when a segment of those who were thus disenfranchised redirected the unjust animosity toward their Issei parents' generation, as possible suspects of disloyalty, as a means of attaining, for themselves, a degree of political immunity from the government. The Issei, thus betrayed not only by their country of choice but by their own progeny as well, were left totally vulnerable to further abuse—materially, physically, financially, psychologically, socially, and politically. Few Nisei came to their aid. Yet the Issei endured, even when their sons marched off to a war in which they (the Issei) would have a questionable stake. *Shikataganai!* They bore it all and yet they prevailed. Such is the silence of true honor. Such is the deception of our cowardly history as written by the JACL.

History itself does not change. It is our perception of it that changes as we peel away layers of deception and self-deception to reveal our true history. But that, it seems, is a legacy we Nisei must entrust to a later generation to confirm. We Nisei in our desperate search for validation from *without* seem to have forsaken our reality from *within* and thereby our true identity as masters of our perceptions and not merely victims of our misperceptions.

Thus, through the freedom of expression with which I have been blessed by the efforts of my father, of which he could not or would not avail himself due to cultural prohibitions, I shall promote the high ethical standards he adopted as a criterion for me and for future generations. Therein the spirit of Hisamitsu will live on.

Hisamitsu, however, was not a patron of the arts. He regarded my interest in the creative arts as a form of infantile indulgence and patiently awaited my "growing up" to deal with matters of the real world. His vision of the stereotypical artist was a disheveled, bearded, unbathed old man in a dusty, dirty attic, in a hopeless state of illusion and delusion, amid the chaos of splattered paint and empty wine bottles. Indeed, no one in the family showed the least interest in my endeavors except perhaps my younger sister Kim. I was tolerated by the others perhaps, but I don't recall ever being encouraged.

This didn't bother me much, however. In fact, it gave me a sense of freedom to pursue whatever ventures I wished, unlike brother Hiroshi, who was expected to bear the responsibility for the family welfare, even though all of us siblings had families of our own by then. So it came as quite a surprise to me when, shortly after Papa's death in 1969, Mama confided to me that Papa had advised her to rely on *me* for her future welfare after he was gone. She never explained the reason for his change of plans for her, and I was never certain she had even heard him correctly, but I was secretly elated that perhaps he was aware all along that he and I shared many of the same dreams and values, even if I lacked his dignity, discipline, and dedication.

But even as Mama confided Papa's advice to her, I had to question the wisdom of his trust in me. Haru and I had been experiencing a growing sense of alienation and having doubts about our marriage, a condition that I'm sure Papa would have found unacceptable had he known. Ironically, his passing would make it less distressing for Haru and me and perhaps was a blessing in disguise for all concerned. A true gentleman to the end.

In any case, by the early 1970s, it became quite evident to Haru and me that our marriage would not last much longer. We both sensed we had been on divergent paths for quite some time and neither of us was ready to make the necessary adjustments to change our respective courses. Thus, we chose to go our separate ways by default—amicably perhaps, but not without trepidation and self-doubt. Such is the perilous path of self-discovery (or self-indulgence; I'm not sure which). In any case, after some costly legal entanglements that were totally uncalled for, created by our greedy and unprofessional legal consultant to line his own pockets, we were finally legally divorced in 1977.

In the interim I had been living in an apartment within walking distance of my office. It occurred to me that this was really the first time I was truly independent. Previously, I had been dependent on my parents to care for all my domestic needs. Then it was the War Relocation Authority. Then it escalated to the federal penal system, under circumstances I regarded as matters of principle. Then it was back to my parents' house briefly before I married and was soon overwhelmed as the sole provider for a growing family. I had somehow managed to shift the responsibility for my existence on others, unmindful that I was a burden on them, but more importantly, cheating myself of the challenge of my own accountability (except perhaps in the case of the welfare of the children). At the ripe old age of fifty-two, I suddenly realized that the opportunity to live an unencumbered bachelorhood, which I had missed in my eagerness to have a family and live a "normal" life, was belatedly at hand.

Indeed, the so-called "normal" life also seemed to have its pitfalls and drawbacks, often stunting the growth of both parties in a relationship through subconscious fears of change. Social convention, in spite of all good intentions, could easily become a prison of one's soul if not one's mind and body. Many a free spirit has been needlessly discouraged by an overly restrictive relationship. Even while detained at Heart Mountain and later at McNeil Island, I felt secure in that my soul was never in jeopardy. In fact, if nothing else, those experiences affirmed my solitary ownership and mastership of my soul. One's conscience is in a sense the language of one's soul, and my conscience was my constant companion and solitary counsel during those dark days.

My first priority, however, was to fulfill my dream of combining my work space with my home space. As a single person, paying full-time rent for both office space and an apartment which I couldn't occupy at the same time seemed rather absurd, especially while professing minimalism.

I located a small bungalow in West Los Angeles that would serve my dual purpose quite well. It had convenient access to major freeways and a major shopping mall within walking distance. It was in a quiet neighborhood of modest homes with very little street traffic, which is unusual in West Los Angeles. In truth, I was attracted to it because not only was it a cute house, but also it had a unique contorted, lopsided sycamore tree that dominated the tiny front yard. The gnarled old tree somehow reminded me of Papa's solitary encounters with his many windmills, thereby imparting a feeling of home to me even before I moved into the house. It would serve as my home and studio for the next fifteen years or more as I encountered my own metaphorical windmills.

———————————

I had recently been introduced to a school of thought about which I became intensely interested. "The Prosperos" is generally based on the premise of teaching one *how* to think as opposed to *what* to think. I mention this, not to expound on its virtues and why I was so attracted to it, but merely because it was there that I met Ruth.

Ruth was a product of the sixties and seventies New Age, antiwar, free speech, and racial equality political movements. She represented a lifestyle to which I was unaccustomed, although I respected the humanitarian ideology behind it. My own priority for man's survival dynamics was the preservation of our natural resources—the discipline of doing more with less and reducing industrial pollution. After many pointless delays, the divorce with Haru was finally resolved. Ruth suggested we could now get married. I needed more time to rediscover myself. After thirty years of marriage and through no one's fault but my own, I was no longer sure of who I was. Further, my relationship with Ruth seemed rather irresponsible given our age and lifestyle differences.

We did get married, however, but it predictably ended with disastrous results. Within fourteen months we separated by mutual agreement.

Freedom is but an illusion when we rely on others to bear our burdens for us.

17

READJUSTMENT

After my brief exposure to our country's corporate greed, which was quite a revelation with many ups and downs—but nonetheless gave me greater insight into a world totally unlike that to which I had been limited—I gradually reentered my own ethnic enclave. I discovered I could relate more easily to the Sansei generation than to my Nisei peer group, who appeared to me to be overly constrained, competitive, and prone to prejudgment—the very blindness that, in others, had caused us so much grief during WWII. These Nisei appeared less interested in the search for truth than in the concealing of it. Many exhibited signs of denial of their wartime experience and avoided all reference to it, claiming it served no purpose to even discuss it. I was reminded anew that the psychological damage that had been wrought on my people had not diminished in over thirty-five years.

I was surprised to discover that singleness was not the rare phenomenon among the Nisei that I had assumed. There were, of course, a few of my peers who never got married, but there were many more who had divorced or were now widows or widowers. There was a very active singles (by choice or circumstance) social presence in Niseidom, and a growing number among the Sansei. The activities ranged from serious political alliances to sports and recreational groups as purely social outlets and for camaraderie. They all, both men and women, denied interest in seeking new partners, but I noticed a fair amount of covert social manipulation and outright competitiveness going on constantly. I found it rather fascinating and sadistically exciting. It was like getting a second (or third) chance

 https://doi.org/10.5876/9781646421848.c017

at happiness, a reprieve from a death sentence or a pardon for having screwed-up the first time (or the second time). But, of course, I wasn't interested in a new partner, either. I hadn't recovered from the last two. Everything was now under control and I had forgotten how important sharing had been to me, at least for the time being. I was too emotionally drained to care. I was just a casual observer, as were all the others.

However, I did join a couple of the social groups in hopes of meeting people with whom to share common interests, mostly fanciful ideas in the realm of the "what ifs" and the "supposings." Somewhat nutty perhaps, but "reality" had proven to be much too grim. I needed relief. The dating scene was enjoyable, but produced nothing of enduring consequence. Perhaps I was unconsciously avoiding serious commitments. I focused more on my work. I found it rather therapeutic solving other people's problems. I wondered if the state of one's garden is somehow a reflection of one's psyche. For me, to get paid for dealing with it became an additional bonus. What treasures we find in the strangest of places!

After several years I met Irene. Irene, I would realize later, was not the usual "meat market" single. Her energies were devoted to the raising of her two children, alone, from their childhood through college, and she had neither time nor interest in socializing. She had reluctantly joined her friend who was a nurse, as was she, at her friend's urging to "circulate." It was at an all-singles picnic.

As I was waiting for a friend to arrive, I noticed Irene sitting alone at a picnic table. So I approached her, introduced myself, and attempted to start a conversation. She looked straight ahead and showed absolutely no interest. "What a snob," I was thinking when I spotted my friend entering through the gate. I was relieved (as was Irene, no doubt) that I could extricate myself from the most humiliating experience I had suffered in a long time. She later explained to me that a couple of boors had approached her just before me, and she was already disgusted with being "hit upon" so crudely.

Disappointed but not discouraged, I saw her again at the Japanese Garden tour at the Tillman Water Reclamation Plant in Van Nuys, California. Noting that she was alone and was toward the back of the crowd, I lagged even farther back so I could observe her. The coast was clear; she had no companion. So I caught up to her and casually remarked on the serenity of the garden and that Van Nuys seemed an unlikely place for the sensitivity of a Japanese garden. The tour guide was much farther ahead and was surrounded by the larger part of our group. This time she at least pretended to be interested. Persistence was beginning to pay off.

Later the group drove to another section of the park, where we picnicked on pre-ordered *bento* lunches [consisting of such items as rice, vegetables, and sashimi]. I sprang for the twenty-five cents extra for our drinks (big-time spender). We found a shade tree a little separate from the rest of the group that had spread blankets to sit on. Suddenly realizing we were being a bit too obvious, we joined those on the blankets, but were careful to sit at the far edge facing away from the others. Rude, to be sure, but I made sure I got my twenty-five cents' worth.

As we left, I promised to give her a call. She later realized she hadn't given me her phone number and hadn't gotten mine, so there was no way to contact me. Not to worry. I had already checked the membership roster and had her phone number as well as her address.

Mama wasn't doing very well. She became increasingly feeble physically, although mentally she was quite alert. We had her move in with Kim and Ted and arranged for hospice care in order to avoid overburdening Kim. Meanwhile Ted, who was still gardening, needed triple bypass heart surgery. He came through the operation quite well, but then against the doctor's orders he went back to work too soon and suffered a serious relapse. Kim was also found to need heart surgery, which she survived but contracted a throat infection while recovering at the hospital. She had complained about it to no avail until a nurse decided to check further and discovered there was indeed a very serious throat condition that had prevented her from swallowing food. Her son, Danny, had her moved to a different hospital immediately, but she died within several days. He never divulged the actual cause of her death to me or, in fact, to anyone else I know.

Shortly thereafter Mama was diagnosed with terminal cancer. Apparently, it was a preexisting condition but was thought to be in remission, so no one had told me. Maybe Kim knew and that was why she wanted Mama close by, so she could care for her. I believe the shock of losing Kim, who was always there for her during every crisis, was more than Mama could bear. I called Corki (Kazumi) in Chicago to express my concerns about Mama's sudden decline, but Corki was still exhausted from attending to Kim and begged off. I knew Em had been taking care of Mama's insurance and other financial matters as well as caring for her own mother, but would be available if needed.

Mama had met Irene a few weeks earlier. There was no question that Irene had gained Mama's approval, not only as a qualified nurse but as a friend (and possibly a mate for me). On meeting a few of my earlier dates, Mama had invariably frowned and turned away.

One Saturday I was staying with Mama for the day. Irene was to join us after she finished working in the morning at a medical clinic. At about noon the doctor stopped by to check on Mama. He suggested I take her to the hospital. I told him I was expecting a friend, so he went ahead to arrange for Mama's admission at the hospital. When Irene arrived, we knew Mama was in pain, and setting aside all formality, Irene attended to Mama's immediate needs, checked her vital signs, and sponge-bathed her, knowing how important that would be to her peace of mind. We quickly got her into my car and Irene followed in hers. I still recall the relief in Mama's eyes the moment she saw Irene. Once Mama was comfortable in the room the doctor had prearranged for her, she dozed off.

I suggested we leave, but Irene, knowing she was only dozing as a result of the admission procedures and blood work that had been done, insisted that we stay. Sure enough, Mama awoke a little confused as to where she was and surprised to see us still there. She insisted she was fine, thanked us (mostly Irene), and suggested we go home.

Others came to visit during the next few days and by Tuesday evening she had become extremely weak. She was also in pain and begged the nurse for some medication. The nurse gave her an injection for her pain and she was immediately comforted. She wanted us to go home, so we gave her a hug and tucked her in. As we waved good-bye at the door, promising to be back the next day, she snuck one hand out from under the covers and her fingers twinkled child-like to gesture good-bye. At two the next morning I got a call from the hospital that she had just slipped away, peacefully.

A few months later that same year, Ted would die. It was not a happy year. And, indeed, forever is a long, long time.

Thankfully, I had Irene to lean on. Earlier I had assured her I was not interested in any long-term commitment. We would just be friends. Irene had agreed, probably thinking I had a lot of nerve implying otherwise. But now, maybe in my grief or out of gratitude, I was beginning to have second thoughts.

We drove to Reedley, a Central California town previously unknown to me, to meet Irene's parents and some of her family. I immediately felt very comfortable with her mother. She had all the qualities of sincerity and warmth I associated with most Issei mothers, although Irene's mother was a Nisei-Kibei and was closer than Irene to my age. Her father, an Issei, was well-versed in English and was much more formal. When we were somewhat separated from the others, he asked Irene, "What are his intentions?" She replied, "He has asked me to marry him." I was taken aback by the abruptness of the question, but I admired his honesty and courage to say exactly what was on his mind—a trait that very few Japanese had acquired and that was traditionally regarded as a cultural no-no.

My feelings for Irene grew deeper, especially after she had demonstrated her compassionate nature when Mama was dying. Irene's training as a nurse accounted for much of this, of course, but there was a personal caring quality about her to which Mama had intuitively responded, whereas in most cases she seemed wary of the several nurses who had been assigned to care for her. Even within the family, Kim was the only one in whom Mama had complete trust, but Kim was no longer there for her.

I was very aware of my own emotional vulnerability, having just lost the two souls I was closest to during my whole life: Mama, whose judgment I could never seem to satisfy, and Kim, whose support was always there, without judgment. They both knew I was doing the best I could in spite of the addled brain with which Mama had provided me.

I had to be careful not to impose onto Irene these expectations to which I had grown accustomed. Our love for each other must be free to express in its own unique way, and our personal expectations must be secondary to the goals of the partnership. We were both unsure of what those goals would entail and of our readiness to make that commitment. We did agree, however, that we both deserved a vacation from all the emotional stress we had undergone. Irene suggested a trip to Hawai'i. Her brother had taken her and her two children there after her divorce and she recalled it as a paradise of sorts. What the heck, we might even get married there, we joked, if it was still the romantic Eden that Irene remembered. It was, and we did! (A word of warning: if you're not serious about getting married, stay away from Hawai'i.)

After a couple of days there, we were married in a Buddhist temple in Honolulu. Since it was all so impromptu, no one was in attendance except a photographer we had managed to grab, the minister, of course, and his wife, who agreed to stand as a witness. She had on bedroom slippers, which was fine with us, but insisted we wait while she ran back to the house to get her shoes and fix her hair when, at that very moment, she noticed the photographer setting up his camera. As I recall, the brief ceremony (in English) was full of mispronounced words (his), giggles, and suppressed laughter (ours). The minister seemed slightly miffed until he saw me reach for my wallet.

We spent the next few days touring the island and all its attractions. Irene could hardly wait to swim in the shallow, clear, and warm waters of Hanauma Bay, while I settled for ogling the bikini-clad beauties on the beach. Many appeared to be young Japanese tourists. By the time Irene came out of the water, her shoulders were beginning to turn pink and my eyeballs were probably a bit red too. By the time we reached the car, her back looked like a well-done lobster. She had difficulty sitting in the seat, even with several towels. She would blister and peel for the next several days, but insisted it was worth it.

We visited the Dole Pineapple facilities, since I had once worked as a design consultant for their Oceanic Properties subsidiary on a 5,200-acre vacation home development along the Northern California coast. It had been my first "big" project after starting my private practice. I had been recommended by my former instructor (and mentor) at Cal Poly, Richard Moore, who later became the director of the design and planning department for Oceanic. I had meant to call Richard, as he lived on a neighboring island, but I may have forgotten in our rush to cover as much ground as we could.

On returning home, Irene's parents were happy that we had gotten married. I think Mama would have been happy, too. Irene's two brothers invited us up to Fresno for a brief champagne celebration and a toast to wish us well. It was Irene's second marriage and my third so we preferred not to make a big thing of it. This one was ours, and ours alone.

FIGURE 17.1.
Newlyweds Irene and
Yoshito in Honolulu,
1989 (photographer
unknown).

Several years before Irene and I met, a camp-era acquaintance happened to mention to me that Michi, my girlfriend of those long-ago camp days, was working at a well-known shop in the Los Angeles suburbs. I had no desire at that time to see her and risk stirring up old wounds. I deliberately avoided the area to further ensure that we wouldn't meet by accident.

Years later, I was involved in a project that would take me into that general neighborhood—which reminded me of her. I wasn't sure whether she still worked there, but a strange compulsion urged me to at least check it out. Naw, I thought, what would be the point? However, the feeling kept nagging at me relentlessly, so one day I decided to stop and inquire.

It had been over forty-four years since I last saw her. That was the day the FBI agent and the US marshal came to my Heart Mountain barrack to arrest me. I wasn't sure I would even recognize her, or she me.

She seemed quite startled to see me. I noticed that she didn't look well. She was no longer the carefree teenager, of course, but seemed wearier than I had expected. There was an awkward moment in which I almost decided it was all a mistake. Nonetheless, I confessed to her my devastation when I received her last letter, but had realized over time how difficult it must have been for her to write it. Now, I just wanted her to know everything was okay.

I held her briefly, then released her. An unexpected wave of relief came over me. I realized that the pain of her rejection I had harbored all these years had also found release. She sobbed quietly and seemed relieved, as if a long-endured burden had been lifted—for both of us. She smiled hesitantly through her tear-filled eyes and for just an instant I saw the perky little teenager I had left at Heart Mountain forty-four years ago.

A few months later her brief obituary appeared in the local ethnic newspaper. Had she been aware of a terminal condition all along, or was it something sudden and unexpected? I never knew and never inquired. All I knew was why the compulsion to see her and release her had been so insistent. Nature's unfailing sense of justice is indeed far superior to that of man's meager efforts. It is said that justice is blind. Could it be that it is man who is blind, and not justice?

18

REBIRTH

Frank Chin is a prominent, if controversial, Chinese American writer and playwright.[89] He has long recognized literature, including folklore, as the key to the understanding, appreciation, and, thereby, the preservation of all ethnic cultures. He has also recognized the dangers of euphemisms such as *assimilation* as cover-ups for the extinction of one's cultural identity. Thus, he was one of the few who were genuinely alarmed when assimilation was promoted as a survival dynamic for Nikkei during and after WWII.

It was inevitable that he would seek out James Matsumoto Omura,[90] who prior to the outbreak of war had published the magazine *Current Life*, and through it promoted the works of Nikkei writers and otherwise encouraged their literary efforts in a negative, if not hostile, media market. James Omura and Frank Chin had common goals, and the magnetism of that commonality was destined to draw them together.

In the summer of 1982, Chin gathered together Omura, Frank Emi and his brother Art, the few draft resisters he could locate, and several interested and influential community notables at the East/West Theater (located on Santa Monica Boulevard at that time). A few of the East/West Players[91] also joined in. That was when I first met James Omura, although I had heard of him during our trial in Cheyenne. I also met Brooks and Sumi Iwakiri,[92] avid supporters of the Heart Mountain Fair Play Committee and the resisters. It may have been the first time I met Frank Chin, also. I had no idea what he had in mind, but I knew something was up.

https://doi.org/10.5876/9781646421848.c018

It took several years, but his efforts would result in the scripted program "Return of the Fair Play Committee," held at Little Tokyo's Centenary Methodist Church. It would be the first public gathering of the FPC and resisters and others who supported our actions during the war years. Frank Chin, jointly with Frank Abe, would subsequently develop the 2000 documentary film *Conscience and the Constitution*, a recounting of the draft resistance movement at Heart Mountain.[93]

I had long ago given up hope that the monstrous chasm that had been created between the Japanese American community and all who protested the inhumane, unconstitutional treatment we were subjected to by the government—abetted by the insidious mind-control tactics of the Japanese American Citizens League—would ever be bridged. Besides, too many had followed the JACL mantra of proving their loyalty on the battlefield to admit they had been duped. I sensed that we didn't have a "Chinaman's chance," but here was Frank Chin doing exactly what we had failed to do for ourselves.

Thus, the long road back to sanity for Japanese America had begun. In truth, the journey had begun at least a decade earlier. A few progressive-minded Nisei and some Sansei, now mature enough to do their own research and draw their own conclusions, began to delve into the constitutional aspects of the various little-known judicial challenges brought by Issei, and later the Nisei (most of which had been adjudicated negatively due to the racial bigotry of those eras).

I had been unaware of the growing resurgence of interest, due largely to my temporary self-imposed exile. I realized I had much catching up to do.

Like a Phoenix rising out of the ashes of the total devastation of the community leadership of the Issei immigrants, a new ethnic identity began to emerge through the dedicated efforts of the new icons and visionaries of Japanese American history: James Omura, Michi Nishiura Weglyn, Harry Ueno,[94] William Hohri,[95] Clifford Uyeda,[96] Frank Chin, Lawson Inada, Aiko and Jack Herzig,[97] and many, many more. Each worked more or less independent of the others, but with the common vision that challenged the misleading, ersatz image of "Quiet Americans" and "Model Minority" created by the self-proclaimed representatives of our ethnic community, the JACL. It occurred in the wake of the former Issei leadership, the demise of which the JACL itself was largely responsible for by virtue of its self-promoting collaboration with government agencies. The wartime JACL, although politically astute in a pragmatic sense, displayed a serious lack of human compassion and moral integrity in assuming leadership of a people for whom the latter attributes were the very foundation of their sense of community.[2] The JACL goal

---

2. Racial prejudice resulted in the denial of equal access to public as well as private facilities to Japanese immigrants. They were thus compelled to rely on others of their own kind for their

was to attain acceptance by the dominant white populace at any price, which most Japanese Americans regarded as degrading. Nonetheless, many acceded to it with the rationale that under the existing conditions of racial animosity it would be key to our future viability in this country. The JACL appeal would be effective only as long as our acceptance of our second-class citizenship status prevailed. To maintain their leadership role, mind control had become the JACL's primary weapon, and a confused, bewildered community would be their target.

Obedience to authority and the avoidance of bringing shame on the family were two cultural conditionings that the Issei generation valued highly. However, the very act of immigrating to America created a moral dilemma for their Nisei offspring, who as American citizens would be taught to question unreasonable authority and were exposed to a generally broader definition of what constituted family shame.

Tragically, with the outbreak of war between America and Japan most Nisei, caught in the confusion of conflicting moral and political directives, resorted to the ancient cultural mandate of Japan in order to prove their loyalty. This occurred, ironically, with the blessing of the US government, which had itself defaulted on the principles of our Constitution—as did the JACL.

This contradiction seems to have escaped the understanding of much of Japanese America. And those who dared act on their commitment to democratic principles were publicly denounced as a threat to our successful *assimilation* into the dominant white society. But assimilation became suspect as the sacrifice seemed to apply only to those of color. In fact, wasn't the perceived unassimilable nature of the Japanese race a key rationale of West Coast bigots in justifying our *en masse* removal?

Disloyalty was never an issue in the minds of the Nisei. We had nothing to prove. But assimilation had been historically denied us through Jim Crow laws that discouraged normal social interaction with the dominant society. But why indeed would we want to assimilate, if assimilation required us to abandon our highly evolved cultural heritage? Fortunately, saner minds would prevail and the postwar era would herald a renewed interest in ancient Eastern philosophy and

---

financial, medical, social, cultural, and recreational needs. *Nihon Machi* (Japan Town) was created to serve those needs. It is a historic symbol of a proud and resourceful people. In denouncing its rebirth after the war, the JACL lacked the sensitivity to respect this legacy. The focus of the new movement, by contrast, would be the legal and moral supremacy of the US Constitution and a citizen's fundamental duty to defend it. The wartime Nikkei legal test cases instigated by Gordon Hirabayashi, Minoru Yasui, Fred Korematsu, Mitsuye Endo, and the several military draft cases (all legal challenges that the JACL vehemently opposed) would become the inspiration and launch pad for the many civil rights efforts that would gradually transform Japanese American thinking. The erstwhile victims of both the government's unconstitutional acts and the ill-conceived JACL support of them would transcend the defeatist mentality and become righteous protagonists in the name of the US Constitution and the fundamental humanitarian principles on which our country is based.

its traditions—not as a replacement for Western thought, but as an enhancement and extension of Western culture.

Perhaps America would lead the world in an era of cultural diversity commensurate with our technical advancement as it would seem destined to become under the humanitarian principles of our Constitution.

During WWII and immediately after, the Issei generation and all their sacrifices had been virtually ignored by younger Japanese Americans. Yet the merit of their influence, even as they slowly faded into oblivion, is evidenced in the resurgence of "Japan Towns" and other ethnic enclaves along the West Coast, and in the popularity of ancient Japanese arts and literature within the general population, and not just limited to our ethnic community. This, in spite of the earlier JACL admonition that such "indulgences" would be counter to the successful *assimilation* (extinction?) of our people as part of the broader American culture. However, simple mathematics demonstrates that optimization is not achieved through subtraction and division; rather, it lies in addition and multiplication. Beware of those who suggest there is a part of you that must be denied.

Thus, only when Nikkeidom was able to cast aside the debilitating JACL mind control were we able to view ourselves as the righteous citizens we always were and proudly share the rich cultural heritage that our Issei forebears had preserved for us in a country rich in its diverse cultures. When Mama and Papa, along with other immigrants from around the world, came to America for all the richness they anticipated finding here, little did they realize that much of that richness was in the culture that they, themselves, were contributing in the very act of their courageous migration. This then is truly the American dream, and it was already in their hearts the minute they embarked on their long journey.

Justification for Executive Order 9066, resulting in the mass removal of Japanese Americans from the West Coast, was largely based on the false claims of General John DeWitt[98] that there was evidence of espionage in radio communications between Japanese Americans and enemy Japanese ships off the West Coast.[99] This claim made it a military necessity that the War Department remove all those of Japanese ancestry from the West Coast. It was thought that all copies of the original document containing DeWitt's claims, and referred to as the *DeWitt Final Report*, had been destroyed by the time the Hirabayashi, Yasui, and Korematsu civil rights cases came to trial. Only the War Department order for restricted movement and final banishment remained in effect and would prevail. However, the Endo case was adjudicated in the plaintiff's favor in late 1944, citing the illegality of detaining loyal citizens without charges. It would be instrumental in the eventual closing of the camps, but not until FDR achieved his historic fourth term in November of 1944.

In 1982 Aiko Herzig-Yoshinaga, a researcher of extraordinary perception and intuition, discovered the sole remaining original edition of the *DeWitt Final*

FIGURE 18.1. Dedication of the former Catalina Prison Camp near Tucson as the Gordon Hirabayashi Recreation Site, 1999. Gordon at center wearing lei; Yoshito at far right (courtesy, Irene Kuromiya).

Report. She noted that the wording was slightly different from what had been submitted to the Supreme Court. The report contained no hard evidence of espionage to claim "military necessity," and the War Department had known it. The government had no justification for issuing E.O. 9066.

To whatever extent the false testimony affected the civil rights cases of Hirabayashi, Yasui, and Korematsu, the Supreme Court reviewed and made the legally appropriate adjustments.[100] But total justice can never be realized for something that should never have happened in the first place. The pain and suffering endured by Japanese Americans as a result of E.O. 9066 can never be indemnified by mere words or monetary compensation.

The independent search for clarification and justice into the many facets of the government's violation of Japanese American civil rights during WWII converged at one point with the common demand in their united claim for redress. This effort was essentially a political resolution which sought congressional recognition of the unconstitutionality of acts committed and to seek restitution thereof. A congressional committee was appointed to first determine the existence of government malfeasance and, if found, to recommend the terms of compensation, if any.

Meanwhile, a separate group, the National Council for Japanese American Redress (NCJAR),[101] filed a class-action lawsuit in the federal court in Washington, DC. The plaintiff for the case was William M. Hohri, and the purpose was to establish a judicial precedent whereby the unconstitutional and illegal aspects of the government's actions would be clearly recorded in the law books, to forever prohibit its repetition involving other racial groups. It also called for a more realistic monetary restitution than the congressional proposal. On the threshold of resolution, however, the class-action lawsuit was impeded by technical delays while Congress passed its redress bill, the Civil Liberties Act of 1988.[102] It imposed a lesser financial burden on the government while at the same time rendering the Hohri challenge moot.[103]

Thus, the redress movement, in spite of the well-intentioned efforts of its supporters, accepted a politically expedient concession in the end and wasn't able to achieve its goal of preventing future mass removal and detention of citizens and lawful residents based solely on ethnicity. Most of Japanese America celebrated our "victory," unaware that we had been outmaneuvered by our wily government and our power-hungry politicians yet again.

In the wake of the government's public apology, the question arose as to whether it would be appropriate for the JACL to likewise extend an apology to the Japanese American community for its part in aiding and abetting the government. Thus in 1989, as earlier noted, the JACL signed a contract with attorney Deborah Lim to research and submit a report on the political activities of the JACL prior to and during WWII. The JACL formed a Presidential Select Committee to oversee the project and to provide Lim with an outline of the subjects to be covered. They granted her access to their national files, including communications with government agencies, unaware of the damning evidence that would be found there.[3]

Upon receiving the report, which for the most part confirmed the very rumors the report was expected to dispel, the committee quickly composed a substitute report to submit to its membership as an "interpretation" of *The Lim Report*. The original question of squaring matters with the Japanese American community was abandoned, and in its place, after much internal conflict, the national JACL held a program of apology to the draft resisters—a group they had publicly denounced during and after the war. The ceremony was held in San Francisco in 2002 and was officially recorded as a "recognition and reconciliation," although it had been publicized as an "apology."[104]

Informally representing the resisters, Frank Emi and I offered statements acknowledging the "apology" and, coincidentally, we both reminded the JACL representatives of their moral obligation to apologize to *all* Japanese Americans for the shameful actions of their wartime predecessors.

Indeed, if the JACL is sincere in its efforts to admit oversight in its failure to recognize the legitimacy of the protests of the draft resisters, wouldn't it seem entirely reasonable that they apologize for their persecution of the Tule Lake segregants also?[105] And what of those who were imprisoned in the DOJ camps based on the questionable claims of the JACL *inus* (spies)? They were separated from their families, and then were later released on the condition that they join their families in the Crystal City camp for "disloyals" for possible deportation of the

---

3. See Deborah K. Lim, *The Lim Report* (Kearney, NE: Morris Publishing, 1990).

FIGURE 18.2. Yoshito on a speaking tour, with Frank Emi, FPC leader, University of Wyoming, 2002 (courtesy, Irene Kuromiya).

entire family. Did not the JACL ignore their pleas for justice? Neither Frank Emi nor I later received any response, verbally or in any form of action, from any JACL representative. So much for sincerity!

Nor was there any further mention of *The Lim Report*. However, the truth is out in the form of the original 95-page report, as well as a later 154-page extended version. There are indeed a few skeletons remaining in the closets of the wartime JACL and the present-day JACL. Their claim of being the "largest and oldest civil rights organization in Japanese America" lacks the moral courage to officially share the truth with its own membership, let alone with the few remaining survivors of the wartime atrocity, those who paid a greater price for the unconscionable stance of the wartime JACL.

As regrettable as the JACL wartime reactionary position was, a blanket condemnation at this late date will do little to rectify the added injustice imposed on those no longer with us. Perhaps the lesson to be learned is that, no matter how good our intentions may seem, we invariably have our blind spots which, too often, affect the well-being of others and may even lead to fatalities—as in the case of the sacrifices of our Japanese American war heroes who hoped to "prove their loyalty."

A review of the many personal stories now available through oral history interviews reveals that each of us, depending largely on our age group in

FIGURE 18.3. Yoshito speaking at the JACL "apology" ceremony, 2002. *Seated, left to right:* Warren Tsuneishi (Military Intelligence Service Language School), Floyd Mori (JACL National Executive Director), Andy Noguchi (JACL, Florin Chapter) (courtesy, Irene Kuromiya).

approximate segments of five or seven years, have a significantly different reaction to specific occurrences we all witnessed prior to, during, and after our imprisonment years. The youngest group was hardly aware they were even in prison. The more active members of the JACL prior to the war were generally in their late twenties and early thirties. Many were college graduates who had expended time, energy, and money to achieve an admirable academic status, only to be shut out by racism of the specialized professions to which they had aspired. Racism to them was a very real and present danger. It would seem perfectly reasonable to deflect hostility with displays of unquestioning obedience and super-patriotism. But they could hardly do it alone. It was essential that they have the government reinforce their efforts, even at the risk of alienating their own people, especially the Issei and Kibei whom they regarded as political liabilities and were therefore expendable.

This is not to condone the actions of the JACL, but it is important that any judgment be tempered with a reasonable understanding of the conditions that often compel human behavior and all its foibles.

Yet, to be of any value to future generations, we who witnessed the catastrophic barrage of violations of citizens' rights, the very principles upon which our Constitution is based and is the heart and soul of our country, must not remain silent. Never again!

In the course of my involvement in the reclamation of our rightful place in democratic America, I have had the extreme honor to interact with a few of the most extraordinary personalities in this psychological and spiritual recovery period of the Japanese American people. Among them, three in particular stand out not only for their inspirational deeds but as enduring avatars of their people in the transcendence of their humanity into the realm of pure principle: James Matsumoto Omura, Michi Nishiura Weglyn, and Ehren Watada, all of whom, in their own time and in their own way, refused to remain silent.

James Omura, the journalist, was long regarded by the JACL leadership as "Public Enemy Number One." To them, the accusation was no doubt righteous and true, but to the public it was nothing more than the usual JACL propaganda. Omura regarded the JACL official acceptance of the government's arbitrary persecution of Japanese Americans as reprehensible, and publicly accused the JACL of pandering to government agencies to attain for themselves preferential treatment. James Omura steadfastly maintained his solitary stand on moral principles. He was the first and perhaps the only Japanese American not in a camp to vehemently and publicly oppose the abridgement of the civil rights of his people. He openly supported the constitutional premise of the Heart Mountain draft resistance and the FPC, and printed their press releases in his editorial column in Denver's *Rocky Shimpo*, the only widely read Japanese American vernacular publication to do so.

James Omura was indicted along with seven members of the FPC for "conspiring to violate the Selective Service Act and counseling others to do so," even though he had never been incarcerated within a camp, much less at Heart Mountain, and never met a single FPC member or resister. He was exonerated [in effect if not in fact] on all charges by virtue of "Freedom of the Press,"[106] but the cost of his legal defense bankrupted him. He was also removed from his editorship of the *Rocky Shimpo*, no doubt as the result of pressure from the JACL. His journalism career came virtually to an end.[107] He had difficulty maintaining *any* job due to the smear tactics of a JACL-controlled media over a confused and vulnerable Japanese American populace. He finally established an independent landscape construction business catering to clients outside the Japanese American community to avoid the senseless harassment.

During the screening of the documentary film *Conscience and the Constitution*, Omura had been staying customarily with Frank Emi and his wife, Itsuko. On one occasion Frank had to leave on a lecture tour and asked Irene and me to take Omura in for a few days. It caught us a bit off guard, as we were unaccustomed to hosting people, especially those I held in such high esteem. But it would prove to be a blessing. It would provide a rare opportunity to get to know James Omura better.

FIGURE 18.4. Yoshito and Irene with Jimmie Omura, 1994 (courtesy, Irene Kuromiya).

Jimmie, as we got to know him, shared much of his personal insights gleaned from his unique life experience, much of which reflected the pain of disappointments and shattered dreams. Yet he was a survivor and his moral integrity remained intact. He spent most of his time in our guest room writing his memoirs until late into the night. Even so, he would always be up early the next morning awaiting his breakfast at the kitchen table, wondering why we had to sleep so long.

Once, he phoned us on a Saturday morning to pick him up at the airport. We surmised he had a meeting somewhere in Los Angeles. On our drive back we asked where he wanted us to take him. "Home, of course," he replied, as if wondering why we had to ask. We were a bit perplexed but were honored that he regarded us as his home away from home. He was welcome any time, we assured him. But a little warning might have been nice.

On still another occasion, we took him to dinner at a nearby Chinese restaurant. We ordered family style with various dishes. One was a lobster with sauce, the lobster which the waiter had displayed beforehand for Jimmie's approval. On being served, Jimmie ignored the other dishes and dug right into the juicy, pungent lobster. He was enjoying it so much we hesitated to interrupt him. Before we knew it, he had finished off the entire serving bowl. With a loud burp, he remarked, "Boy, that was good!"

"Oh, really?" we responded in unison, "Why don't you try some rice to go with it? And the chicken is quite tasty too." He just shrugged off our sarcasm with another loud burp.

Once, when he was ready to return to his home in Denver, we noticed on the TV set that the weather had turned quite cool there. It had been very warm when he arrived so he had on only a light shirt and no jacket. Irene found one of my favorite sweaters and insisted he take it along, just in case. Several days later we heard he had been in an auto accident, so we called the hospital to see if he was okay. He said he was fine except for a few bruises, but was afraid my sweater was a total loss. Irene immediately went shopping for a new one for him, relieved that he was otherwise okay.

Even before I had met Jimmie, I knew from his writings that he was a man of integrity. But like Papa, Jimmie never spoke of his high moral standards or of always following his conscience. He merely lived by them. That is, no doubt, why I knew he was a man of impeccable integrity. He reminded me of Papa. Further, Papa's nickname was also Jimmie—a concession to whites who had difficulty pronouncing Hisamitsu. It was like having Papa back again, but only briefly, because Jimmie Omura would die in 1994.

Michi Nishiura Weglyn's *Years of Infamy* was originally published in 1976 (it is currently available from the University of Washington Press).[108] An extraordinary account of the Japanese American experience during WWII, it was the first thoroughly researched, historically accurate document to be written by a Japanese American about her own people, an account that was relatively free of the insidious JACL mind-control repression that had overwhelmed most of Japanese American academia. It was extraordinary because Michi was not a professional writer, historian, or a recognized member of academia. She just wrote what was in her heart, based on extensive research. Few, if any, Japanese Americans at that time had the courage or compulsion to do so.

I wouldn't meet Michi until 1993, at the California State Polytechnic University, Pomona, where an endowed chair in multicultural studies was established in the name of Walter and Michi Weglyn. She was not aware of the draft resistance at Heart Mountain or of the FPC when writing her book. Apparently, none of her many advisers thought this subject matter was important enough to be included as a part of Japanese American history. At any rate, when she realized that a few of us resisters lived in the Los Angeles area, she requested the school president, Bob Suzuki, to arrange for our presence at the ceremony. She set aside a private time after the ceremony to meet each of us personally and to learn more about our wartime protest. Appropriately, Jimmie Omura was also there, as were quite a few of our other supporters.

In 1998, for the Day of Remembrance ceremony, Michi was to be honored with the Fighting Spirit Award by the NCR/R (National Coalition for Redress/Reparations)[109] of Los Angeles. The program would be jointly sponsored with the Resisters of Conscience. I had planned a photo exhibit of Michi's life, having received several photos, drawings, and documents from her for that purpose. I inquired at the JACCC (Japanese American Cultural and Community Center) about exhibit space and aid in putting the exhibit together, but the cost far exceeded our meager budget. I tried the JANM (Japanese American National Museum) and again got nowhere. Apparently, "community service facility" wasn't what I had presumed. Everyone was on the payroll and even the space, props, and furnishings had rental tags on them, some by the hour. I asked for volunteers from both the NCR/R and the resisters, but got no response. Finally, on a friend's suggestion I called a perfect stranger, a Mas Yamashita, who happened to be an art director for a private firm and an ardent fan of Michi's, no doubt based on her art work for the Perry Como Show. Further, he had access to the equipment we would need and was eager to help as long as we covered his out-of-pocket expenses. Because of the lack of space (or funds for the space), limited resources, and now limited time, we reduced the exhibit to a mere three portable panels to be displayed in the lobby of the theater where the ceremony would take place. I had to apologize to Michi, but Michi, being the gracious lady that she was, assured me she was extremely honored and appreciated our efforts.

Later that evening the NCR/R and resisters held a private dinner reception for Michi. Irene and I were seated at a table away from the entrance door. Suddenly, I felt Michi's presence. I looked for her, but she hadn't even entered the room yet. Her distinctive, pervasive aura had preceded her, and once she entered the room, I felt the glow of her presence energize its entirety. I don't know if I was the only one to be affected in this way, but no one spoke of it, at least not to me, so I just shrugged it off as my imagination. But the strange feeling never left me.

It wasn't long after that that she would suffer some very serious health complications. She had been quite frail since childhood. Walter had constantly feared for her health, but it was he who would go first, by a few years.

Michi and I exchanged letters and talked via the phone on several occasions during her final months. Her weakened condition allowed for only a brief sharing of thoughts, but we agreed that our spiritual nature was our true identity and that our physical manifestation was the means through which we relate to a dimensional world that is essentially an illusion. Illusions end once they serve their purpose in the dimensional realm, and the spirit moves on to further enhance universal consciousness. I'm not sure I understood everything we babbled about, but it seemed to comfort her, and I felt much closer to her. All the while, I knew it might be the last time I would hear her voice.

The image of Michi in her incarnate form will be forever preserved in all her elegance in her star performance as an outraged, righteous citizen in Frank Abe's

Conscience and the Constitution. But those who were fortunate enough to know her personally will cherish her memory in their hearts as a gracious spiritual entity that transcended the mundane limits of the human condition, and yet who remained connected to it beyond her last breath.

In November 2006 First Lieutenant Ehren Watada refused to deploy his troops into battle in Iraq. His refusal was based on his research of our political involvement with that country which had led to the armed conflict. He found no legal or moral justification for the US attack on that nation. Iraq was not the enemy. It was not responsible for the terrorism that brought down the Twin Towers in the World Trade Center. It did not conceal or possess weapons of mass destruction, as claimed by the war-mongers in Washington, DC, and the Pentagon. So Watada could not in good conscience deploy his troops into a civilian population already devastated by the ill-advised reactionary aggression of our government. Conscience sometimes comes at a high price, as many of us had discovered sixty-two years earlier while protesting conscription into military service after being deprived of our civil liberties in a concentration camp.

Ehren Watada would face not only a court-martial and prison time, but also censure from his own people who feared his actions would reflect negatively on their hard-won image of unquestioning patriotism—an image they had bartered for with their blood on the battlefields of Europe.

I never had the honor of meeting Lieutenant Watada face to face, but through his writings and in the clarity of his impromptu statements made during a brief telephone conference with Frank Emi and me, I detected an extremely well-organized, sincere, and deeply committed intelligence from whence his words emerged. It was clear to me that Lieutenant Watada was endowed with a wisdom beyond his youth, with the courage and perseverance to follow his commitment wherever it would lead him. It was obvious he didn't need advice from two doddering old men who somehow failed to pursue to a reasonable conclusion their own legal challenge to government misfeasance during WWII, and thereby failed to establish a clear, legal precedence for citizen's rights.

Nevertheless, he graciously thanked us for our support and made it quite clear that he regarded the issue as a private matter at that point and was confident that all would work out as it should. He was not seeking public acclaim for his actions. It was truly a matter of personal integrity as dictated by an uncompromising conscience. We assured him that we understood.

I had hardly realized how exhausted I had become, speaking in circles about the illusions Japanese America had created to escape the ugliness of what we feared had entrapped us. It was *truth* that we ran from and there was no threat, only freedom, freedom from fear itself. But we chose the myths as if they would assure the world of our credibility. Then came Watada and his bold attempt to rid his people of the many illusions, some of which he himself had accepted at one time but no longer held himself hostage to any more. He was inspired to delve deeply, not only with his mind, but also into his heart and soul because that is where his conscience resided. That is when the phoenix emerged from the over half-century of debris of wrong-thinking in our community.

After a full century in this country, has Japanese America finally discovered its real history? It was always there, of course, but are we prepared to embrace the newfound reality of it and the eternal promise it holds? Ehren Watada may not lead us to it, but he has already shown us the way.

19

RESOLUTION

The validity of the incarceration camp draft resistance as a civil rights issue was officially recognized by a few civil rights organizations in the early 1990s.

- The Japanese American Bar Association, in March 1993, awarded the members of the Heart Mountain Fair Play Committee a certificate of recognition for our civil rights stance during WWII. Robin Toma, Esq., hosted the event. The ceremony was attended mainly by the immediate families of the resisters because the Japanese American community had not yet perceived our wholesale victimization as essentially a civil rights issue in spite of the highly publicized civil rights confrontations of the 1960s and 1970s.

- In February 1995, the Pacific Southwest District of the JACL held a ceremony acknowledging the resisters' stand during WWII with an apology for the wartime JACL's opposition to it. It was primarily promoted by Sansei civil rights advocates Trisha Murakawa and Ruth Mizobe. They did not have the full support of their chapter, but they did command a majority. They may have lost a few members due to the then "controversial" nature of the proposal.

- In June 1995, the Southern California Chapter of the American Civil Liberties Union held a garden party for all Japanese American resisters from all the camps in recognition of our defense of civil rights. Ramona Ripson and Trisha Murakawa hosted the event.

It became increasingly apparent that, in spite of the endorsement of noted civil rights organizations, we were not reaching our community peers. I believe it was Frank Emi who suggested we focus more on the younger generations and develop a program suited to their quest for historical knowledge rather than to argue with those who had already committed themselves to the notion that demonstrating our loyalty was the key to social acceptance. Are we still fighting the war? The veterans seem to think so.

Of course, as earlier noted in chapter 18, Frank Chin had already embarked on this course of educating the youthful public by providing the few resisters who were willing to talk the opportunity to do so.

In April 1994, William Hohri (of NCJAR fame) and Yuriko Hohri moved from Chicago to Los Angeles, where William had grown up prior to the war. William was aware of the contents of *The Lim Report* as key to the healing of Japanese America by virtue of the well-researched facts therein. A prolific writer, William expressed his thoughts through his newsletter, *The Epistolarian*. He had quite a substantial following among the intellectual elite of Japanese America. He regarded *The Lim Report* as substantiating the claims of the resistance movement, both morally and perhaps legally. Based on this premise, William composed and conducted a reading recounting the wartime resistance by recruiting a few of us former resisters and other volunteers from the community. It was titled *A Question of Who We Are*. Our initial performance was on February 22, 1995, at California State University, Fullerton, hosted by Dr. Arthur Hansen, and then followed during the ensuing two months by other Southern California performances at the Centenary United Methodist Church in Los Angeles' Little Tokyo, Loyola Marymount University in Westchester, and Occidental College in Eagle Rock. I noticed that the younger people in the mixed audiences seemed genuinely inspired and openly asked questions, while the older ones, my peer group, appeared skeptical and remained silent.

William also wrote a thought-provoking column for the *Rafu Shimpo* titled "Ramblers Nemesis," in which he often referred to the resistance movement.

Moreover, he wrote two books addressing the draft resistance as a civil rights issue: *Resistance*[110] and *The Lim Report*. The former contains the personal accounts of four Heart Mountain Fair Play Committee members with comments by William Hohri on how their actions coincide, in principle, with the findings in *The Lim Report*. The latter, although attributed to Deborah K. Lim, seems to have been written by William Hohri (for legal or technical reasons no doubt, or just as a matter of professional protocol) as an explanation of the report in layman terms for public consumption. Both books are essential contributions in the understanding of the Japanese American wartime experience. Unfortunately, *Resistance* is no longer in print. I am uncertain about the availability of *The Lim Report*.

In 2001 the Heart Mountain Wyoming Foundation sponsored a conference and teacher-training conference at the Little America Hotel in Cheyenne, Wyoming.

The event, held June 21–24, which was open to the public, was titled "Protest and Resistance: An American Tradition," and it focused on the Heart Mountain draft resisters of conscience and the constitutional basis for our actions. The panel consisted of a few resisters and several prominent historians and educators such as Dr. Arthur Hansen, professor of history and Asian American studies at California State University, Fullerton, and Eric Muller, professor of law at the University of North Carolina.

Lawson Inada, a professor of English at Southern Oregon University, and the then Poet Laureate for the State of Oregon, emceed the entire event. Lawson had earlier published a book of poetry titled *Drawing the Line*, which featured a poem of the same title that was dedicated to me.[111] Yes, to me! I was overwhelmed and a bit embarrassed as I had never before been so honored.

"Divided Community" is a ninety-minute reading scripted by noted playwright Frank Chin. It is based on his 2002 book, *Born in the USA*.[112] He apparently felt it would be best if it was produced and performed by Japanese Americans as it is about the experience of Americans of Japanese ancestry in this country. He selected Momo Yashima,[113] a seasoned actress, to fulfill the dual role of narrator and production manager. She is the sister of late actor Mako[114] and daughter of the noted artist Taro Yashima.[115] Heart Mountain resisters Frank Emi, Mits Koshiyama,[116] and I played ourselves, while Paul Tsuneishi,[117] a Military Intelligence Service (MIS) veteran, played himself and filled in as co-narrator. As for Ralph Brannen, he played the parts of various government agents and JACL leader Mike Masaoka.[118]

Not only was Paul Tsuneishi an MIS member, but also a former governor of the JACL's San Fernando chapter. Unaware of the draft resistance movement at the Heart Mountain camp in which he was an inmate, it was only after the war that Paul learned of the civil rights premise of the protest which his father had supported. Paul joined us in our effort to clarify to our racial-ethnic community the validity of the resistance movement the JACL had so maligned.

We held about ten performances at various colleges and universities and at our local Japanese American National Museum (JANM) in Los Angeles. Momo arranged to have the program recorded on a disc in order to reach a broader public and, most especially, for educational purposes, which was fortunate as Mits would die within the year, and Frank, a couple of years later. Paul soon became incapacitated so it left Momo and me to field the flurry of questions that would invariably arise at subsequent showings. Whatever became of Kiyoshi Okamoto, the founder of the Fair Play Committee? Nobody knew, and few seemed to care—except for his grandniece Marie Masumoto. After her retirement as a research assistant at JANM, she painstakingly researched his whereabouts, ultimately discovering his burial plot in the Los Angeles County Paupers Cemetery adjacent to Evergreen Cemetery in the Boyle Heights district of the City of Los Angeles. It was marked by a simple four-by-six-inch concrete block with no name or date—just a reference number to identify it in the county log book. He had died on December 28, 1974, at eighty-five years of age.

So this was the demise of the infamous, bombastic, soapbox orator of East First Street of prewar Lil' Tokyo, who later became the notorious instigator of constitutional debate at the Heart Mountain camp and would-be savior of its youths. Here lay his ashes not far from the heavily traveled First Street and neighboring the often-visited Evergreen Cemetery by *Niseidom*. Whatever became of him, indeed!

Marie was granted special permission to replace the cement block with a polished granite plaque engraved with Kiyoshi Okamoto's name and dates of his birth and death, more in keeping with the extraordinary man he was. A few of his relatives, a few resisters, Dr. Arthur Hansen, and Frank Chin attended a brief but long-overdue ceremony in honor of Kiyoshi Okamoto, a true champion of civil rights. Sadly, he had been ignored and abandoned by the many who owed him so much.[119]

In 2014, I was invited to speak to a small group of college-age members of the Kansha program, sponsored by the JACL's Chicago chapter. It was held in conjunction with their annual educational tour of Lil' Tokyo and its community facilities, culminating with the annual pilgrimage to the site of the former Manzanar concentration camp in eastern California's Owens Valley. Our informal discussion centered on the wartime draft resistance, an aspect of Japanese American history that was relatively new to them. They were aware of the persecution imposed on their earlier West Coast counterparts, but knew little about our response to it, other than the highly publicized feats of our fighting men. Thus, the issue at hand was not so much of why we resisted, but why others did not.

I was initially introduced to the Kansha program by its director, Bill Yoshino, in 2012, and then reinvited in 2013 and in 2014, each time with a new group of members. I found the sessions quite encouraging and they compelled me to reassess my long-held distrust of the JACL for the duplicity of their wartime predecessors. These youths were of an entirely different breed.

The National Consortium on Racial and Ethnic Fairness in the Courts held their twenty-sixth annual meeting in Cody and Heart Mountain, Wyoming, in June 2014. The consortium is a group of judges, attorneys, law professors, and other professionals involved in our country's judicial system. They are of various ethnicities and both genders and represent all facets of our judicial system. They presumably selected Heart Mountain because that is where the largest organized draft resistance case in US history occurred and also for the racist aspect of the trials themselves. The Heart Mountain Wyoming Foundation co-sponsored and co-hosted the event since the consortium members were from different parts of the country, whereas many of the foundation members resided nearby.

One of the featured events was titled "Heart Mountain: Conscience, Loyalty and the Constitution," a reenactment of the two 1944 trials, the trial of the sixty-three and the trial of the Fair Play Committee leaders. Both reenactments were based on the original court transcripts. The members of the consortium and members of the foundation played the various roles as assigned by the author, the Honorable Dennis Chin (and coauthor Kathy Hirata-Chin). I happened to be the only authentic player—playing myself.

It was about seventy years to the day since the real mass trial, so to me the cycle was complete. As the performance concluded, I felt an overwhelming sense of closure. I was saddened, however, that none of my fellow resisters were there—nor was my father and mother or my sister Kim. However, some family members were at my side. Thus, it symbolized a legacy of sorts being passed on to future generations. Hopefully, this story serves the same purpose for all who have suffered injustice due to ignorance and intolerance. To them, this story perhaps represents a new beginning rather than an end.

There is indeed hope in the future of Japanese Americans, especially with the growing influx of the Hapa generation (offspring of ethnically mixed parentage) as a symbol of the integration and enhancement of all cultures as evidence of a true democracy. Even the term "Japanese American" will become meaningless as it gradually transcends into simply "American" with no inference of superiority or inferiority. Welcome to the REAL America!

EPILOGUE

TRIUMPH OVER DECEPTION

Deception in its many forms is generally regarded as a morally questionable act with intent to trick or mislead in order to gain unfair advantage in a given situation. It is regarded in most if not all civilized societies as a less than honorable means by which to defraud others to one's own advantage, whether it be a business transaction or nations involved in deadly combat over territorial mandates or issues of political ideology. In any case, however, it may be regarded as morally acceptable fair game as long as the conflict of interest is a mutually recognized condition so that various forms of deception are therefore to be expected. Under those conditions, such action would not necessarily be regarded as dishonorable.

It is when the deception occurs without reasonable provocation between those with common and shared goals that any form of deception becomes questionable in view of the state of trust that prevailed prior to the act of deception. Therefore, the deception constitutes a violation of an established trust rather than merely a matter of tactical expedience. It is the element of trust existing between two parties that is the crucial factor that determines the moral integrity of any act of deception. Quantitatively, the number of people affected by the violation of trust should also become a determinant in the seriousness of the violation. Thus, when we speak of deception it is the violation of the presumed trust that we find most disturbing, and not necessarily the act of deception in and of itself.

When Hisamitsu discovered the mishandling of corporate funds in the soda water partnership, it was the trust between old friends that was betrayed. A redistribution of funds could easily have been negotiated to everyone's satisfaction and

 https://doi.org/10.5876/9781646421848.c020

FIGURE 20.1. Return to Heart Mountain, 1995 (courtesy, Irene Kuromiya).

the matter forgotten—or would it be? To Hisamitsu, it was not simply a matter of the money. It was the violation of an unspoken, but very real trust, and it involved the honor of all five partners. But rather than join the pretense of forgiveness while knowing the distrust still remained unresolved (which would be yet another act of deception), he chose, as a matter of honor, to remove himself from the partnership and forego his dreams of becoming a successful businessman.

When President Roosevelt (as alleged by historical researcher Robert B. Stinnett in his 1999 Free Press book *Day of Deceit: The Truth about FDR and Pearl Harbor*), conspired to provoke an enemy attack to justify US entry into WWII, knowingly sacrificing many American lives in the process, he betrayed the trust of all Americans. The well-documented details of the conspiracy are not yet widely known, but have been publicly available for some time, and, one hopes, will become common knowledge in the very near future.[120] Impeachment would have seemed appropriate, except that the state of war that FDR had covertly provoked would probably have protected him from such retribution. Instead, he was rewarded with a historic fourth term as president of the United States. Such is the irony of our wartime history.

When FDR signed E.O. 9066, which led to the removal of all those of Japanese ethnicity from the West Coast under the guise of military necessity, for conditions he himself had provoked, was he not compounding the initial deception that created the supposed threat in the first place?

When the War Relocation Authority implemented the confinement of American citizens without due process, it violated the trust of all Americans and the provisions of the US Constitution and Bill of Rights. Dillon Myer and the War Relocation Authority that he directed should have been held accountable for aiding and abetting the false imprisonment and detention of 120,000 ethnic Japanese. Did following government orders, despite one's conscience (if they did indeed have one), constitute a reasonable defense?

When certain members of the wartime JACL acted as government agents and cast suspicion on others of Japanese ethnicity to gain for themselves favorable government sanctions at the expense of their own people, they violated the trust of the very people they claimed to represent. The various members who caused the arrests and imprisonment of community leaders should have been held accountable for casting suspicion without tangible evidence that any crime had even been committed, and been forced to pay restitution for libel and defamation of character. The JACL owes an apology to the prisoners of the various Department of Justice camps, the Crystal City family camp, and the Tule Lake Segregation Center, for character assassination, libel, and accusations of disloyalty. The JACL owes *all* of Japanese America an apology for falsely claiming to represent the interests of Japanese Americans while conspiring with our government to surrender our civil and human rights.

When the JACL endorsed the mandatory induction of citizens from the camps into racially segregated military units on the pretext of "proving their loyalty," they in effect preempted every citizen's right of free choice to serve or not to serve according to his conscience while under specific conditions of duress unique to his situation in the unspoken trust between each citizen and his government. The JACL, through its threats of social ostracism, did indeed abrogate that trust.

The JACL should apologize for aiding and abetting the constitutionally questionable mandatory drafting for military service of those imprisoned in concentration camps while their constitutional rights were suspended. The JACL should further be held morally accountable for those soldiers drafted from the camps who became casualties of WWII. But neither that nor any of the above will likely ever happen.

The Japanese American community has long indulged in the self-deception that all acts consistent with government dictates automatically attest to one's loyalty, that obedience to authority in and of itself was proof of one's loyalty. Contrarily, disobedience to such dictates or even the questioning of their wisdom was regarded as proof of one's disloyalty. Not so! The basic tenants of our democracy in its many expressions reveal that many in the Japanese American community, including its leadership, were pathetically ignorant of the basic principles of our democracy.

———————————————

The effectiveness of deception ultimately depends on our willingness to accept it as truth. We are victims only to the extent we allow the deception to prevail and, thereby, inadvertently become a part of the deception.

Due to the efforts of a handful of Nisei of conscience, along with several astute Sansei and Yonsei [fourth-generation Japanese Americans] scholars who were skeptical of the apparent inconsistencies in the wartime legacy to which they became heirs, and professional writers, historians, educators, and scholars of various ethnicities, likewise questioning the inconsistencies and omissions in the then available accounts of Japanese American wartime history, a widespread search to find the missing pieces ensued. It became apparent that government agencies as well as the JACL found it desirable to delete or sanitize certain aspects of our and our country's wartime history. Thus, it seems the cover-up is yet a further deception, compounding the insult of the original deception.

For those of us who lived through the harrowing experience of the injustice, inhumanity, and humiliation imposed upon us, the resultant righteous disbelief, anger, and outrage will not be easily forgotten. But we know now it was all part of the betrayal of trust into which we so naïvely bought.

Beyond the betrayal was an extraordinary era of heroic faith in humankind and our confidence in the ultimate triumph of the principles of human dignity inherent in the US Constitution and the Bill of Rights. Ehren Watada exemplifies the living, breathing embodiment of this hope and symbolizes what I refer to as the *Real* America for future generations.

I hope that after almost 100 years since Hisamitsu and Hana embarked on their honeymoon voyage to a new land of promise, the promise is about to be fulfilled, not for them perhaps, but for their grandchildren, great-grandchildren, and for generations to come.

Truth was and always had been their constant companion. Honesty is the essence of honor, and the painfully honest nature of Hisamitsu Kuromiya marked him as an honorable man. Although he had struggled with hard times through much of his life, as did many of his fellow immigrants who held dreams of a new life in a new world, never did he submit to poverty or to despair. Even in the face of *shikataganai*, his faith was in *Truth* as the only reality. But knowing that the Truth was not always evident, he remained confident that the reality was not necessarily the appearances that masquerade as the reality in times of stress. *Gambare* was his byword and would ultimately lead to the liberation of Truth. It was a triumph of patience and perseverance. Thus, to Hisamitsu and those of his generation it was a silent victory. Its realization occurred after many of them were gone; but it was a victory nonetheless, and true valor is, of course, its own reward.

The truth is that which is so.
That which is not the truth is not so. Therefore, Truth is all there is.
The Prosperos

Beyond the betrayal lies the true America.

AFTERWORD

"DRAWING THE LINE"

LAWSON FUSAO INADA

For Yosh Kuromiya

I.
Yosh is drawing the line.
It's a good line, on paper,
and a good morning
for just such an endeavor—

and the line seems to find
its own way, flowing
across the white expanse

like a dark, new river . . .

II.
Yes, Yosh is drawing the line.
And you might say he's simply
following his own nature—

he's always had a good eye,
a fine sense of perspective,
and a sure hand, a gift

 https://doi.org/10.5876/9781646421848.c021

for making things ring true,
and come clearer into view.

III.
So the line makes its way,
on paper, charting a clear
course like a signature,

starting from the left
and toward the bottom end,
logically and gradually
and gracefully ascending

to the center, where it takes
a sharp turn upward, straight
toward the top before it
finds itself leveling off
to the right again, descending

slightly for a while before
dropping straight down, coming
to a rest near the bottom,

bending, descending gradually
and gracefully as it began, but

at the other side of the space . . .

IV.
No sooner said than done.
Yosh relaxes for the moment,
blinks his eyes, realizing

his intensity of focus, almost
like prayer, a sunrise meditation.

V.
Ah, another beautiful morning!
Time to move on, see what the day
provides by way of promise . . .

And as for the drawing, well,
the line is drawn, on paper—

other dimensions can come later . . .

VI.

Yosh, although a young man,
a teenager, is naturally
calm and confident by nature.

Thus, when he draws a line,
it tends to stay drawn.
He may make adjustments
but doesn't make mistakes.

That's just the way he is—
trusting his own judgment
as a person, as an artist.

As a result, he is a most
trusted friend, judging
from the many friends who
count on him, rely on him,
respect what he has to say . . .

That's just the way he is—
good-hearted, as they say:
"If you need a favor, ask
Yosh; he'll go out of his way . . ."

VII.

Still, though, you've got to draw the line
somewhere—and as the saying goes,

so goes Yosh. And his friends know
certain things not to ask of him.

What "everybody does" just may not go
with Yosh, the set of beliefs, the sense
of integrity, values, he got from his folks.

VIII.

As for this drawing in his sketchbook,
you might well ask: "What is it?"

At this stage, it's just a line—
a line that goes sideways, up, over,
down, descending to the other margin.

Is it just a line? An abstract design?
Or might it stand for something?

At first glance, it looks to be a line
charting the progress of something
that goes along slowly, rising
a bit to indicate, oh, maybe a normal
growth rate or business-as-usual,

when all of a sudden it jumps, reflecting
a decisive turn of events which lasts
a while before resuming

what might be assumed to be a more
regular course of activity concluding

at what may represent the present
on the journey from the then to the now . . .

That's what graphs show, the flow
of activity, the rise and fall of events
often out of our hands, so it can become
gratifying to simply resume the bottom
line of normalcy again, starting over
at square one, back to the drawing board . . .

That is, it could have been worse.
The line could have been broken, snapped,
or bottomed out into nothing, going
nowhere fast like the slow and steady
line monitoring a silent patient . . .

Or, the line could have turned back
into itself into a dead-end maze,
a meaningless mass of angles and tangles . . .

Ah, but if you asked an observant child,
the answer might be: "Well, it just looks
like the bottom of my baby sister's mouth—
'cause when she smiles, she only has one tooth!"

And if you asked Yosh, he'd simply say,
in his modest way: "Oh, that's just Heart Mountain."

IX.
Maybe you had to be there.
For if you were, you would not only
not have to ask, but you would
appreciate the profile, the likeness

of what looms large in your life
and mind, as large as life staring
you in the face day by day by day

and so on into night, where it is so
implanted in your sight and mind
that the ancient promontory assumes
a prominence in your mildest dreams,
and even when the dust billows, or clouds
cover it, blowing snow and sleet and rain,

you can't avoid it, you can count on it,
Heart Mountain. Heart Mountain
is still there. And you're here.

X.
Ah, but it is, after all,
just a mountain—one of many,
actually, in this region,
in this range, and if anything
distinguishes it, it's just
its individual shape and name.

And the fact that it stands
rising up out of the plains
so close you can touch it,
you can almost but not quite

get there on a Sunday picnic,
your voices echoing in the evergreen forest on its slopes . . .

As it stands, it is a remote
monument to, a testament to
something that stands to be
respected from a distance,

accessible only in dreams,
those airy, carefree moments
before the truth comes crashing
home to your home in the camp . . .

XI.
Yosh can take you there, though,
by drawing the line, on paper.

And Yosh, with his own given name,
is somewhat like the mountain—

an individual, certainly, but also
rather common to this region.
He's just so-and-so's kid,
or just another regular teenager
engaged in whatever it takes these days . . .

But this morning, it was different.
He was out there at the crack of dawn,
pacing around over by the fence,
blowing into his hands, rubbing
his hands, slapping, clapping
his hands together as if in preparation

to undertake something special
instead of doing the nothing he did—

that is, he just got to his knees
and knelt there, facing the mountain.

Knelt there. Knelt there. Is he praying?
But now he's writing. But writing what?

Then, as sunlight struck the mountain,
and the ordinary idle elder
and the regular bored child
approached Yosh, they could tell
from the size of the wide sketchpad
that he was drawing—but drawing
what? Well, that's obvious—but what for?

XII.
Seeing the drawing was its own reward.
Boy, look at that! He's got it right!
You've got to admire him for that.

And, boy, if you really look at it—
in this sunrise light, under this
wide, blue sky—why, it really is
a beautiful sight, that majestic
hunk of rock they call Heart Mountain.

And to top it off, this talented guy
sure accentuates the positive, because
he *didn't* include the posts and wire.

XIII.
Yosh, smiling, greeting, is striding
toward the barracks. There's a line
at the mess hall, a line at the toilets.

Better check in with the folks. Mom's
all right, but Dad's never adjusted.
I may or may not show him the drawing.

It depends. He likes me to stay active,
but this might be the wrong subject.
It might rub him wrong, get him
in a mountain-mood of reminiscing
about California, the mountains of home.

And, heck, those were just hills
by comparison, but they've taken on
size in his eyes; still, when I fill in
the shading, the forest, tonight, maybe
he can appreciate it for just what it is:

Heart Mountain, in Wyoming, a drawing
by his dutiful son here with the family
doing its duties—kitchen duty, latrine duty . . .

I'll do my duties; and I've got my own duty, my
right, to do what I can, to see this through . . .

XIV.
The sketchbook drops to the cot.
Brrr, better go get some coal.
It's the least I can do—not worth
much else, me, without a real line
of work. But this art might get me
someplace—maybe even a career
in here. Doing portraits of inmates.

But out there is *in here* too, related—
it's a matter of perspective, like lines
of lineage and history, like the line
between me and the fencepost, between

me and the flagpole, between stars,
stripes, the searchlight, and the guy
on duty in the guardtower, maybe
like me, from California, looking
up at the airplane making a line
of sound in the sky, searching
for the right place in a time of peace . . .

Yes, if I had a big enough piece
of paper, I'd draw the line
tracing the way we came, smooth
as tracks clear back to California,

and in the other direction, the line
clean out to the city of Philadelphia
and the Liberty Bell ringing testimony
over Independence Hall and the framing
of the Constitution. Yes, it's there,
and I can see it, in the right frame of mind . . .

XV.
No, you have no right
to imprison my parents.

No, you have no right
to deny us our liberty.

Yes, I have my right
to stand for our justice.

Yes, I have my right
to stand for our freedom.

XVI.
And this is where Yosh
drew the line—

on paper, on the pages
of the Constitution.

XVII.
The rest is history.
Arrested, judged,
sentenced, imprisoned

for two years
for refusing
induction under

such conditions:
"as long as my
family is in here . . ."

Eventually arrives
a few sentences
of presidential

pardon, period.
But history
doesn't rest,

as Yosh gives
testimony,
drawing the line,
on paper, again.

XVIII.
This time, though, he's a free man
with a free mind and a very clear
conscience, having come full circle
to this clear spring at Heart Mountain.

And Heart Mountain, of course,
is still here, timeless and ever-
changing in the seasons, the light,
standing, withstanding the test of time.

And this time Yosh is free to roam
his home range like an antelope,
circling the mountain, seeing all sides
with new visions, wide perspectives:

from here, it comes to a narrow peak;
from here, it presents the profile
of a cherished parent, strong, serene;
from here, yes, it could be a tooth;
and from anywhere, forever, a heart.

Yes, that's about the truth of it—
once a heart, always a heart—

a monumental testament under the sky.

This time, though, Yosh is strolling
over a freshly plowed and fenceless field
with that very same sketchbook, searching
through the decades to find that rightful
place in relation to the mountain, wanting
to show his wife where the drawing happened,

where that quiet young man sank to his knees
in reverence for the mountain, in silent
celebration for that vision of beauty
that evoked such wonder, such a sunrise
of inspiration, wisdom, and compassion

that the line drew itself, making its way
with conviction in the direction it knew
to be right across the space, on paper,

and yes, yes, the heart, the eye, the mind
testify this is right, here, Yosh, hold
up the drawing, behold the mountain, trust
the judgment upholding truth through time
as the man, the mountain, the profile make
a perfect fit in this right place and time

for Yosh to kneel again, feel again, raise
his radiant eyes in peace to face the radiant
mountain, Heart Mountain, Heart Mountain—

and begin, again, with confidence, to draw the line!

APPENDIX A

"CIVIL RIGHTS"

Editorial in *Wyoming Eagle*, June 13, 1944

THIS NEWSPAPER never has commented, editorially, on the merits of any legal action during the time that it was being heard or before it was adjudicated by any court. That is and will continue to be the policy of The Wyoming Eagle.

Nevertheless, we feel free to call attention to the case involving 63 Japanese-Americans now on trial before Judge T. Blake Kennedy in the federal court for the district of Wyoming.

This is a case which is of national importance and which probably will attract more attention in Washington and other metropolitan areas than it will in Cheyenne or anywhere else in the state outside of Heart Mountain and Park County.

The 63 Japanese-Americans (citizens of the U.S.A.) are charged with violation of the Selective Service Act, said violation alleged to consist of failure to submit to a pre-induction physical examination. Conviction on such a charge could make them liable to very severe penalties in the forms of fines and imprisonment. So, it is reasonable to assume that they or their advisers thought they had a legal argument to sustain their action.

At issue in the case is the civil liberties of citizens as guaranteed by the federal constitution and the degree to which these civil liberties may temporarily be abrogated by a government at war which under the constitution and by act of Congress is presumed to have been granted emergency war-time powers.

https://doi.org/10.5876/9781646421848.c022

Probably no federal court has been called upon to hear a more "vital" case or one in which the issues are more momentous than the case now being heard by Judge Kennedy. Able counsels are representing both the government and the 63 defendants. Despite the importance of the case, however, it will not excite the interest of the average man or attract the number of spectators as would a murder trial or a spicy divorce case. But the legal fraternity throughout the nation and statesmen will have their ears attuned to the proceedings in federal court in Cheyenne this week. Until the court has weighed the evidence and arguments and has handed down his decision, editorial comment is strictly out of order.

APPENDIX B

"NISEI SERVICEMEN'S RECORD REMEMBERED"

BILL HOSOKAWA

Newspaper column in *Pacific Citizen*, June 13, 1988

There have been efforts of late to glorify the very few who, for whatever reason, sought to disrupt the orderly recruitment of Nisei troops in World War II. Not many listened to them then, and not many do so today. Yet, it is a tribute to the tolerance of our nation that acts of conscience are respected. Let's let it go at that. On this day [Memorial Day], the glory, the love, the appreciation was reserved for those who had faith, and were willing to make any sacrifice to demonstrate it.

https://doi.org/10.5876/9781646421848.c023

APPENDIX C

"THE FOURTH OPTION"

YOSHITO KUROMIYA

Essay in *A Matter of Conscience: Essays on the World War II Heart Mountain Draft Resistance Movement*, edited by Mike Mackey (Powell, WY: Western History Publications, 2002)

After war with Japan was declared, we of Japanese descent were notified by the government that U.S. citizens and noncitizens alike were restricted to an 8:00 PM to 6:00 AM curfew. We were also prohibited from traveling more than five miles from our homes. This did not apply to those of German or Italian descent, even though we were also at war with those countries. Nonetheless, we complied.

In the spring of 1942, we were to be sent to an "assembly center" at the Pomona Fair Grounds. There was much confusion as to the reason for this. Were we suspected as potential saboteurs? Or were we to be detained for our own protection? We were, however, assured that this was merely a precautionary wartime measure, and all citizens' rights and interests would be reinstated in due time. Meanwhile, it was our patriotic duty to abide by these temporary measures in the interest of national security. So said our self-appointed "leaders," the Japanese American Citizens League. So again, we complied.

Later that same year, we were to be transported further inland. This new location was in Wyoming, a place called Heart Mountain. We had had no hearings, and there had been no accusations nor proof of any wrong-doing. The same questions again arose. But, during our brief stay in Pomona, many began suggesting that in

https://doi.org/10.5876/9781646421848.c024

spite of our citizenship, somehow the Constitution and Bill of Rights did not apply to us. Our future survival in a country, which now viewed us as the enemy, had become our primary concern. We felt that we had to demonstrate our loyalty and dedication to this country for our very survival. So again, we complied.

Heart Mountain was a grim and inhospitable strip of prairie. It was located between two movie-like western towns, Cody and Powell. Both seemed to turn their backs on the prison camp hastily constructed on land nobody wanted. This orphan-like cluster of tar-papered barracks in the middle of nowhere seemed to express its own self-hate through its guard towers armed with weapons pointed inward, and placed at intervals along a barbed-wire fence.

It took a few weeks to orient myself to my new home, but as the everyday survival needs became more commonplace, the full import of the betrayal by our government began to sink in. I finally had to face the reality I tried so desperately to avoid. Because of the trust we had placed in our government and the cowardly, misguided leadership of our JACL, we had become war-prisoners in our very own country.

Early in 1943, the infamous "loyalty questionnaire" was circulated, causing much confusion, disbelief, and outrage. The Heart Mountain Congress of American Citizens warned that the "questionnaire" could be a precursor to imposing the military draft onto those in the camps. If answered carelessly, it could be interpreted as a willingness to be inducted into an already formed, racially segregated army unit.

I naïvely reasoned that perhaps this was yet another clumsy attempt by the government to determine our trustworthiness, a prelude to our clearance and release. Besides, if I answered "No" out of anger or spite, I might jeopardize whatever was left of my citizenship status. Also, it might tend to justify the government's wholesale detention program as a reasonable wartime contingency.

I finally heeded the warning of the Congress of American Citizens and answered with a *conditional* "Yes" on question 27, as to my willingness to serve in the armed forces, and "Yes" to 28, forswearing allegiance to the Emperor of Japan, even though I had never sworn allegiance to him in the first place.

The Congress of American Citizens was right, of course. Early in 1944, without further hearings nor explanations, my draft classification was changed from 4-C to 1-A. It was a relief to know that I was no longer considered sinister, but the condition of the prior reinstatement of my civil rights seemed to have been ignored.

Shortly thereafter, I received a notice to report for a physical exam prior to induction into the army. I regarded the notice as yet another insult, the first being the curfew, which now seemed so long ago.

What of my family still detained in this infernal prison camp? What of our suspended Constitutional rights? What of our past cooperation with the government in surrendering those rights in the name of "national security?" What of the democratic principles which had been denied us—the very principles we were then asked to defend on foreign soil?

I thought, "NO! This is MY country! This is MY Constitution! This is MY Bill of Rights!

I am here finally to defend them. I regret I had surrendered my freedom. I will not continue to surrender my dignity nor the dignity of the U.S. Constitution!" Thus, after receiving the notice to report for the pre-induction exams, I REFUSED TO COMPLY!

Had the mainland United States been threatened with probable invasion, I would not have taken this stand. But to join in the killing and maiming in foreign lands, not because they were the enemy, but ostensibly to prove my loyalty to a government who imprisoned me and my family without hearings or charges, I felt would be self-serving, irresponsible, and totally without conscience. Indeed, the real threat to our democracy was at my very doorstep.

Subsequently, I, along with 62 others, was indicted, tried, and found guilty of violating the Selective Service Act. We were sentenced to three years in prison. An appeal to a higher court was turned down. We were also denied parole, as an early release might encourage others still in the camps to defy the draft. However, after completing two years of our sentence, we were released on good behavior. The war had ended by then, the camps were closed, and we were no longer considered a threat.

A year and one-half after our release, we were *unexpectedly* granted a presidential pardon, erasing all criminal records and reinstating full citizenship rights.

After 57 years of introspection, and with the saner vision of hindsight, I have gained some insights about those events and the on-going misconceptions about the entire incarceration debacle that still plagues the Japanese American community. The inmate reaction to governmental abuses seemed to fall generally into three conflicting categories. There were those who believed in cooperation and sacrifice without question as a means of regaining the trust and acceptance of our government and the public at large, as proffered by the JACL. Their position seemed to imply that the camps were, in fact, sanctuaries, given the ugly wartime hysteria that prevailed "outside." Any spectacle, such as a court challenge questioning the constitutionality of the camps and other on-going infringements of our civil rights, would only cause unwanted notoriety and bad publicity which they felt we could ill-afford. They endorsed conspicuous acts of patriotism, regardless of their sincerity, in order to project an image of unfaltering loyalty.

On the other hand, there were the so-called "dissidents," the "No-Nos" and those who had become disenchanted with the government's professed "ideals and good intentions." They were basically, anti-administration and anti-JACL. Some were openly pro-Japan, although most were not. Many were Kibei, and a few were WWI veterans outraged with the treatment they received in spite of their being previously proven loyalty. They held in common a righteous anger and resentment resulting from years of racial injustice and had apparently given up all hope of ever attaining equity under what they perceived as a racist government.

The vast majority, however, for personal reasons, vacillated somewhere between the two extremes, committing themselves to neither position. They remained generally ineffective victims with a wait-and-see attitude, cautious and prone to finger-pointing, with an overall intolerance of those who dared to take a stand. They were, and still remain, smugly cloaked in the anonymity of the "Quiet American."

All three groups, in their own way had, in essence, abandoned that which should have been their greatest asset and source of inspiration, the U.S. Constitution—the first, out of a misguided patriotic fanaticism; the second, out of anger and despair; and the third, out of a culturally ingrained blind deference to authority, no matter what the circumstances.

In that climate of confusion, despair, and paralysis, pitting victim against victim, neighbor against neighbor, and brother against brother, the Heart Mountain Fair Play Committee, which was formed in early 1944, provided a fourth option, one which demanded absolute faith in the principles of the U.S. Constitution, while challenging, in the courts, government policies which were blatantly in violation of those principles. Indeed, what appeared initially as a reasonable fourth option, emerged after careful study, as a citizen's *inescapable primary duty*—the spirit of which lay at the very foundation of our country. It was, indeed, more than a simple option.

We lost our case, of course, and in a sense, so did the Constitution and democracy itself. But through subsequent acts like the presidential pardon, the success of the *coram nobis* cases, and the passage of the Civil Liberties Act of 1988 with the historic acknowledgment by the government of its massive civil rights violations, I feel our actions in placing our faith in the U.S. Constitution and the basic principles of our democracy have been more than vindicated. As the saying goes, "With so much manure, there HAD to be a pony in there somewhere." Happily, I think we found the pony.

APPENDIX D

CHRONOLOGY OF WWII AND POST-WWII EVENTS AND ACTIVITIES

This chronology was created by Yoshito Kuromiya and included in the original manuscript of his memoir.

December 7, 1941	Japan attacks US naval fleet at Pearl Harbor, Hawai'i.
December 8, 1941	United States declares war on Imperial forces of Japan and joins Allied forces in Europe.
February 19, 1942	President Franklin D. Roosevelt signs Executive Order 9066 leading to the exclusion of all people of Japanese descent from the West Coast states and incarceration in concentration camps without benefit of due process.
January 29, 1943	Loyalty questionnaire imposed on prisoners in detention camps.
February 1943	Congress of American Citizens formed at the Heart Mountain camp as an open forum to discuss citizens' rights in the context of the mandatory questionnaire.
January 14, 1944	Selective Service Act reinstated to those eligible in the detention camps.
January 26, 1944	The Heart Mountain Fair Play Committee (an outgrowth of the Congress of American Citizens) is formed to challenge the conscription of those held in government custody and the legality of the camps themselves.
May 10, 1944	A federal grand jury issues indictments against 63 Heart Mountain draft resisters.

June 26, 1944   District Court Judge T. Blake Kennedy deems all 63 as guilty, disregarding civil rights issues, and sentences all to three-year federal prison terms.

October 23, 1944   The trial of seven leaders of the Fair Play Committee (FPC) and James Omura is held in Cheyenne, Wyoming. All seven are convicted, but later released on appeal. James Omura, English language editor of the Denver-based *Rocky Shimpo* is exonerated.

December 18, 1944   Mitsuye Endo Supreme Court case deems it illegal to detain citizens without specific charges. Camp closures begin in the following year.

March 12, 1945   The appeal of the Heart Mountain 63 draft resisters fails.

July 1946   Release of the Heart Mountain 63 draft resisters from federal prison in recognition of good behavior.

December 24, 1947   Presidential pardon granted by Harry S. Truman restoring all citizen rights to WWII draft resisters of conscience.

January 27, 1952   The McCarran-Walter Act grants the opportunity for citizenship to Issei through naturalization.

December 1955   Rosa Parks refuses to relinquish her seat to a white man on a Montgomery, Alabama, bus.

1957   *No-No Boy*, novel by John Okada, is published.

1976   *Years of Infamy*, book by Michi Nishiura Weglyn, is published.

November 28, 1978   Day of Remembrance (DOR) first observed at former assembly center in Puyallup, Washington; conceived by Frank Chin, Lawson Inada, and Frank Abe to promote Japanese American redress.

May 1979   The National Council for Japanese American Redress (NCJAR), spearheaded by William Hohri in Chicago, is formed.

December 19, 1981   "The Last Organized Resistance" by Frank Chin is published in a *Rafu Shimpo* Holiday Supplement.

November 10, 1982   Aiko Herzig-Yoshinaga and Jack Herzig recover the original *DeWitt Final Report*, giving evidence contrary to the claim of military necessity for the exclusion and detention of Japanese Americans. The discovery is instrumental in the success of redress and leads to the Korematsu, Hirabayashi, and Yasui Supreme Court decisions being vacated.

December 1982   *Rafu Shimpo* runs a Frank Chin article on draft resistance in a Holiday Supplement.

November 10, 1983   Writ of *coram nobis*: Korematsu decision vacated.

February 2, 1986   Writ of *coram nobis*: Hirabayashi and Yasui decisions vacated.

August 10, 1988   Civil Liberties Act of 1988 signed by President Ronald Reagan provides a government apology for civil rights violations and monetary compensation to Japanese Americans who had been incarcerated. Established as an entitlement in November of 1989 through the efforts of US Senator Daniel Inouye of Hawai'i.

October 31, 1988	Supreme Court disallows the NCJAR class-action lawsuit on a procedural technicality.
1990	Original *Lim Report* submitted to Japanese American Citizens League (JACL) under private contract.
October 1, 1991	Manzanar reunion at Westin Bonaventure Hotel, Los Angeles. Yoshito Kuromiya first meets William Hohri, who is present to speak on *The Lim Report*. Hideki Obayashi distributes unofficial copies of the report.
February 21, 1993	Performance of *Return of the Fair Play Committee* at the Centenary United Methodist Church in Los Angeles, scripted by Frank Chin.
March 14, 1993	Japanese American Bar Association (JABA) recognizes Heart Mountain resisters and FPC for their civil rights protest, Robin Toma presiding.
June 13, 1993	Michi and Walter Weglyn Endowment instituted at California State Polytechnic University, Pomona; ceremony conducted by Bob Suzuki, president of Cal Poly.
February 5, 1994	*Principled Dissent*, Oakland Museum, recognition of Heart Mountain resisters, moderated by Dr. Clifford Uyeda.
February 5, 1994	*Valor & Sacrifice*, Florin JACL, Daruma Award to Amache resisters, Gordon Hirabayashi, guest speaker.
February 19, 1994	National Coalition for Redress/Reparations (NCR/R) presents its Fighting Spirit Award to James Omura at the Japanese American Cultural and Community Center (JACCC) George Aratani Theater.
April 1994	William and Yuriko Hohri move from Chicago, Illinois, to Lomita, California.
November 14, 1994	Family Expo at the Los Angeles Convention Center: WWII display of documents on the Heart Mountain resistance, by Frank Emi, Takashi Hoshizaki, and Yoshito Kuromiya.
February 19, 1995	Pacific Southwest District JACL recognizes Heart Mountain resisters in Los Angeles at JACCC, awarded by Ruth Mizobe and Trisha Murakawa; first JACL chapter to recognize the legitimacy of draft resistance.
February 22, 1995	Dramatic reading at California State University, Fullerton, Dr. Art Hansen presiding. *The Lim Report* revisits government-JACL conspiracy during WWII and resistance. "A Question of Who We Are" scripted and narrated by William Hohri, read by William Hohri, Frank Emi, Traci Kiriyama, Yoshito Kuromiya, Aki Maehara, Wilbur Sato, Ryan Yokota, and Kedric Wolfe.
March 12, 1995	"A Question of Who We Are" presented at Centenary United Methodist Church, Los Angeles.
March 22, 1995	"A Question of Who We Are" presented at Loyola Marymount University.
April 10, 1995	"A Question of Who We Are" presented at Occidental College.

April 15, 1995	Talk on Heart Mountain and draft resistance in Los Angeles at Japanese American National Museum (JANM) with Frank Emi, Takashi Hoshizaki, and Yoshito Kuromiya—first JANM-sponsored program focusing on resisters.
May 18, 1995	Northwest College, Powell, Wyoming, hosts symposium on the Heart Mountain camp and the draft resistance, at which copies of *The Lim Report* are distributed.
June 3, 1995	American Civil Liberties Union (ACLU) honors Heart Mountain FPC and draft resisters of conscience, Fred Okrand at *Garden Party*.
July 23, 1995	Lawson Fusao Inada reads from *Drawing the Line*, his book of poems, at Lannan Center, Los Angeles.
May 18, 1996	NCR/R and California State University, Long Beach (CSULB), host symposium on internment and military service, with Frank Emi and Yosh Kuromiya.
June 15, 1996	Filming for *Conscience and the Constitution* at Heart Mountain site in Cody, Wyoming.
August 10, 1996	Dedication of Wall Brick to James Omura at the Southern California Research Library, Los Angeles.
February 20, 1998	Day of Remembrance (DOR)/NCR/R/Resisters present Michi Weglyn with the Fighting Spirit Award.
February 1999	DOR/NCR/R present Heart Mountain FPC and draft resisters of conscience with the Fighting Spirit Award.
November 7, 1999	Dedication of former Catalina Prison Camp in Tucson, AZ, as the Gordon Hirabayashi Recreation Site.
May 23, 2000	*Conscience and the Constitution* film showing at the East West Theater in Los Angeles.
September 23, 2000	*Conscience and the Constitution* showing at Laemmle Theater, Santa Monica.
October 12, 2000	"Unveiling Truth" panel held at Long Beach City College, with Frank Emi, Takashi Hoshizaki, and Yoshito Kuromiya.
December 2000	*Conscience and the Constitution* showing at University of California, San Diego.
2001	Publication of *Resistance*, edited by William Hohri with contributions by Mits Koshiyama, Yoshito Kuromiya, Takashi Hoshizaki, and Frank Seishi Emi.
June 21–24, 2001	Resisters conference at Little America Hotel in Cheyenne, Wyoming.
2002	*The Lim Report* is published for public consumption on the critical aspects of the report.
April 22, 2002	Speaking tour at Webb School, La Verne, CA, with Frank Emi and Yoshito Kuromiya.
May 11, 2002	National JACL apology at San Francisco, promoted by Andy Noguchi and the JACL's Florin, CA, chapter.

June 3, 2002	Speaking tour at University of California, Santa Barbara, with Frank Emi and Yoshito Kuromiya, moderated by Professor Diane Fujino.
June 28, 2002	Pasadena City College symposium, with Frank Emi, Takashi Hoshizaki, and Yoshito Kuromiya, moderated by Professor Robert Lee.
April 26, 2003	Talk by Frank Emi and Yoshito Kuromiya, sponsored by Sandy Ellege at University of Wyoming, Laramie, WY.
March 24, 2004	Final "Ramblers Nemesis" column by William Hohri appears in *Rafu Shimpo*.
November 5–6, 2004	Symposium organized by Eric Muller, "Judgments Judged and Wrongs Remembered," on the US government's civil rights transgressions during WWII, is held at JANM and cosponsored by the University of North Carolina and the University of California, Los Angeles (UCLA).
June 3, 2005	*Divided Community*, a personalized reading organized by Momo Yashima and based on Frank Chin's documentary novel *Born in the USA*.
November 19, 2005	*Divided Community* reading organized by Momo Yashima is held at Centenary United Methodist Church in Los Angeles.
March 11, 2006	*Divided Community* reading organized by Momo Yashima is held at JANM.
May 2, 2006	*Divided Community* reading organized by Momo Yashima is held at UCLA.
October 7, 2006	Ehren Watada, National Coalition of Redress/Reparations at JACCC on the Significance of the Watada story as viewed by WWII resisters Frank Emi and Yoshito Kuromiya.
January 27, 2007	Phone conference with Ehren Watada, Frank Emi, Paul Tsuneishi, and Yoshito Kuromiya.
February 22, 2007	*Divided Community* reading for high school students, coordinated by Momo Yashima, is held at JANM.
February 24, 2007	*Divided Community* reading for general public, coordinated by Momo Yashima, is held at JANM.
March 3, 2007	*Divided Community* reading for Vietnam veterans, coordinated by Momo Yashima, is held at the home of Mike Nakayama.
March 30, 2007	*Divided Community* reading, coordinated by Momo Yashima, is held at George Nakano Theatre, Torrance, CA.
April 21, 2008	George Nozawa dies at age 85 in San Jose, CA.
April 23, 2008	*Divided Community* reading, coordinated by Momo Yashima, is held at California State University, San Bernardino.
May 19, 2008	*Divided Community* reading, coordinated by Momo Yashima, is held at California Polytechnic State University, San Luis Obispo.

June 25, 2008	Memorabilia is donated, via Noriko Sanefuji, to Smithsonian Institution.
July 4–6, 2008	JANM-sponsored national conference is held in Denver, CO.
August 22, 2008	Taping begins for *Divided Community* documentary film.
February 6, 2009	Mits Koshiyama dies at age 83 in San Jose, CA.
April 14, 2009	Japanese American speakers for high school seniors at JANM: Jim Makino of the 442nd Regimental Combat Team, Cedric Shimo, 1800th Battalion military resister of conscience, and Yoshito Kuromiya, Heart Mountain draft resister of conscience.
August 21, 2009	Discovery of gravesite of Kiyoshi Okamoto (died in 1974 at age 85) at Evergreen Cemetery, Los Angeles, identified through research by his grandniece, Marie Masumoto.
January 30, 2010	Japanese American history series at JANM: Don Seki of the 442nd Regimental Combat Team.
March 12, 2010	Japanese American history series at JANM: Hitoshi Sameshima, Military Intelligence Service, and Helen Tsuyuki.
July 10, 2010	Interview with Frank Chin and Lawson Inada at the home of Yoshito and Irene Kuromiya, Alhambra, CA.
November 12, 2010	William Hohri dies at age 83 in Los Angeles.
November 12, 2010	Interview with Brian Yagi at Miyako Inn, Little Tokyo, Los Angeles.
December 1, 2010	Frank Emi dies at age 94 in San Gabriel, CA.
January 2, 2012	Gordon Hirabayashi dies at age 83 in Edmonton, Alberta, Canada.
February 3, 2012	*Divided Community* screened at Pitzer College, Claremont, CA.
May 12, 2012	*Conscience and the Constitution* screened at JANM with panel consisting of Frank Abe, Takashi Hoshizaki, and Yoshito Kuromiya.
July 21, 2012	*Divided Community* documentary film screening with a panel consisting of attorney Deborah Lim, Ken Inouye of the JACL, Dr. Art Hansen, and Yoshito Kuromiya; moderated by Momo Yashima.
2012, 2013, 2014	Informal discussions with JACL youth under Kansha Program from Chicago.
June 2014	"National Consortium on Racial and Ethnic Fairness in the Courts" held at Heart Mountain and Cody, WY.

NOTES

1. For a succinct depiction of "The Age of Aquarius," see the University of Miami's posting on it, http://scholar.library.miami.edu/sixties/aquarius.php (accessed on September 20, 2019). See also Ralph Metzner, "Consciousness Expansion and Counterculture in the 1960s and Beyond," *Maps Bulletin* 19 (Spring 2009): 16–20, https://maps.org/news-letters/v19n1/v19n1-pg16.pdf (accessed on September 20, 2019).

2. Garrett Eckbo and his *Landscape for Living* are discussed in chapter 13.

3. For detailed information about Michi Nishiura Weglyn (1925–1999), see Sharon Yamato, "Michi Nishiura Weglyn," *Densho Encyclopedia*, http://encyclopedia.densho.org/Michi_Nishiura _Weglyn/ (accessed on September 5, 2019).

4. See "The Prosperos," Encyclopedia.com, https://www.encyclopedia.com/science/ encyclopedias-almanacs-transcripts-and-maps/prosperos (accessed on September 3, 2019). See also Zuerrnnovahh-Starr Livingstone, "The Prosperos Are Holding a Key to Self-Realization," January 9, 2016, *Educate-Yourself: The Freedom of Knowledge, The Power of Thought*, http://educate -yourself.org/zsl/The-Prosperos-Are-Holding-A-Key-Tool-To-Self-Realization09jan16.shtml (accessed on September 3, 2019).

5. For bibliographic information on these films and books, see the selected bibliography.

6. For biographical data on James Omura (1912–1994), see Arthur A. Hansen, "James Omura," *Densho Encyclopedia*, http://encyclopedia.densho.org/James_Omura/ (accessed on September 3, 2019).

7. For information on Ehren Watada (1978–), see "Ehren Watada," *Wikipedia*, https://en .wikipedia.org/wiki/Ehren_Watada (accessed on September 5, 2019). See also Jeremy Brecher and Brendan Smith, "Ehren Watada: Free at Last," *The Nation*, October 26, 2009, https://www .thenation.com/article/ehren-watada-free-last/ (accessed on September 5, 2019).

8. For a very similar yet fuller version by Kuromiya of the situation described here, see appendix C of the present volume.

9. Since the Union Station in Los Angeles was not opened until 1939, the station in question was either the La Grande Station, which opened in 1893, or (more likely) the Central Station, which opened in 1914.

10. See the following sources: Hillary Jenks, "Home Is Little Tokyo: Race, Community, and Memory in Twentieth-Century Los Angeles" (PhD diss., University of Southern California, 2008); Lon Kurashige, *Japanese American Celebration and Conflict: A History of Ethnic Identity and Festival, 1934–1990* (Berkeley: University of California Press, 2002); and Ichiro Mike Murase, *Little Tokyo: One Hundred Years in Pictures* (Los Angeles: Visual Communications / Asian American Studies Central Inc., 1983). See also Scott Tadao Kurashige, *The Shifting Grounds of Race: Black and Japanese Americans in the Making of Multiethnic Los Angeles* (Princeton, NJ: Princeton University Press, 2010); and Martha Nakagawa, "Little Tokyo / Bronzeville, Los Angeles, California," *Densho Encyclopedia*, http://encyclopedia.densho.org/Little_Tokyo_/_Bronzeville%2C_Los_Angeles%2C _California/ (accessed on August 31, 2019).

11. The paperback edition of Robert B. Stinnett's *Day of Deceit: The Truth about FDR and Pearl Harbor* (New York: Simon and Schuster, 2001) provides two back-cover blurbs drawn from reviews that appeared in the liberal *New York Times* ("It is difficult after reading this copiously documented book, not to wonder about previously unchallenged assumptions about Pearl Harbor.") and the conservative *Wall Street Journal* ("Fascinating and readable. Exceptionally well-presented."). The first of these reviews, written by Richard Bernstein and published on December 15, 1999, contends that in spite of Stinnett's seventeen-year search for documentary evidence to prove his book's conclusion—i.e., that not only was the alleged "surprise attack" on Pearl Harbor on December 7, 1941, not a surprise to President Franklin D. Roosevelt, but also that the Roosevelt administration's attempt to provoke Japan into military action had been its principal policy for the entire previous year—Stinnett has produced no "smoking guns" on the subject and has failed "to take account of less radical explanations for the data he has uncovered." As for the December 7, 1999, review of *Day of Deceit* in the *Wall Street Journal* by Bruce Bartlett, the author of *Coverup: The Politics of Pearl Harbor, 1941–1946* (New York: Arlington House, 1979), he observes that while Stinnett has unearthed a great deal of invaluable documentation that indicts Roosevelt for "provoking the Pearl Harbor attack and failing to warn his military commanders there [at Pearl Harbor] when he knew that an attack was imminent," his case against Roosevelt "remains circumstantial," leaving "a reasonable doubt" as to its validity. In short, Bartlett's bottom line is that Stinnett has found some guns with "warm barrels," but no smoking guns.

Many other reviewers aside from Bernstein and Bartlett have taken the measure of Stinnett's book. Richard Young, whose review appeared in the April 1999 issue of *Naval History*, maintains that, notwithstanding the 200,000 documents that Stinnett allegedly reviewed to "prove" that Roosevelt was aware of the impending attack on Pearl Harbor and deliberately hid that fact from the world, his "hopelessly flawed research convincingly proves just the opposite: Roosevelt did not know." Like other conspiracy writers, avers Young, Stinnett failed to take into account that for such a conspiracy as he depicted to have happened, it would have necessarily involved the knowing complicity of huge numbers of people, "from civilian and military heads, to their staffs, radio intercept operators, code-breakers, and even the watch-standers at Pearl Harbor on that morning [of December 7, 1941]." Michael Hull, in contrast, roundly applauds *Day of Deceit*'s research findings and convincing narrative, summing up his January 2001 review in *World War II* with this laudation: "Highly detailed, reasoned and literate, Stinnett's book is a triumph of historical scholarship and a valuable contribution to the record of World War II." In his March–April 2003 review in *Military History*, Richard L. Milligan ends his terse commentary on Stinnett's book with this equivocating sentiment: "I recommend this book, but not because I agree with its conclusions, but because it provides information about a subject that will be discussed and debated long into the future." Mark D. Mandeles, in his overwhelmingly negative review in the June 2000 issue of *Naval History*, climaxes it with this dismissive remark: "In the end, Stinnett's conspiracy thesis is more suitable to television's X-Files than to understanding the actions of civilian and military officials in the months before U.S. entry into World War II." As for David Kahn's November 2, 2000, *New York Review of Books* review, after situating *Day of Deceit* within earlier revisionist treatments of the same subject by the likes of Charles Beard, onetime president of the American Historical Association, and John Tolan, a former Pulitzer Prize–winning author, it asserts that Stinnett "has spent a decade and a half but has come up with the most irrational of the revisionist books." Kahn goes on to bemoan the fact that, unfortunately, "Stinnett is such a passionate believer in conspiracy that he is unwilling to consider the countervailing evidence." For Kahn, therefore, *Day of Deceit* is doomed to experience as sorry a fate as previous books within the same genre. Justus D. Doenecke, in his June 2002 review of *Day of Deceit* for the *Journal of American History*, the journal of record for US history, limits himself to only a few key fallacies in Stinnett's argument, declaring that space does not allow for a detailed refutation. His closing paragraph, however, captures the crux of his disdain for the volume under review: "Parties conspiring to withhold information include not only the president but Chief of Staff George Marshall, Chief of Naval Operations Harold Stark, Admiral [Walter S.] Anderson [director of naval intelligence], who became battleship commander at Pearl Harbor, the intelligence officers Edwin Layton and Irving Mayfield, and the cryptographer Joseph John Rochefort. The vastness of such a conspiracy falls of its own weight." Robert C. Whitten's review of *Day of Deceit*, which appeared in Winter 2001 in the *Journal of Political and Military Sociology*, is a decidedly mixed appraisal. "In short," wraps up Whitten, "Stinnett makes a convincing case that Roosevelt knew that war was coming in the Pacific and roughly when, but he did not convince this reviewer that the President knew about the Pearl Harbor attack before it occurred. These reservations aside, *Day of Deceit* is an important addition to the literature of the workings of our political establishment on the eve of the war." In contrast, Edward J. Drea's review of *Day of Deceit* in the April 2000 issue of the *Journal of Military History* is an unmixed indictment. He attacks Stinnett's book in a series of volleys, calling it a "bad book," declaring that its "methodology is as flawed as the author's logic," charging that "Stinnett deluges the reader with extensive end notes, mostly very lengthy and expository in nature, that obfuscate his errors," and accusing Stinnett both of "lacking documentary evidence to support his predetermined conclusions" and resorting to "vicious innuendo to slander President Franklin D. Roosevelt, General George C. Marshall, and the United States Navy as the perpetrators of a heretofore cleverly concealed government." Drea then climaxes his case against *Day of Deceit*: "The book also has a great deal of fill because frankly Stinnett has little to say. In short, the meretricious style relies on distortion and ignorance to fabricate a case. This kind of publication gives military history a bad name."

The question that is of the utmost significance in the present context about Robert B. Stinnett's exceedingly controversial book is simply this: Why did Yoshito Kuromiya believe so convincingly in its core conspiratorial message, which implied that President Roosevelt, in withholding critical information from commanders in the field so as to "ensure an uncontested overt Japanese act of war," had by so doing sacrificed the lives of 2,273 American soldiers and sailors at Pearl Harbor? The answer to this enigmatic question, of course, will never be known. However, it can be speculated that perhaps what made Kuromiya favorably disposed toward Stinnett's thesis was his having himself experienced Roosevelt's act, through his February 19, 1942, issuance of Executive Order 9066, of sacrificing in one fell swoop the civil and human rights and dignity of 120,000 Americans of Japanese ancestry in the name of national security.

12. Pasadena Junior College is now Pasadena City College.

13. See Cherstin Lyon, "Japanese American Citizens League," *Densho Encyclopedia*, http://encyclopedia.densho.org/Japanese%20American%20Citizens%20League/ (accessed on August 28, 2019).

14. See Brian Niiya, "Executive Order 9066," *Densho Encyclopedia*, http://encyclopedia.densho.org/Executive_Order_9066/ (accessed on August 31, 2019). See also Michael Ray, "Executive

Order 9066," *Encyclopedia Britannica*, https://www.britannica.com/topic/Executive-Order-9066 (accessed on August 31, 2019).

15. In the words of Eric L. Muller, "JACL did not pre-commit to cooperating with Executive Order 9066; JACL argued against mass removal and only offered cooperation when it became clear that mass removal was in the works." From Muller's 2015 critique of Kuromiya's final draft of the manuscript (see "Editor's Note" in this volume); hereafter cited as Muller critique.

16. See Konrad Linke, "Pomona (detention facility)," *Densho Encyclopedia*, http://encyclopedia .densho.org/Pomona_%28detention_facility%29/ (accessed on August 28, 2019). See also Francis Feeley, *A Strategy of Dominance: The History of an American Concentration Camp, Pomona, California* (New York: Brandywine Press, 1995).

17. For the most compelling and complete treatment of Chinese railroad workers, see Gordon H. Chang's *Ghosts of Gold Mountain: The Epic Story of the Chinese Who Built the Transcontinental Railroad* (New York: Houghton Mifflin Harcourt, 2019).

18. A very useful overview of the Heart Mountain Relocation Center is Mieko Matsumoto's "Heart Mountain," *Densho Encyclopedia*, https://encyclopedia.densho.org/Heart_Mountain/ (accessed on August 28, 2019).

19. See Greg Robinson's exquisite entry on Miné Okuba (1912–2001) in the *Densho Encyclopedia*, http://encyclopedia.densho.org/Mine_Okubo/ (accessed on August 28, 2019).

20. For detailed information on the Heart Mountain landform, see "Heart Mountain (Wyoming)," *Wikipedia*, https://en.wikipedia.org/wiki/Heart_Mountain_%28Wyoming%29 (accessed on August 28, 2019).

21. See Aiko Herzig-Yoshinaga, "Words Can Lie or Clarify: Terminology of the World War II Incarceration of Japanese Americans," https://www.nps.gov/tule/learn/education/upload/Words _Can_Lie_or_Clarify.pdf (accessed on August 28, 2018).

22. As observed by Eric L. Muller, "It's not correct that aliens in Justice Department captivity were not permitted to communicate with their families. Louis Fiset's *Imprisoned Apart: The World War II Correspondence of an Issei Couple* (Seattle: University of Washington Press, 1997) documents an extensive correspondence between an interned alien in a Justice Department camp and his wife in a WRA (War Relocation Authority) camp." Muller critique.

23. For a definitive treatment of Tule Lake as both a relocation center and a segregation center, see Barbara Takei, "Tule Lake," *Densho Encyclopedia*, http://encyclopedia.densho.org/Tule %20Lake/ (accessed on August 28, 2019). See also Takei's forthcoming volume on Tule Lake, coauthored with Roger Daniels, with the proposed title of "America's Worst Concentration Camp."

24. See Stephen Mak, "Crystal City (detention facility)," *Densho Encyclopedia*, http:// encyclopedia.densho.org/Crystal_City_%28detention_facility%29/ (accessed on August 28, 2019). See also Jan Jarboe Russell, *The Train to Crystal City: FDR's Secret Prisoner Exchange Program and America's Only Family Internment during World War II* (New York: Scribner, 2015).

25. As opined by Eric L. Muller, "It's not altogether clear that the detention of a person who is a citizen of a belligerent nation in wartime is a 'human rights violation.' Countries have done this for a long time; the United States authorized it by statute in the 1790s. I believe that detention of enemy aliens of belligerent nations is not contrary to international law even today, so long as the detention meets certain standards." Muller critique.

26. See Roger Daniels, "Words Do Matter: A Note on Inappropriate Terminology and the Incarceration of the Japanese Americans—Part 1 of 5," February 1, 2008, Japanese American National Museum, *Discover Nikkei*, http://www.discovernikkei.org/en/journal/2008/2/1/words-do -matter/ (accessed on August 29, 2019).

27. A succinct and valuable overview of the *Heart Mountain Sentinel* is afforded by Patricia Wakida in "Heart Mountain Sentinel (newspaper)," *Densho Encyclopedia*, https://encyclopedia .densho.org/Heart_Mountain_Sentinel_(newspaper)/ (accessed on August 29, 2019).

28. See Eric L. Muller, "Heart Mountain Fair Play Committee," *Densho Encyclopedia*, http:// encyclopedia.densho.org/Heart_Mountain_Fair_Play_Committee/ (accessed on August 29, 2019).

29. For a trenchant account of the 1943 loyalty questionnaire, see Cherstin M. Lyon, "Loyalty Questionnaire," *Densho Encyclopedia*, https://encyclopedia.densho.org/Loyalty_questionnaire/ (accessed on August 29, 2019).

30. Information on the Heart Mountain Congress of American Citizens is perhaps best related by its chief organizer, Frank T. Inoyue (1920–1995), in his "Immediate Origins of the Heart Mountain Draft Resistance Movement," in *Remembering Heart Mountain: Essays on Japanese American Internment in Wyoming*, ed. Mike Mackey (Powell, WY: Western History Publications, 1998), 121–139. See also Arthur A. Hansen, "Protest-Resistance and the Heart Mountain Experience: The Revitalization of a Robust Nikkei Tradition," chap. 5 in *Barbed Voices: Oral History, Resistance, and the World War II Japanese American Social Disaster* (Louisville, CO; University Press of Colorado: 2018), 200–204.

31. For biographical information on Inouye, see his "Immediate Origins." See also Inouye's unpublished memoir, "Odyssey of a Nisei: A Voyage of Self-Discovery," Department of Special Collections, Library, University of Cincinnati. Thanks are extended to University of Cincinnati Professor Emeritus Roger Daniels for alerting me to the existence of this manuscript and arranging to have it copied and made available to me.

32. Biographical information on Robert Kiyoshi Okamoto (1889–1974) is provided in *Nisei Naysayer: The Memoir of Militant Japanese American Journalist*, ed. Arthur A. Hansen, chap. 5, n. 66, 313–314 (Stanford, CA: Stanford University Press, 2018). See also Chizu Omori, "Kiyoshi Okamoto, an Unsung Hero of the Camp Resistance Movement," *Nichi Bei Weekly*, January 20, 2011, https://www.nichibei.org/2011/01/rabbit-ramblings-kiyoshi-okamoto-an-unsung-hero-of-the -camp-resistance-movement/ (accessed on August 29, 2019).

33. Relevant data on Paul Nakadate (1914–1964) is contained in Brian Niiya, "Paul Nakadate," *Densho Encyclopedia*, https://encyclopedia.densho.org/Paul%20Nakadate/ (accessed on August 29, 2019). See also Sharon Yamato, "Unraveling Family Mysteries: Paul Nakadate and the Heart Mountain Fair Play Committee," January 13, 2015, Japanese American National Museum, *DiscoverNikkei*, http://www.discovernikkei.org/en/journal/2015/1/13/5623/ (accessed on September 14, 2010).

34. Eric L. Muller states, "Yosh's statements about how the government used the answers to the questions on the loyalty questionnaire to determine loyalty significantly misrepresent how government agencies actually processed the questionnaires." Muller critique. Muller points out that his *American Inquisition: The Hunt for Japanese American Disloyalty in World War II* (Chapel Hill: University of North Carolina Press, 2007) describes this process in detail.

35. As viewed by Eric L. Muller, "The questionnaire was *not* 'a citizen's waiver of any claims against the government of civil rights infringements and a vow to obey governmental dictates no matter how unreasonable.' This may have been Yosh's perspective on the questionnaires, but words like 'waiver of claims' and 'vow to obey . . . dictates' are assertions about the factual nature and effect of the questionnaires that are not factual." Muller critique.

36. See Robert Shaffer, "Tolan Committee," *Densho Encyclopedia*, http://encyclopedia.densho .org/Tolan_Committee/ (accessed on September 15, 2019). See also "Whereas: Stories from the People's House: House Select Committee Investigates Japanese Evacuation and Relocation" (blog post), May 8, 2018, United States House of Representatives, *History, Art & Archives*, https://history .house.gov/Blog/2018/May/5-8-tolan-committee/ (accessed on September 15, 2019).

37. See Hansen, ed., *Nisei Naysayer*, for pertinent information about the life and editorial career of James Matsumoto Omura. In regard to Kuromiya's reference to "the Gestapo," Eric L. Muller offers this objection: "The suggestion that the WRA was 'the Gestapo' is certainly provocative, and may well be Yosh's experience of the WRA, but as a matter of fact the analogy simply cannot be sustained. The differences between the Gestapo's handling of the supposed enemies of the German

Reich and the WRA's handling of the Japanese Americans in their custody are too numerous to state, and dwarf whatever similarities might support an analogy. They certainly can't support the claim of equation that Yosh makes here." Muller critique.

38. For a well-crafted and compact biography of Frank Seishi Emi (1916–2010), see Esther Newman, "Frank Emi," *Densho Encyclopedia*, http://encyclopedia.densho.org/Frank_Emi/ (accessed on August 29, 2019). See also Gann Matsuda, "Two Views on Frank Seishi Emi: A True American Hero," December 8, 2010, Japanese American National Museum, *DiscoverNikkei*, http://www.discovernikkei.org/en/journal/2010/12/8/frank-emi/ (accessed on August 29, 2019).

39. For a brief biography of Guntaro Kubota (1903–1967), see Brian Niiya, "Guntaro Kubota," *Densho Encyclopedia*, http://encyclopedia.densho.org/Guntaro%20Kubota/ (accessed on August 29, 2019). See also Hansen, ed., *Nisei Naysayer*, chap. 5, p. 322, n. 118.

40. See the entry on resettlement by Megan Asaka in the *Densho Encyclopedia*, https://encyclopedia.densho.org/Resettlement/ (accessed on September 15, 2021).

41. For a life portrait of Kiyoshi Kuromiya (1943–2000), see Hugh Ryan, "themstory: Kiyoshi Kuromiya, the AIDS Activist Who Marched with Martin Luther King, Jr.," December 4, 2017, *them*, https://www.them.us/story/themstory-kiyoshi-kuromiya (accessed on August 30, 2019). See also Greg Robinson, "Kiyoshi Kuromiya: A Queer Activist for Civil Rights," in *The Great Unknown: Japanese American Sketches* (Boulder: University Press of Colorado, 2016), 241–244.

42. Joe Grant Masaoka (1909–1970) was incarcerated in 1942 at the Manzanar Relocation Center in eastern California, where he was employed by the War Relocation Authority as a documentary historian. From 1942 to 1951 he was the regional director of the Japanese American Citizens League in Denver, Colorado, and he also established the JACL regional office in San Francisco.

43. See Gil Asakawa's well-informed entry on Minoru "Min" Yasui (1916–1986) in the *Densho Encyclopedia*, http://encyclopedia.densho.org/Minoru_Yasui/ (accessed on August 30, 2019).

44. But, as rectified by Eric L. Muller, "the 63 resisters and the members [leaders] of the Fair Play Committee were indicted at the same time." Muller critique.

45. See Greg Robinson, "War Relocation Authority," *Densho Encyclopedia*, https://encyclopedia.densho.org/War_Relocation_Authority/ (accessed on August 30, 2019).

46. Michigan-born Thomas Blake Kennedy (1874–1957), an 1897 graduate of Syracuse University College of Law, was named in 1921 as a federal judge in the US District Court for the District of Wyoming, whose appeals are heard by the US Court of Appeals for the Tenth Circuit.

47. A Denver, Colorado–based lawyer, Samuel David Menin (1906–1995) was known as a courtroom battler, in both a figurative and literal sense. In March 1940 he physically tangled with another lawyer, O. Otto Moore, in a Denver courtroom, during a case pitting the two men as legal representatives for rival old-age pension organizations. See "O. Otto Moore, Samuel Menin Trade Punches," *Greeley Daily Tribune*, March 8, 1940. Moreover, Menin was not a stranger to wartime draft evasion cases. In June 1942 he unsuccessfully defended in Denver a member of a religious sect who sought an exemption both from the army and noncombatant service. For additional information on Menin's background and role in the July 1944 Cheyenne federal mass trial for the sixty-three Heart Mountain draft resisters, see Muller, *Free to Die for Their Country*, 103 and 108–110.

48. For more on this courtroom ploy and Kuromiya's critical assessment of it, see Muller, *Free to Die for Their Country*, 109, 187–188.

49. For a biographical snapshot of Carl L. Sackett (1867–1972), see Muller, *Free to Die for Their Country*, 96–97.

50. See Daryl C. McClary, "McNeil Island and the Federal Penitentiary, 1841–1981," April 17, 2003, Essay 5238, History Link.org, https://www.historylink.org/File/5238 (accessed on August 30, 2019). See also "McNeil Island Corrections Center," *Wikipedia*, https://en.wikipedia.org/wiki/McNeil_Island_Corrections_Center (accessed on September 14, 2019).

51. Eric L. Muller, explaining why Omura was acquitted while the leaders of the Fair Play Committee were convicted in their October–November 1944 conspiracy trial at the federal court in Cheyenne, Wyoming, writes: "It is often asserted that the jury acquitted him [Omura] because he was a journalist exercising his First Amendment right to freedom of the press, but the historical record suggests that the jury's real reason was that they simply did not believe the [US] government had presented enough evidence to link him with the other defendants' conspiracy." Muller, "Heart Mountain Fair Play Committee."

52. For a resplendent portrait of Wakako Yamauchi (1924–2018), see Patricia Wakida, "Wakako Yamauchi," *Densho Encyclopedia*, http://encyclopedia.densho.org/Wakako_Yamauchi/ (accessed on August 30, 2019).

53. The meaning of the term is treated in-depth in "Conscientious Objector," *Wikipedia*, https://en.wikipedia.org/wiki/Conscientious_objector (accessed on August 31, 2019).

54. See Cherstin M. Lyon's astute entry on Gordon Hirabayashi (1918–2012) for the *Densho Encyclopedia*, http://encyclopedia.densho.org/Gordon_Hirabayashi/ (accessed on August 31, 2019). See also Gordon Hirabayashi, with James A. Hirabayashi and Lane Ryo Hirabayashi, *A Principled Stand: The Story of Hirabayashi v. United States* (Seattle: University of Washington Press, 2013).

55. For an incisive summary of the Minidoka Relocation Center, see Hanako Wakatsuki, "Minidoka," *Densho Encyclopedia*, https://encyclopedia.densho.org/Minidoka/ (accessed on August 31, 2019).

56. See Michael Huefner, "Topaz," *Densho Encyclopedia*, http://encyclopedia.densho.org/Topaz/ (accessed on August 31, 2019).

57. This explanation is challenged by Eric Muller in a below note. Muller critique.

58. See the superlative entry on A. L. Wirin (1900–1978) by Greg Robinson and Brian Niiya, "A. L. Wirin," *Densho Encyclopedia*, http://encyclopedia.densho.org/A.L._Wirin/ (accessed on August 31, 2019).

59. This explanation is challenged by Muller: "Yosh misstates the reasoning of the US Court of Appeals for the Tenth Circuit in reversing the convictions of the members [leaders] of the Fair Play Committee. The court held (in an attempt at plain, rather than legal, language) that the trial judge should have instructed the jury that a defendant's good-faith desire to create a legal test case (by urging others to resist the draft) could serve as an innocent motive." Muller critique.

60. Muller takes exception to this contention of Kuromiya's: "Yosh mistakenly states that no attempt was made to obtain further appellate review of the Tenth Circuit's rejection of the resisters' appeal of their conviction in the *Fujii case*. An application was made by A. L. Wirin [attorney for the FPC leaders] to the US Supreme Court to grant a writ of certiorari to review the Tenth Circuit's decision. The Supreme Court on May 28, 1945, denied that application. Wirin then petitioned for a rehearing of the matter (basically a last-ditch request to convince the court that it missed something very important when it denied review), which the Court denied on June 18, 1945. So, I see no evidence that the FPC leadership actually slighted the rank-and-file resisters." Muller critique.

61. See Brian Niiya, "Ex parte Mitsuye Endo (1944)," *Densho Encyclopedia*, https://encyclopedia.densho.org/Ex%20parte%20Mitsuye%20Endo%20(1944) (accessed on August 31, 2009). See as well Niiya's equally beneficial entry on Mitsuye Endo (1920–2006), "Mitsuye Endo," *Densho Encyclopedia*, https://encyclopedia.densho.org/Mitsuye_Endo/ (accessed on August 31, 2019).

62. This narrative is discounted by Muller: "Yosh expresses disapproval of the fact that the appeal did not seek to avail itself of the helpful Supreme Court decision in *Ex parte Endo*, decided in December of 1944. But the briefs to the 10th Circuit Court of Appeals in Yosh's case did cite the *Endo* case a number of times." Muller critique.

63. See Iris Yokio, "Little Tokyo: 75th Anniversary for Union Church," *Los Angeles Times*, February 7, 1993, https://www.latimes.com/archives/la-xpm-1993-02-07-ci-1802-story.html (accessed on August 31, 2019).

64. See "Union Station (Los Angeles)," *Wikipedia*, https://en.wikipedia.org/wiki/Union_Station_%28Los_Angeles%29 (accessed on August 31, 2019); and "South Pasadena Station," *Wikipedia*, https://en.wikipedia.org/wiki/South_Pasadena_station (accessed on August 31, 2019).

65. For an expertly rendered source on this unit, see Franklin Odo, "442nd Regimental Combat Team," *Densho Encyclopedia*, http://encyclopedia.densho.org/442nd_Regimental_Combat_Team/ (accessed on August 31, 2019).

66. On the significance of Japanese American gardeners before and after World War II in Southern California, see Naomi Hirahara, *Green Makers: Japanese American Gardeners in Southern California* (Los Angeles: Southern California Gardeners' Federation, 2000).

67. See Glen Kitayama's well-documented entry on the Manzanar Relocation Center, "Manzanar," *Densho Encyclopedia*, https://encyclopedia.densho.org/Manzanar/ (accessed on August 31, 2019). For information on the gardens at Manzanar, see Ronald J. Beckwith, "Landscape Gardens and Gardeners at Manzanar War Relocation Center," January 25, 2008, Japanese American National Museum, *DiscoverNikkei*, http://www.discovernikkei.org/en/journal/2008/1/25/landscape-manzanar/ (accessed on August 31, 2019); and Lauren Walser, "Restoring the Historic Gardens of Manzanar," November 2, 2015, National Trust for Historic Preservation, https://savingplaces.org/stories/restoring-the-historic-japanese-gardens-of-manzanar#.XWrYRihKiUk (accessed on August 31, 2015).

68. Although unbeknownst to Kuromiya, the appeal did, in fact, occur. See chapter 9 and the note containing Muller's comment.

69. Pasadena's pre–World War II Japanese American community is discussed in "Pasadena," *California Japantowns*, http://www.californiajapantowns.org/pasadena.html (accessed on August 31, 2019). For information on the late-war/postwar resettlement experience of Japanese Americans in Pasadena, see also Brian Niiya's entry on Esther Takei Nishio (1925–2019) in the *Densho Encyclopedia*, http://encyclopedia.densho.org/Esther%20Takei%20Nishio/ (accessed on August 31, 2019).

70. See Suzie Ling, "Three Generations of the Kuromiya Family of Monrovia," copied for the most part from the 2016 *Monrovia Historical Museum Newsletter*, http://ppolinks.com/monrovia/Kuromiya%20Family2.pdf (accessed on August 31, 2019).

71. See Charlotte Brooks, *Alien Neighbors, Foreign Friends: Asian Americans, Housing, and the Transformation of Urban California* (Chicago: University of Chicago Press, 2009).

72. See "1947 December 24: Truman Pardons 1,523 WW II Draft Resisters," *Today in Civil Liberties*, http://todayinclh.com/?event=truman-pardons-1523-ww-ii-draft-resisters (accessed on September 7, 2019). As noted, this pardon extended well beyond the Japanese American resisters. See also Muller's comprehensive contextual treatment of Truman's presidential pardon in *Free to Die for Their Country*, 181–183. According to Muller, Truman established a board to review the cases of World War II draft violators and appointed US Supreme Court Justice Owen J. Roberts to preside over it. A. L. Wirin, the defense attorney for the Heart Mountain Fair Play Committee, acted as a witness during the board's proceedings and made a formal request for amnesty on behalf of the draft resisters. In turn, the board, upon deliberation, chose to honor this request. Accordingly, President Truman granted them a "full pardon, including all of their political rights."

73. Actually, the FPC leadership did not betray Kuromiya and the other Heart Mountain draft resisters; nor did the FPC fail all of Japanese America and the US Constitution. For an explanation of precisely why not, see chapter 9 and the note containing Muller's comment.

74. For a balanced historical account of this organization, see "Native Sons of the Golden West," *Wikipedia*, https://en.wikipedia.org/wiki/Native_Sons_of_the_Golden_West (accessed on September 1, 2019).

75. For information about the Crown City Gardeners Association in the context of Southern California gardening associations in the post–World War II period, see Martha Nakagawa, "Gardena Valley Gardeners Association to Disband," *Rafu Shimpo*, January 5, 2016, https://www

.rafu.com/2016/01/gardena-valley-gardeners-association-to-disband/ (accessed on September 1, 2019).

76. See the Japanese American National Museum's publicity announcement, "Southern California Gardeners' Federation: Fifty Years," pertaining to its 2007 exhibition, "Landscaping America: Japanese American Gardeners and Their Gardens," http://www.janm.org/exhibits /gardenersfed/ (accessed on September 1, 2019).

77. Southern California–based landscape architect Raymond E. Page (1895–1992) was best known for his work at the Pickfair Estate, the Beverly Hills home of Hollywood film legends Mary Pickford and Douglas Fairbanks. The Landscape Architecture Foundation sponsors the annual Raymond E. Page Scholarship.

78. For a biography of Garrett Eckbo (1910–2000), see Los Angeles Conservancy, "Garrett Eckbo," https://www.laconservancy.org/architects/garrett-eckbo (accessed on September 1, 2019).

79. See Robert Riley's review of *Landscape for Living* in the *Harvard Design Magazine*, no. 6 (Fall 1998): 76–78, http://www.harvarddesignmagazine.org/issues/6/landscape-for-living-by -garrett-eckbo (accessed on September 1, 2019).

80. For information on William Charles Carr (1890–1978), see "William C. Carr papers, 1941–1962," UCLA Library, Special Collections, Charles E. Young Research Library, *Online Archive of California*, https://oac.cdlib.org/findaid/ark:/13030/tf6g50073j/ (accessed on September 2, 2019). See also Susie Ling, "Thank You, Carr Family" (blog post), May 21, 2015, *Thinking Aloud*, https:// susieling.wordpress.com/2015/05/21/thank-you-carr-family/ (accessed on September 2, 2018). Originally printed in *Rafu Shimpo*, November 21, 2014.

81. For a 1958 example of the landscape design work done by the Eckbo, Dean and Williams firm, see John Chase, "Eckbo, Dean and Williams," AIA California Council, http://www.aiacc.org /tag/eckbo-dean-and-williams/ (accessed on September 2, 2019).

82. Thomas D. Church, *Gardens Are for People: How to Plan for Outdoor Living* (New York: Reinhold Pub. Corp., 1955); Garrett Eckbo, *Urban Landscape Design* (New York: McGraw-Hill, 1964).

83. For an assessment of EDAW, see Tooru Miyakoda, *EDAW, The Integrated World: Landscape Design and Sustaining Environments* (Tokyo: Process Architecture Co., 1994).

84. See "Francis Dean: The Art of Modern Landscape Architecture," https://env.cpp.edu/la /event/francis-dean-exhibition-reception-and-panel-discussion (accessed on September 2, 2019). This exhibition on Dean was held at the Huntley Gallery, California State Polytechnic University, Pomona, October 21, 2017–January 11, 2018.

85. See Brian Niiya, "Lim Report," *Densho Encyclopedia*, http://encyclopedia.densho.org/Lim _Report/ (accessed on September 2, 2019). See also Frank Abe, " 'The Lim Report' Now Back Online: The Mueller Report of Its Time" (blog post), May 4, 2019, resisters.com, http://resisters .com/2019/05/04/the-lim-report-now-back-online-the-mueller-report-of-its-time/ (accessed on September 2, 2019).

86. For an authoritative account of the Japanese American movement for redress and reparations, see Alice Yang, "Redress Movement," *Densho Encyclopedia*, https://encyclopedia.densho.org /Redress_movement/ (accessed on September 2, 2019).

87. Kuromiya's feelings here are at variance with historical reality, for the Fair Play Committee leaders, through the efforts of their defense attorney, A. L. Wirin, did indeed appeal the convictions of the Heart Mountain draft resisters. See, in this connection, chapter 9 and the note containing Muller's comment.

88. See "Old Pasadena," *Wikipedia*, https://en.wikipedia.org/wiki/Old_Pasadena (accessed on September 3, 2019).

89. See the entry for Frank Chin (1940–) in *Wikipedia*, https://en.wikipedia.org/wiki/Frank _Chin (accessed on September 3, 2019). See also "Guide to the Frank Chin Papers," University of California, Santa Barbara, Davidson Library, Department of Special Collections, California Ethnic

and Multicultural Archives, https://www.library.ucsb.edu/sites/default/files/attachments/special
-collections/cema/chin_frank/Chin_Frank_Archives_guide.pdf (accessed on September 3, 2019).

90. See Hansen, "James Omura."

91. See "East West Players," *Wikipedia*, https://en.wikipedia.org/wiki/East_West_Players
(accessed on September 3, 2019).

92. For pertinent information on Brooks Iwakiri (1921–2003) and Sumi Iwakiri (1927–2007), see
Frank Abe, "In Memoriam: Sumi Iwakiri" (blog post), December 17, 2007, resisters.com, http://
resisters.com/2007/12/ (accessed on September 3, 2019).

93. For information on Frank Abe (1951–), particularly in relation to his award-winning
Conscience and the Constitution documentary film, see Brian Niiya, "Conscience and the
Constitution (film)," *Densho Encyclopedia*, http://encyclopedia.densho.org/Conscience_and_the
Constitution%28film%29/ (accessed on September 5, 2019). See also Bruce Rutledge, "A Flair for
the Dramatic: Frank Abe Talks about the First Day of Remembrance, the Fight for *No-No Boy*, and
More," *North American Post*, July 11, 2019.

94. For a biographical portrait of Harry Ueno (1907–2004), see Arthur A. Hansen, "Harry
Ueno," *Densho Encyclopedia*, http://encyclopedia.densho.org/Harry_Ueno/ (accessed on
September 5, 2019).

95. An exceedingly illuminating entry for William Hohri (1927–2010) by Martha Nakagawa
appears in the *Densho Encyclopedia*, http://encyclopedia.densho.org/William%20Hohri/ (accessed
on September 5, 2019).

96. See Greg Robinson's penetrating entry for Clifford Uyeda (1917–2004) in the *Densho
Encyclopedia*, http://encyclopedia.densho.org/Clifford_Uyeda/ (accessed on September 5, 2019).

97. For information on Jack Herzig (1922–2005) and Aiko Herzig-Yoshinaga (1924–2018), see
"Jack and Aiko Herzig Papers, Collection 451," UCLA Asian American Studies Center, http://
www.aasc.ucla.edu/herzig451/ (accessed on September 5, 2019). See also Thomas Fujita-Rony,
"Aiko Herzig-Yoshinaga," *Densho Encyclopedia*, http://encyclopedia.densho.org/Aiko_Herzig
-Yoshinaga/ (accessed on September 5, 2019).

98. See Brian Niiya's exemplary entry on General John DeWitt (1880–1962) in the *Densho
Encyclopedia*, http://encyclopedia.densho.org/John_DeWitt/ (accessed on September 5, 2019).

99. Eric Muller rejects this point: "Executive Order 9066 was not 'largely based on' claims about
espionage in radio communications." Muller critique.

100. This information, according to Muller, is incorrect: "There was no 'false testimony,' and the
Supreme Court did not review the Hirabayashi, Yasui, and Korematsu cases in the 1980s." Muller
critique.

101. See Martha Nakagawa, "National Council for Japanese American Redress," *Densho
Encyclopedia*, http://encyclopedia.densho.org/National_Council_for_Japanese_American
_Redress/ (accessed on September 5, 2019).

102. See Sharon Yamato, "Civil Liberties Act of 1988," *Densho Encyclopedia*, http://encyclopedia
.densho.org/Civil_Liberties_Act_of_1988/ (accessed on September 5, 2019).

103. Muller finds this observation to be flawed: "The Civil Liberties Act of 1988 did not *moot*
the *Hohri* opinion. *Hohri* was decided in 1986, *before* the Civil Liberties Act was passed." Muller
critique.

104. This 2002 "apology" of the Japanese American Citizens League is deftly covered by Cherstin
M. Lyon in "JACL Apology to Draft Resisters," *Densho Encyclopedia*, http://encyclopedia.densho
.org/JACL%20apology%20to%20draft%20resisters/ (accessed on September 5, 2019).

105. This action has now been achieved. See J. K. Yamamoto, "JACL National Council Passes
Resolution Apologizing to Tule Lake Resisters," *Rafu Shimpo*, September 3, 2019, https://www
.rafu.com/2019/09/jacl-national-council-passes-resolution-apologizing-to-tule-lake-resisters/
(accessed on October 25, 2019).

106. Muller, "Heart Mountain Fair Play Committee," discusses Omura's purported acquittal on the grounds of freedom of the press

107. In the latter half of 1947, Omura did serve as the editor for Denver's *Rocky Shimpo*. For an analysis of his editorials during this interval of time, see Arthur A. Hansen, "Return to the Wars: Jimmie Omura's 1947 Crusade against the Japanese American Citizens League," in *Remapping Asian American History*, ed. Sucheng Chan, chap. 7, 127–150 (Walnut Creek, CA: AltaMira Press, 2003). For the content of Omura's 1947 editorials, see Arthur A. Hansen, ed., "*Rocky Shimpo* Editorials, May 16, 1947–December 15, 1947, by James M. Omura," Suyama Project, UCLA Asian American Studies Center, http://www.aasc.ucla.edu/storybooks/suyama/omura_shimpoeditorials .aspx (accessed on September 5, 2019).

108. See Michi Weglyn, *Years of Infamy: The Untold Story of America's Concentration Camps* (Seattle: University of Washington Press, 1996).

109. See Brian Niiya, "National Coalition for Redress/Reparations," *Densho Encyclopedia*, http:// encyclopedia.densho.org/National_Coalition_for_Redress/Reparations/ (accessed on September 5, 2019). For a recent full-scale study of this organization, see Nikkei for Civil Rights & Redress, *NCRR: The Grassroots Struggle for Japanese American Redress and Reparations* (Los Angeles: UCLA Asian American Studies Press, 2018). See also the review of this volume by Arthur A. Hansen, "Documenting an Evolving Movement," Japanese American National Museum, *DiscoverNikkei*, http://www.discovernikkei.org/en/journal/2018/8/15/NCRR/ (accessed on September 5, 2019).

110. See William Minoru Hohri, with Mits Koshiyama, Yosh Kuromiya, Takashi Hoshizaki, and Frank Seishi Emi, *Resistance: Challenging America's Wartime Internment of Japanese-Americans* (Lomita, CA: The Epistolarian, 2001).

111. See Lawson Fusao Inada's afterword in the present volume for the complete poem.

112. See Frank Chin, *Born in the USA: A Story of Japanese America, 1889–1947* (Lanham, MD: Rowman & Littlefield, 2002).

113. For information on Momo Yashima (1948–), see Japanese American National Museum, "Momo Yashima," *DiscoverNikkei*, http://www.discovernikkei.org/en/journal/author/yashima -momo/ (accessed on September 6, 2019).

114. For a biographical profile of Mako Yashima (1933–2006), see "Mako," Hollywood Walk of Fame, https://walkoffame.com/mako/ (accessed on September 6, 2019).

115. See the entry for Taro Yashima (1908–1994) by an unidentified author in the *Densho Encyclopedia*, http://encyclopedia.densho.org/Taro_Yashima/ (accessed on September 6, 2019).

116. For an obituary of Mits Koshiyama (1924–2009), see Kenji Taguma, "Remembrance for Mits Koshiyama," resisters.com, http://resisters.com/category/fair-play-committee/mits-koshiyama/ (accessed on September 6, 2019).

117. For a life review of Paul Tsuneishi (1923–2014), see Phil Shigekuni, "Senior Moments: Eulogy for Paul Tsuneishi," *Rafu Shimpo*, October 29, 2014, https://www.rafu.com/2014/10/senior -moments-eulogy-for-paul-tsuneishi/ (accessed on September 6, 2019).

118. Shio Imai provides a balanced appraisal of the controversial career of Mike Masaoka (1915–1991) in his entry for the *Densho Encyclopedia*, https://encyclopedia.densho.org/Mike _Masaoka/ (accessed on September 6, 2019).

119. See Chizu Omori, "Rabbit Ramblings: Kiyoshi Okamoro, an Unsung Hero of the Camp Resistance Movement," *Nichi Bei Weekly*, January 20, 2014, https://www.nichibei.org/2011/01/rabbit -ramblings-kiyoshi-okamoto-an-unsung-hero-of-the-camp-resistance-movement/ (accessed on September 6, 2019).

120. See chapter 3 and the accompanying note that provides a bibliographical exploration of Robert B. Stinnett's *Day of Deceit*.

SELECTED BIBLIOGRAPHY

The references below are restricted to books, articles, and documentary films that directly illuminate the World War II draft resistance movement at the Heart Mountain Relocation Center. Pertinent sections within books are not individually denoted as references, only the titles of the books in which these sections appear.

BOOKS

Chan, Sucheng, ed. *Remapping Asian American History*. Walnut Creek, CA: AltaMira Press, 2003.

Chin, Frank. *Born in the USA: A Story of Japanese America, 1889–1947*. Lanham, MD: Rowman & Littlefield, 2002.

Chin, Frank, Jeffrey Paul Chan, Frank Chin, Lawson Inada, and Shawn Hsu Wong, eds. *The Big Aiiieeee! An Anthology of Chinese American and Japanese American Literature*. New York: Penguin Books, 1991.

Daniels, Roger. *Concentration Camps USA: Japanese Americans and World War II*. New York: Holt, Rinehart and Winston, 1971.

Fiset, Louis, and Gail M. Nomura, eds. *Nikkei in the Pacific Northwest: Japanese Americans and Japanese Canadians in the Twentieth Century*. Seattle: University of Washington Press, 2005.

Hansen, Arthur A. *Barbed Voices: Oral History, Resistance, and the World War II Japanese American Social Disaster*. Louisville, CO: University Press of Colorado, 2018.

Hansen, Arthur A., ed. *Japanese American World War II Evacuation Oral History Project, Part 4: Resisters*. Munich: K. G. Saur, 1995.

Hansen, Arthur A., ed. *Nisei Naysayer: The Memoir of Militant Japanese American Journalist Jimmie Omura*. Stanford, CA: Stanford University Press, 2018.

Hohri, William Minoru, ed., with Mits Koshiyama, Takashi Hoshizaki, and Frank Seishi Emi. *Resistance: Challenging America's Wartime Internment of Japanese-Americans*. Lomita, CA: The Epistolarian, 2001.

Mackey, Mike, ed. *A Matter of Conscience: Essays on the World War II Heart Mountain Draft Resistance Movement*. Powell, WY: Western History Publications, 2002.

Mackey, Mike, ed. *Remembering Heart Mountain: Essays on Japanese American Internment in Wyoming*. Powell, WY: Western History Publications, 1998.

Muller, Eric L. *Free to Die for Their Country: The Story of the Japanese American Draft Resisters in World War II*. Chicago: University of Chicago Press, 2001.

Murray, Alice Yang. *Historical Memories of the Japanese American Internment and the Struggle for Redress*. Stanford, CA: Stanford University Press, 2008.

Nelson, Douglas W. *Heart Mountain: The History of an American Concentration Camp*. Madison: State Historical Society of Wisconsin, for the Department of History, University of Wisconsin, 1976.

Nomura, Gail M., Russell Endo, Stephen H. Sumida, and Russell C. Leong, eds. *Frontiers of Asian American Studies: Writing, Research, and Commentary*. Pullman: Washington State University Press, 1989.

Pearson, Bradford. *The Eagles of Heart Mountain: A True Story of Football, Incarceration, and Resistence in World War II America*. New York: Simon & Schuster, 2021.

ARTICLES

Emi, Frank. "Resistance: The Heart Mountain Fair Play Committee's Fight for Justice." *Amerasia Journal* 17 (1991): 47–51.

Hansen, Arthur A. "James Matsumoto Omura: An Interview." *Amerasia Journal* 13 (Fall 1986): 99–113.

Hansen, Arthur A. "The 1944 Nisei Draft at Heart Mountain, Wyoming: Its Relationship to the Historical Representation of the World War II Japanese American Evacuation." *OAH Magazine of History* 10 (Summer 1996): 48–60.

FILMS

Abe, Frank, dir. *Conscience and the Constitution*. Documentary. Seattle: Resisters.com Productions, 2000.

Omori, Emiko, dir. *Rabbit in the Moon*. Documentary. Hohokus, NJ: New Day Films, 1999.

Yashima, Momo, dir. *A Divided Community: 3 Personal Stories of Resistance*. Documentary. Self-marketed, 2012.

INDEX

Note: page numbers in italics refer to figures. Those followed by n refer to notes, with note number.

ABOUT THE AUTHOR

Yoshito Kuromiya and Eric Muller in front of resister's
exhibit at Heart Mountain Interpretive Center, Cody,
Wyoming, 2014 (courtesy, Paul R. Parker).

YOSHITO KUROMIYA (1923–2018), a second-generation Japanese American born and
raised in the San Gabriel Valley of Southern California, had his Pasadena Junior College
education aborted when he and his family, along with other West Coast Americans of
Japanese ancestry, were summarily evicted from their homes and communities and
unjustly imprisoned in American-style concentration camps. After detention at Pomona
Assembly Center in Los Angeles County, Kuromiya was incarcerated at Wyoming's Heart
Mountain Relocation Center. In early 1944 the twenty-one-year-old Kuromiya joined
the camp's Fair Play Committee (FPC), an inmate organization protesting on civil rights
grounds the US government's military draft of American citizens of Japanese ancestry. As one of sixty-three FPC members refusing pre-induction physical examinations,
Kuromiya was arrested, tried at a Cheyenne federal court in Wyoming's largest mass
trial, and sentenced to three years' imprisonment at Washington's McNeil Island Federal
Penitentiary. In late 1947, President Harry S. Truman granted full pardons to Kuromiya

and all other WWII draft resisters. In the postwar period, Kuromiya attended California State Polytechnic University, Pomona, and then compiled a highly successful career as a landscape architect. From the early 1980s to his 2018 death, he championed the wartime dissent and historical legacy of the Heart Mountain Fair Play Committee, the World War II Japanese American draft resisters, and the courageous wartime role played by Nisei journalist James Matsumoto Omura in support of constitutional rights and social justice.

ABOUT THE CONTRIBUTORS

Arthur Hansen. (Photograph by Frank Abe.)

ARTHUR A. HANSEN (b. 1938), a third-generation American of Irish-Norwegian descent, was born in Hoboken, New Jersey, and came of age in Santa Barbara, California. He earned all of his academic degrees at the University of California, Santa Barbara, and is now a professor emeritus of history and Asian American studies at California State University, Fullerton (CSUF). During his CSUF tenure, which extended from 1966 to 2008, he was the founding director of both the Center for Oral and Public History and its Japanese American Project. He was also the recipient of the CSUF College of Humanities and Social Sciences' Outstanding Teacher Award and Outstanding Professor Award. Between 1991 and 1995 he edited for publication the six-volume *Japanese American World War II Evacuation Oral History Project*. From 2001 to 2005, he served as the senior historian at the Japanese American National Museum. In 2007 the Association for Asian American

Studies presented him its Distinguished Lifetime Achievement Award. Most of his scholarly writings have focused on the resistance that Japanese Americans mounted against their community's World War II oppression by the US government and the Japanese American Citizens League. In 2018 he published two books on this theme—an edited one, *Barbed Voices: The Memoir of Militant Japanese American Journalist Jimmie Omura*, and an authored one, *Barbed Voices: Oral History, Resistance, and the World War II Japanese American Social Disaster.*

From left to right: Lawson Inada, Irene Kuromiya, Frank Chin (in back), and Yoshito Kuromiya (courtesy, Sam Chew Chin).

LAWSON FUSAO INADA (b. 1938), a third-generation Japanese American poet, was born and raised in Fresno, California. During World War II he was confined with his family in the Fresno Assembly Center and in two other American-style concentration camps in Arkansas (Jerome Relocation Center) and Colorado (Amache Relocation Center). He received his post-secondary education at Fresno State University, the University of Iowa, and the University of Oregon. After teaching in the English Department at the University of New Hampshire for three years, in 1966 he became a professor of English at Southern Oregon University, where he taught poetry and completed his academic career with the rank of emeritus professor of English. Inada's major volumes of poetry are *Before the War: Poems as They Happened* (1971); *Legends from Camp* (1992); and *Drawing the Line* (1997). In 1974, along with Frank Chin, Jeffery Paul Chan, and Shawn Wong, he coedited *Aiiieeeee! An Anthology of Asian American Literature*, which was followed up in 1991 by the same editors with *The Big Aiiieeeee! An Anthology of Chinese American and Japanese American Literature*. In 2000, Inada edited and wrote the introduction to a collection of personal documents, art, propaganda, and stories titled *Only What We Could Carry: The Japanese American Internment Experience*. Additionally, he has served as the narrator for two films, *Children of the Camps* (1999) and *Conscience and the Constitution* (2000), and has been the subject of three other pioneering Asian American video works, the Alan Kondo–directed *I*

Told You So (1974), *What It Means to Be Free* (2001), and *Legends from the Camps* (2004). The winner of an American Book Award in 1994, he was named Oregon's Poet of the Year in 1991 and later served as the poet laureate of Oregon from 2006 to 2010.

ERIC L. MULLER (b. 1962), a second-generation American of German-Jewish ancestry, was born in Philadelphia, Pennsylvania, and grew up in Cherry Hill, New Jersey. A Phi Beta Kappa graduate of Brown University in 1984, he received his J.D. from Yale Law School in 1987. After clerking for US district judge H. Lee Swanson in Newark, New Jersey, and then practicing in the litigation department of a law firm in Manhattan, he joined the US Attorney's Office in Newark, where he served as assistant US attorney in the Criminal Appeals Division from 1990 to 1994. Following several years of adjunct teaching at Seton Hall Law School in Newark, while still in government practice, Muller accepted a full-time teaching position in 1994 at the University of Wyoming College of Law, where he specialized in criminal law and procedure and constitutional law; in 1997, as a capstone to his appointment, he was named the College of Law's Outstanding Faculty Member. In 1998 Muller joined the faculty of the University of North Carolina School of Law, where he is presently the Dan K. Moore Distinguished Professor in Jurisprudence and Ethics. During his tenure at this law school, he has served as associate dean for faculty development, chair of the Board of Governors for the University of North Carolina Press, and director of the Center for Faculty. In addition, he has twice, in 2010 and 2011, been the recipient of the Frederick B. McCall Award for Teaching Excellence. His publication record includes articles in such prestigious publications as the *University of Chicago Law Review*, the *Harvard Law Review*, and the *Yale Law Journal*. All three of his major books focus on the World War II Japanese American incarceration experience: *Free to Die for Their Country: The Story of the Japanese American Draft Resisters of World War II* (2001); *American Inquisition: The Hunt for Japanese American Disloyalty in World War II* (2007); and *Colors of Confinement: Rare Kodachrome Photographs of Japanese American Incarceration in World War II* (2013).